T0212157

IFIP Advances in Information and Communication Technology

573

Editor-in-Chief

Kai Rannenberg, Goethe University Frankfurt, Germany

Editorial Board Members

TC 1 – Foundations of Computer Science
 Luís Soares Barbosa, University of Minho, Braga, Portugal
TC 2 – Software: Theory and Practice
 Michael Goedicke, University of Duisburg-Essen, Germany
TC 3 – Education
 Arthur Tatnall, Victoria University, Melbourne, Australia
TC 5 – Information Technology Applications
 Erich J. Neuhold, University of Vienna, Austria
TC 6 – Communication Systems
 Burkhard Stiller, University of Zurich, Zürich, Switzerland
TC 7 – System Modeling and Optimization
 Fredi Tröltzsch, TU Berlin, Germany
TC 8 – Information Systems
 Jan Pries-Heje, Roskilde University, Denmark
TC 9 – ICT and Society
 David Kreps, University of Salford, Greater Manchester, UK
TC 10 – Computer Systems Technology
 Ricardo Reis, Federal University of Rio Grande do Sul, Porto Alegre, Brazil
TC 11 – Security and Privacy Protection in Information Processing Systems
 Steven Furnell, Plymouth University, UK
TC 12 – Artificial Intelligence
 Eunika Mercier-Laurent, University of Reims Champagne-Ardenne, Reims, France
TC 13 – Human-Computer Interaction
 Marco Winckler, University of Nice Sophia Antipolis, France
TC 14 – Entertainment Computing
 Rainer Malaka, University of Bremen, Germany

IFIP – The International Federation for Information Processing

IFIP was founded in 1960 under the auspices of UNESCO, following the first World Computer Congress held in Paris the previous year. A federation for societies working in information processing, IFIP's aim is two-fold: to support information processing in the countries of its members and to encourage technology transfer to developing nations. As its mission statement clearly states:

> IFIP is the global non-profit federation of societies of ICT professionals that aims at achieving a worldwide professional and socially responsible development and application of information and communication technologies.

IFIP is a non-profit-making organization, run almost solely by 2500 volunteers. It operates through a number of technical committees and working groups, which organize events and publications. IFIP's events range from large international open conferences to working conferences and local seminars.

The flagship event is the IFIP World Computer Congress, at which both invited and contributed papers are presented. Contributed papers are rigorously refereed and the rejection rate is high.

As with the Congress, participation in the open conferences is open to all and papers may be invited or submitted. Again, submitted papers are stringently refereed.

The working conferences are structured differently. They are usually run by a working group and attendance is generally smaller and occasionally by invitation only. Their purpose is to create an atmosphere conducive to innovation and development. Refereeing is also rigorous and papers are subjected to extensive group discussion.

Publications arising from IFIP events vary. The papers presented at the IFIP World Computer Congress and at open conferences are published as conference proceedings, while the results of the working conferences are often published as collections of selected and edited papers.

IFIP distinguishes three types of institutional membership: Country Representative Members, Members at Large, and Associate Members. The type of organization that can apply for membership is a wide variety and includes national or international societies of individual computer scientists/ICT professionals, associations or federations of such societies, government institutions/government related organizations, national or international research institutes or consortia, universities, academies of sciences, companies, national or international associations or federations of companies.

More information about this series at http://www.springer.com/series/6102

Ilias O. Pappas · Patrick Mikalef ·
Yogesh K. Dwivedi · Letizia Jaccheri ·
John Krogstie · Matti Mäntymäki (Eds.)

Digital Transformation for a Sustainable Society in the 21st Century

I3E 2019 IFIP WG 6.11 International Workshops
Trondheim, Norway, September 18–20, 2019
Revised Selected Papers

 Springer

Editors
Ilias O. Pappas 🆔
University of Agder
Kristiansand, Norway

Norwegian University of Science
and Technology
Trondheim, Norway

Yogesh K. Dwivedi 🆔
Swansea University
Swansea, UK

John Krogstie
Norwegian University of Science
and Technology
Trondheim, Norway

Patrick Mikalef 🆔
Norwegian University of Science
and Technology and SINTEF
Trondheim, Norway

Letizia Jaccheri 🆔
Norwegian University of Science
and Technology
Trondheim, Norway

Matti Mäntymäki 🆔
University of Turku
Turku, Finland

ISSN 1868-4238   ISSN 1868-422X   (electronic)
IFIP Advances in Information and Communication Technology
ISBN 978-3-030-39636-7   ISBN 978-3-030-39634-3   (eBook)
https://doi.org/10.1007/978-3-030-39634-3

© IFIP International Federation for Information Processing 2020, corrected publication 2020
This work is subject to copyright. All rights are reserved by the Publisher, whether the whole or part of the material is concerned, specifically the rights of translation, reprinting, reuse of illustrations, recitation, broadcasting, reproduction on microfilms or in any other physical way, and transmission or information storage and retrieval, electronic adaptation, computer software, or by similar or dissimilar methodology now known or hereafter developed.
The use of general descriptive names, registered names, trademarks, service marks, etc. in this publication does not imply, even in the absence of a specific statement, that such names are exempt from the relevant protective laws and regulations and therefore free for general use.
The publisher, the authors and the editors are safe to assume that the advice and information in this book are believed to be true and accurate at the date of publication. Neither the publisher nor the authors or the editors give a warranty, expressed or implied, with respect to the material contained herein or for any errors or omissions that may have been made. The publisher remains neutral with regard to jurisdictional claims in published maps and institutional affiliations.

This Springer imprint is published by the registered company Springer Nature Switzerland AG
The registered company address is: Gewerbestrasse 11, 6330 Cham, Switzerland

Preface

During the 18th International Federation of Information Processing (IFIP) Conference on e-Business, e-Services, and e-Society (I3E), which was held in Trondheim, Norway, during September 18–20, 2019, we made efforts to offer the opportunity for discussing up-to-date topics under the broad umbrella of e-Business, e-Services, and e-Society. Nonetheless, there are specific topics that require increased attention. This was accomplished by hosting several workshops in parallel with the main conference.

The workshops allow the researchers to present their working ideas and ongoing projects, while at the same time offer the opportunity to discuss research ideas with a highly focused audience. Based on the feedback received during the presentations and the workshops activities, the authors had the opportunity to edit the workshop articles for the current publication.

Four workshops took place during the 18th IFIP I3E 2019 conference. We were proud to host DTIS, TPSIE, 3(IT), and CROPS. Each workshop focused on different topics, with all being connected to the main theme of the I3E 2019 conference "Digital Transformation for a Sustainable Society in the 21st Century." They focused on Digital Transformation for an Inclusive Society (DTIS), Trust and Privacy Aspects of Smart Information Environments (TPSIE), Innovative Teaching of Introductory Topics in Information Technology (3IT), and CROwd-Powered e-Services (CROPS). A message from the chairs of each workshop is included below.

We would like to express our gratitude to everyone who made the I3E 2019 workshops successful. First of all, our workshop chairs, the members of the workshop Program Committees, authors of submitted papers, invited speakers, and finally all workshop participants.

November 2019

Ilias O. Pappas
Patrick Mikalef
Yogesh K. Dwivedi
Letizia Jaccheri
John Krogstie
Matti Mäntymäki

Conference Organization

Conference Chairs

Ilias O. Pappas	University of Agder and Norwegian University of Science and Technology (NTNU), Norway
Patrick Mikalef	Norwegian University of Science and Technology (NTNU) and SINTEF, Norway
Yogesh K. Dwivedi	Swansea University, UK
Letizia Jaccheri	Norwegian University of Science and Technology (NTNU), Norway
John Krogstie	Norwegian University of Science and Technology (NTNU), Norway

Program Committee Chairs

Ilias O. Pappas	University of Agder and Norwegian University of Science and Technology (NTNU), Norway
Patrick Mikalef	Norwegian University of Science and Technology (NTNU) and SINTEF, Norway
Yogesh K. Dwivedi	Swansea University, UK
Letizia Jaccheri	Norwegian University of Science and Technology (NTNU), Norway
John Krogstie	Norwegian University of Science and Technology (NTNU), Norway
Matti Mäntymäki	University of Turku, Finland

Contents

Innovative Teaching of Introductory Topics in Information Technology - 3(IT)

CROwd-Powered e-Services - CROPS

Digital Transformation for an Inclusive Society - DTIS

DTIS 2019 Workshop - Message from the Chairs

The use of Information and Communication Technologies for promoting involvement of minority groups (gender, race, etc.) in specific working fields as well as for inclusion of people with special needs (i.e. people with disabilities, people in risk of social exclusion, elderly people) is growing year after year. According to recent studies, by 2024 the assistive technologies market will surpass $24 billion.

The inclusion of people with special needs can be understood as a sequence of stages:

1. diagnosis
2. education
3. self-achievement

Many professionals are involved in this process, such as psychologists, teachers, or occupational therapists. In the recent years, technologies of support are becoming more and more popular, and results and approaches from technology fields can be applied at the different stages.

From a demographic point of view, there is a huge difference in gender between the professionals involved in the process and researchers/developers involved in the design and development of technologies of support. Historically, the professions involved are related to knowledge areas where women have had a dominant position, while technology has been historically a men dominated area. This arises the motivation of promoting women participation in ICT for inclusion. Even though women make up half of the total gaming population, their place and role in gaming culture and industry is not well understood.

We wanted to share best-practice experiences of successful initiatives, as well as discuss empirical outcomes and novel designs to build up and strengthen the community of interest in inclusion and the impact of gender. Besides building an international community, the workshop aimed to identify challenges and opportunities related to digital transformation to promote inclusion and reduce the gender gap; presented research and experiences related to the following questions:

- How can we improve the inclusion of people with special needs by digital transformation (DT)?
- How can we make DT so flexible and adaptable that people with special needs can participate and make use of it?
- How can we arise the position of women in the process of shaping DT? Traditionally, software is designed by men to men. But female contributions, preferences, and approaches should be included, shared, and promoted as well.

In this workshop, we invited researchers and practitioners to discuss why and how DT for a sustainable society in the 21st century should be shaped in order to improve inclusion of people who do not participate or participate less in DT processes than mainstream user groups.

The workshop received 11 submissions, and the Program Committee selected 4 for presentation at the workshop. The session also included three invited presentations, from three expert researchers in the area, as well as a panel discussion.

September 2019

Javier Gomez
Letizia Jaccheri
Özlem Özgöbek
Gunnar Hartvigsen

DTIS Organization

Workshop Chairs

Javier Gomez	Universidad Autónoma de Madrid, Spain
Letizia Jaccheri	Norwegian University of Science and Technology (NTNU), Norway
Özlem Özgöbek	Norwegian University of Science and Technology (NTNU), Norway
Gunnar Hartvigsen	University of Tromsø - The Arctic University of Norway, Norway

Program Committee

Jannicke Baalsrud Hauge	Bremen Institute for Production and Logistics (BIBA), Germany, and Royal Institute of Technology (KTH), Sweden
Elisa Rubegni	University of Lancaster, UK
Eva-Sophie Katterfeldt	Universität Bremen, Germany
Nadine Dittert	Universität Bremen, Germany
Petar Jercic	Blekinge Institute of Technology, Sweden
Juan Carlos Torrado	Universidad Autónoma de Madrid, Spain
Germán Montoro	Universidad Autónoma de Madrid, Spain
Gabriela Marcu	University of Michigan, USA
Paula Alexandra Silva	University of Aveiro, Portugal
Masood Masoodian	Aalto University, Finland
Kshitij Sharma	NTNU, Norway
Serena Lee-Cultura	NTNU, Norway

Everybody Rock Your Equity: Experiences of Organizing a Women in Computing Event with Role Models for Diversity and Inclusion

Virginia Grande[1]([✉])[iD], Clara Benac Earle[2][iD], Cristina Manresa-Yee[3][iD],
Elena Gómez-Martínez[4][iD], Laura M. Castro[5][iD], Patricia Pons[6][iD],
and Raúl Corobán[7]

[1] Uppsala University, Uppsala, Sweden
virginia.grande@it.uu.se
[2] Universidad Politécnica de Madrid, Madrid, Spain
cbenac@fi.upm.es
[3] Universitat de les Illes Balears, Palma, Spain
cristina.manresa@uib.es
[4] Universidad Autónoma de Madrid, Madrid, Spain
mariaelena.gomez@uam.es
[5] Universidade da Coruña, A Coruña, Spain
lcastro@udc.es
[6] Universitat Politècnica de València, Valencia, Spain
ppons@dsic.upv.es
[7] Vrije Universiteit, Amsterdam, The Netherlands
r.coroban@student.vu.nl

Abstract. This paper describes the experiences of organizing an event to celebrate women in computing in Spain. We present how the idea of the event was conceived and what the aims with its organization are from its conception, including providing a network and role models for the participants based on role model theory. We then explain how these aims have been implemented for each of the four editions of the event, and we include data for them. Finally, we compile recommendations for readers interested in launching an event of these characteristics and we reflect on the work to be done in the future.

Keywords: Gender · Events · Role models

1 Introduction and Background

One of the current concerns in computing education in the Western world is the underrepresentation of certain groups among students and faculty. In the case of women, enrolment tends to be low and progress to improve this situation is

© IFIP International Federation for Information Processing 2020
Published by Springer Nature Switzerland AG 2020
I. O. Pappas et al. (Eds.): I3E 2019 Workshops, IFIP AICT 573, pp. 5–16, 2020.
https://doi.org/10.1007/978-3-030-39634-3_1

slow [10]. Recruiting processes have been studied in order to address this issue and one of the drawn conclusions is the need of role models [24]. Researchers in computing education have worked on the implementation and analysis of this strategy, e.g. [12,14,17,23], particularly to broaden participation [9,11,21].

Besides interventions aimed at the education system such as the ones mentioned above, other initiatives have been launched to address the lack of diversity in the area. In the US these initiatives were created in the 80's–90's [19]. These women wanted to support their younger counterparts and the focus was on how to keep one's identity as a woman while being in a male–dominated environment. From the numbers above we see that this uneven ratio in gender is still ongoing in the West, and indeed the initiatives continue in different countries. Some of the motivations for the volunteers' participation in this kind of project are providing a support network and positive role models in the same group to others [15].

The term role model is loosely defined and thus used in different ways [13]. While it is often used in computing education research, there is little work in how the phenomenon of role modelling works, what it involves, etc. Here we follow Grande's model [16], where a role model in engineering is defined as "a person who embodies a seemingly attainable achievement and/or an aspect (competency, character attribute, or behaviour) which, through its imitation or avoidance, may help another individual achieve a goal." A role model that represents an achievement is an example of reaching one of the goals that the person emulating them desires to achieve. The completion of this goal comes from outside of the role model themselves, it is given by others, e.g. winning an award. If what the role model represents is a goal achieved that is inherent to the role model, such as their being an honest person or having a particular skill, they represent an aspect. In events to celebrate women in computing, as concerns this paper, we should find both types of role models. And, following the definition, their achievement or aspect needs to seem attainable by those observing them.

It is important that there is diversity among the potential role models, as aspects as gender and ethnicity increase the positive effect of the role model [22,25], and we need different role models depending on the different stages we can be at in our careers [13]. Another kind of diversity refers to the professional identities that potential role models represent. Peters has studied how students in computing may narrow along their studies their view of how it is possible to be a part of the computing community, by favouring those identities that seem more accepted by others [20]. It is crucial then that role models represent different areas in computing and that those with influence support the role models that represent identities less dominant in computing [18].

This paper describes the experiences of organizing an event that has the aim of creating a local community that celebrates women in computing in Spain. In the next section we present how the idea of the event was conceived and what the aims with its organization are from its conception, including providing participants with different kinds of role models. We then explain in Sect. 3 how these aims have been implemented for each of the four editions of the event, and we include data for them. Finally, we compile recommendations for readers interested in launching an event of these characteristics and we reflect on the work to be done in the future.

The view of gender used in this paper is as non-binary. According to this view, it is not possible to describe the gender of the participants by using just "male" or "female". Moreover, only each individual can say with which gender they identify. We did not deem necessary to request gender as part of the participation form for either audience nor speakers. Thus, when we refer to a particular gender in this paper we are assuming this gender based on the gender that is traditionally assigned to names in Spanish culture, which in turn the participants provided in the registration form. Note that when we say e.g. women we use it as short for "those who identify as women". We would also like to emphasize that we show data related to gender, and focused on the female participants, to analyse the actual inclusion of members of all genders. This analysis is limited due to the reasons just stated.

2 Origin and Aims of the Event "Informática para tod@s"

The Association for Computing Machinery (ACM) is a well-known computing society, the goal of which is "to bring together computing educators, researchers, and professionals to inspire dialogue, share resources, and address the field's challenges" [5]. Within ACM, the ACM Women's Council (ACM-W) "supports, celebrates, and advocates internationally for full engagement of women in all aspects of computing" [1]. One key activity of ACM-W are the ACM-W Celebrations of Women in Computing, local conferences targeted at students and professionals. Each celebration is unique and adapts to the local culture and environment, but common activities include poster sessions, presentations about work in computing, career fairs, and industry and graduate school panels. ACM Women Europe (ACM-WE) is "a standing committee of ACM Europe and works to fulfill the ACM-W mission in Europe" [3]. ACM-W supports the creation of new celebrations and provides financial and conference services support to these conferences. The main ACM-WE Celebration of Women in Computing is called womEncourage. It is an annual event targeted at individuals in Europe. The location for each year is chosen so that different areas of Europe are reached. The first womEncourage celebration took place in Manchester (UK) in 2014, followed by Uppsala (Sweden), Linz (Austria), Barcelona (Spain) and Belgrade (Serbia). The 2019 womENcourage celebration will take place in Rome (Italy). In addition to the womENcourage celebrations, ACM-W supports local (country or regional level) similar celebrations. Celebrations are tracked on an annual basis from July to the same month the following year. For the 2018–2019 period, 23 local celebrations have taken place or are scheduled around the world, in countries such as Azerbaijan (with the official language of the event being Azerbaijani), Serbia (in Serbian), Chile (in Spanish), Canada (in English), Turkey (in Turkish) and Ukraine (in Ukranian and English) [2].

One of the authors, Virginia Grande, has been involved in the ACM for over a decade. She started as a volunteer in her local ACM Student Chapter [4] at the Universidad Politécnica of Madrid (UPM). From here she was part of a committee to support chapter members across Europe, which included a collaboration with ACM-WE. In 2015, she was one of the two Chairs of the womENcourage celebration in Uppsala. She contacted another of the authors, Dr. Clara Benac, a lecturer at UPM, to be part of that womENcourage celebration, which she did as Posters's Co-chair. After the success of womENcourage 2015, Grande approached Benac with the idea of starting a local Spanish ACM Celebration of Women in Computing. Benac then contacted another of the authors, Dr. Laura Castro from the Universidade da Coruña (UDC) who had collaborated with Benac in some European research projects. To maximize exposure to students of the event-to-be, Grande proposed to contact the ACM-W Student Chapter from the Universidad Politécnica de Valencia (UPV). The students Patricia Pons, Raúl Corobán and Carolina Marín readily joined the team, and proposed Valencia as the first location for the celebration. Thus, the first "Informática para tod@s (IPT)" took place the first of July 2016 at UPV. Lecturer Dr. Silvia Terrasa was the local organizer, closing the first IPT team. In the following section we explain the growth of the team and the evolution of the conference organization in general terms. Here we want to emphasize that from its origins the IPT organizing committee has been formed by professionals and students from different regions in Spain. This is important because, as a celebration at a national level, different regions should be represented. Notice that we put special care in saying that this is a celebration in Spain but not of Spanish people: our target audience includes any individual who is located in Spain and/or speaks Spanish (so that they can follow the event), regardless of their country of origin, citizenship, cultural background or gender. As for the different stages of career development, besides contributing to better quality for the organization due to more varied representation, this aligns with the role model theory that diversity in this aspect is important too [13].

As organizers, we wanted to send a clear message that diversity is important for us. Thus, as mentioned above the name chosen for the celebration was "Informática para tod@s" (IPT). In Spanish, most words have a gender, i.e., are either "feminine" or "masculine". The plural masculine is used to refer to a set which may contain masculine and feminine words. "Todos" means everyone, while "todas" is used for a group of only female individuals. In Spain, it has become common to use the "@" symbol to include feminine and masculine words (among other inclusive language practices, none of them yet to be recognized by the Spanish Language Academy or RAE by its acronym in Spanish [7]). Thus, by using "tod@s" we stress the inclusion of all genders. But gender is not the only aspect considered in terms of diversity. Besides the cultural aspects mentioned above, we target attendees and organizers from different educational and professional backgrounds, from all areas of computing, from young people to retirees, and always asking for all kinds of food restrictions to accommodate for those with varied belief systems and needs. We also aim to take care of accessibility for both the venue and the website of the celebration, including support for parents, e.g. lactation rooms. In terms of topics covered, the decision is to organize a mix of presentations about work in computing and activities that address awareness of gender-related issues. The topics in computing should be carefully selected to foster the view that many professional identities are welcome in this community and are represented by different role models.

While ACM provides funding for the celebrations (half from ACM itself and half from Microsoft Research), our aim is to find other sources of funding whenever possible and recognize the support given by these sources. As an example, one of the higher expenses tends to be the venue, which may be covered by a public institution, e.g. for the first edition, the hosting university kindly supported the event by letting us use their facilities, and financing some of the expenses. We featured them as a supporter of the event in the merchandising materials.

This effort in looking for more funding comes from the goal of having free registration for all attendees. Our believe is that this is particularly important for students (and it is encouraged by ACM-W). We have also included professionals and others who may not have a financial situation that allows them to afford a regular conference fee. For the same reason, there is a goal to establish and maintain a travel grant system aimed at students, particularly those presenting posters, so that those who want to present their work (or listen to others) may have the financial means to participate in IPT.

3   Evolution of IPT

In this section we present how we have worked to reach the aims stated above during each of the four editions of IPT and data to support these claims. The aims listed were:

1. regional diversity in terms of event location and location of members of the organizing team
2. role models in different career stages
3. variety in areas of computing represented
4. send a message of inclusion, that the event is open to everyone regardless of gender, country of origin, needs, beliefs, etc.
5. accessibility of venue and website
6. financial support for participants: free registration and some travel grants
7. to support the previous aim, find sources of funding other than ACM whenever possible

Thanks to the enthusiasm of the IPT community, it has been possible to address aim 1 in terms of venue location with participants from an edition that volunteer for local arrangements of the next one. This is crucial to facilitate attendance to the event from different regions in Spain. Spain is politically and administratively organized in 17 regions referred to as "Comunidades Autónomas". Since 2016 each IPT edition has taken place in a different "Comunidad Autónoma". IPT2016 was in Valencia, followed by IPT2017 in Palma de

Fig. 1. Map with IPT locations as of 2019.

Mallorca (Universidad de les Illes Balears, UIB), IPT2018 was held in Madrid, and IPT2019 in A Coruña (Universidade da Coruña, UDC). Figure 1 depicts the four locations IPT has had in its four editions so far.

As for the volunteers in the organizing committee, an example of the variety of institutions can be found in the list of affiliations in this paper, which are a subset of the actual volunteer team. Notice that location in Spain is not a requirement. Grande is a PhD student in Sweden, while other organizers have been doing their exchange studies, internships or work in different countries, such as student Corobán (in charge of graphic design for all editions) in the Netherlands or Google engineer Alma Castillo (2019 Co-chair) in the UK. This can be seen as another take on how the event is targeted at those with some connection to Spain and/or the Spanish language, and not necessarily Spanish citizens located in Spain. It also shows an aspect of aim 2 for role models in different areas and career stages.

The organizing committee of each new IPT edition combines experienced members (participants from previous editions) with new organizers. From the beginning there have always been two General Chairs. After the first edition, it was decided to choose two Chairs whose background and experience came from academia and industry respectively, to encourage the participation of educators, students, researchers, and professionals and offer different perspectives of computing and better address aims 2 and 3 regarding different role models and professional identities represented through them. Table 1 shows the names and affiliations of the Chairs for each edition, classified as academia (university) or industry (company).

In the first three editions, all of the general Chairs had experience in organizing conferences and/or related competencies gained during their professional careers. This changed in the 2019 edition when one of the Chairs, (now Dr.) Patricia Pons, was a PhD student. She has been a member of the IPT organizing committee from the beginning. Pons started as a student by coordinating the student volunteers in 2016, later took charge of the poster track and in general showed skills and attitudes that led the organizing team to invite her to co-chair the 2019 edition while she approached her PhD graduation. As the rest of the Chairs before her, Pons's work was excellent and an example of what can be achieved when non-senior volunteers are trusted with responsibility.

In every year of IPT there have been different kinds of role models, of which we name a few here. While Pons is another example of a role model showing her development through different stages (in this case, of her PhD), she also represents the two kinds of role models that Grande's model [16] includes. Pons is an achievement role model, as IPT participants can see her achievements in IPT as her roles in the organization that have been posted for every edition on the event website [8]. She is also an aspect role model, as she is a concrete example of competencies, behaviours and attitudes that can be emulated by both professionals and students, e.g. her presentation skills showed in her different roles as a speaker in IPT, her proactiveness inspiring other members of the organizing team. Corobán's outstanding contribution to IPT, described below, is an example of how men can be part of a team that aims to celebrate women, regardless of the gender of the volunteer themselves. Lobo, who we also mention again below, exemplifies that people in computing do not necessarily have a background solely in the area: she is a student in Computer Science and Business, currently in Dublin. As for examples of skills related to being in computing but not exclusively of the area, PhD student Nerea Luis has been mentioned in Spanish media often for her impact in local policies and in general abilities to discuss computing with those who are not trained in the field. There were also five pregnancies along the editions during which parents and the rest of the committee adapted the work when needed so that everyone continued to participate (not only in the organization but attending the event itself).

As described in Sect. 1, the success of a role model needs to seem attainable. Observers need to be able to understand how they could get there themselves. Thus, for all editions of IPT we made sure that there were plenty of networking opportunities that involved contact with potential role models, in this case the

Table 1. IPT chairs

	Chairs	University	Company
IPT2016	Clara Benac	UPM	
	Laura Castro	UDC	
IPT2017	Paloma Moreda	UA	
	Susana Morcuende		People are not resources
IPT2018	Cristina Manresa	UIB	
	Inés Huertas		Datatons
IPT2019	Patricicia Pons	UPV	
	Alma Castillo		Google

examples described here but also speakers and others. In 2019 we made more emphasis in presence in media, which included interviews to the organizing committee expressing their views on gender and computing, why there were part of IPT, etc. Other interviews were conducted with speakers and other participants. Since 2018 we have recorded talks with the permission of the speakers, so that they can be watched after the event by the participants and those interested who could not make it to that year's edition.

The participation in the event and the format chosen for the program of each edition illustrate efforts towards aims 3, 4, and 6, i.e. all areas of computing are deemed as relevant, and everyone should feel welcome and supported financially if needed and possible. The oral presentations every year have included topics such as artificial intelligence, human-computer interaction, working in computing with a social sciences background, and reflections on issues related to gender in the field, such as a presentation on the challenges of working as an engineer and motherhood. From the first edition of IPT, students have been invited to submit posters about their work in any area of computing and not necessarily finished projects, so that they can receive feedback and recognition. Initially it was a poster session with posters hanged in the corridor panels and discussed during the breaks, but in later editions we chose to have lightning talk presentations for each poster as part of the only track of the event, to increase the visibility of the work and their authors. For this reason, and the addition of a career fair from the 2018 edition, the event has been extended from one to two days in length.

Table 2 shows the evolution of IPT regarding the number posters, oral presentations and the inclusion of a round table or a career fair. The round tables themes have been: "What would I be doing tomorrow? Job opportunities for all" (Valencia), "Reinventing yourself in computing" (Palma), "Factors and options for professional and personal development" (Madrid) and "Initiatives for women in STEM" (A Coruña). The career fair was added as the organizing team grew, and has featured both local and international organizations, for profit and NGOs.

IPT has grown year-on-year, with each edition delivering higher numbers of oral presentations (including keynotes), attendees and sponsors. While IPT is open to everyone interested in celebrating the role of women in computing, female participation has been predominant in all editions, as shown in Table 3.

Table 2. IPT program evolution in numbers

	Place	Posters	Oral presentations	Round table	Career fair
IPT2016	Valencia (Valencian Community)	5	3	Yes	No
IPT2017	Palma (Balearic Islands)	12	4	Yes	No
IPT2018	Madrid (Community of Madrid)	8	6*	Yes	Yes
IPT2019	A Coruña (Galicia)	12	12†	Yes	Yes

*One invited keynote
†Two invited keynotes

Table 3. IPTs' participation

	Attendees	Women	Travel grants to students
IPT2016	40	30	4 (3 women)
IPT2017	50	39	7 (5 women)
IPT2018	70	50	7 (6 women)
IPT2019	101	70	7 (6 women)

Fig. 2. IPT 2019 poster.

We have always managed to achieve our goal 6 of financial support for the registration: it has always been free for all participants. The funding received (through ACM or by Spanish companies) was mainly used to cover (i) travel expenses (number of grants given in each edition, see Table 3) of speakers, poster presenters, organizers and students, (ii) other costs like catering or printed material, e.g. accepted posters were printed at the venue as additional support to the students who may not have the chance to print them themselves. The travel grants have been mainly given to individuals in Spain but we have also granted one for a person in Tunisia and another in Peru.

As sources of funding other than ACM, the universities involved in each edition (UPV, UIB, UPM, UDC) were very supportive. They let us use their facilities and/or cover some of the expenses. Note that the Madrid edition was the only one which did not take place at a University. A more central facility provided by the Madrid city council was used instead. From 2019, a committee member had the specific role of sponsors outreach. Student Marta Lobo was very successful in attracting external funding that allowed us to improve the financial support for participants aforementioned. Sponsors were featured in the material promoting the event, including the website.

All the graphical material has been created by Corobán with a focus on inclusion. For instance, Fig. 2 shows the poster used to announce IPT2019. Here and in material such as different Calls for Participation (CFP), Corobán included depictions of participants of different gender expressions, skin colour, body type and age, among others. He also took the chance to include parents of small children mingling with other participants as another example of sending a message of inclusion represented in aim 4. Not forgetting those with different impairments, besides the depictions in the graphical material (a complete compilation of which can be found in [6]), the website [8] followed accessibility guidelines and the venues were chosen considering appropriate access for different levels of mobility and well-connected for easier travel.

4   Conclusions and Future Work

In this paper we have presented our experience during the last four years organizing an event for women in computing with an interdisciplinary approach that uses role models of different kinds to inspire the computing community in Spain. This section compiles several recommendations for those interested in organizing a similar event, based on the lessons learned during the four editions of IPT.

The different role models that participate in the event may have a positive impact not only on the participants but also on the organizers, as shown previously with the example of Patricia Pons. While among the participants we have had people from different countries, unfortunately so far, the citizenship represented in the organizing committee is only Spanish. Bringing other perspectives to the table, such as the one provided by someone from a different country or culture, is something for which to aim. Another initiative to refine our selection of role models and their characteristics will be to compile more precise data on demographics: at the moment we are aware of the participation in IPT of attendees and speakers from different career stages and paths, regions, ages, genders, etc. because these individuals themselves mention it in our registration form or in exchanges with the organization. We are planning on a formal compilation of data for IPT 2020 so that we can better study how the community we target the event to looks and with what kind of role models we can aim to provide them. A similar approach will be included in a feedback form after the event to better evaluate the impact of IPT again in terms of the specific case of our demographics and role modeling (at the moment there is a common generic feedback form for all ACM Celebrations).

The hosting institution and organizations that collaborate with the event may gain visibility, which can translate into new members. This has happened, for example, for local groups in the 2019 edition. The event can also foster collaborations between groups that are not in the same geographical area but meet there.

The program aims to provide a learning experience for the participants mainly in two ways. The activities about gender and computing encourage the attendees to reflect on the role of women in computing, particularly in Spain, and learn about opportunities for female students and professionals, such as grants and other networks and events. The presentations about work in computing aim to be informative for all kinds of participants: speakers are informed of the audience being partly students, partly professionals from industry and academia, and the content is adapted accordingly.

There are several points we consider for future editions. One of our aims is to keep a controlled size: we deem important to keep the balance between providing our attendees with an interesting network while maintain the total amount of participants within a range that fosters interaction during breaks and networking activities.

Overall, our experience has been that an event like IPT has a positive effect on not only participants (due to the learning opportunities that the program offers plus the chances to meet roles and other contacts) but also organizers. We recommend to both professionals and students that they investigate how they can get involved in a similar initiative in their region.

Acknowledgements. The authors would like to thank the members of the organizing committees of all the editions of IPT, and all of the people who made these events possible by participating as audience, speakers, sponsors and other roles.

References

1. ACM-W. https://women.acm.org
2. ACM-W Celebrations. https://women.acm.org/2018-2019-celebrations/
3. ACM-WE Europe. https://europe.acm.org/acm-we
4. ACM Chapters. https://www.acm.org/chapters/about-chapters
5. Association for Computing Machinery ACM. https://acm.org
6. Corobán's Graphical Material for IPT 2019. https://projects.invisionapp.com/boards/VC3QZ01F93J
7. Real Academia de la Lengua Española, RAE. http://www.rae.es/
8. Website IPT. https://ipt.acm.org/

9. Aish, N., Asare, P., Miskioglu, E.E.: People like me increasing likelihood of success for underrepresented minorities in STEM by providing realistic and relatable role models. In: 2017 IEEE Frontiers in Education Conference (FIE), pp. 1–4. IEEE (2017)
10. Barr, V.: Gender diversity in computing: are we making any progress? Commun. ACM **60**(4), 5 (2017). https://doi.org/10.1145/3056417
11. Black, J., Curzon, P., Myketiak, C., McOwan, P.W.: A study in engaging female students in computer science using role models. In: Proceedings of the 16th Annual Joint Conference on Innovation and Technology in Computer Science Education, pp. 63–67. ACM (2011)
12. Clayton, D., Lynch, T.: Ten years of strategies to increase participation of women in computing programs: the central Queensland University experience: 1999–2001. SIGCSE Bull. **34**(2), 89–93 (2002)
13. Gibson, D.E.: Developing the professional self-concept: role model construals in early, middle, and late career stages. Organ. Sci. **14**(5), 591–610 (2003)
14. Goode, J.: Increasing diversity in K-12 computer science: strategies from the field. In: ACM SIGCSE Bulletin. vol. 40, pp. 362–366. ACM (2008)
15. Grande, V.: Perspectives on volunteering for initiatives for women in computing: a case study. In: 2015 IEEE Frontiers in Education Conference (FIE), pp. 1–4. IEEE (2015)
16. Grande, V.: Lost for words! Defining the language around role models in engineering. In: 2018 IEEE Frontiers in Education Conference (FIE) (FIE 2018), San Jose, USA, October 2018
17. Grande, V., Daniels, M.: A diversity lens on the last decade of the FIE conference: role models for the engineering community. In: 2017 IEEE Frontiers in Education Conference (FIE) (FIE 2017) (2017)
18. Grande, V., Peters, A.K., Daniels, M., Tedre, M.: "Participating under the influence": how role models affect the computing discipline, profession, and student population. In: 2018 IEEE Frontiers in Education Conference (FIE) (FIE 2018), San Jose, USA, October 2018
19. Patitsas, E., Craig, M., Easterbrook, S.: A historical examination of the social factors affecting female participation in computing. In: Proceedings of the 2014 Conference on Innovation & Technology in Computer Science Education, pp. 111–116. ACM (2014)
20. Peters, A.K.: Students' experience of participation in a discipline - a longitudinal study of computer science and IT engineering students. ACM Trans. Comput. Educ. (TOCE) **19**(1), 5:1–5:28 (2018). https://doi.org/10.1145/3230011
21. Scott, A., Martin, A., McAlear, F., Koshy, S.: Broadening participation in computing: examining experiences of girls of color. ACM Inroads **8**(4), 48–52 (2017)
22. Stout, J.G., Dasgupta, N., Hunsinger, M., McManus, M.A.: STEMing the tide: using ingroup experts to inoculate women's self-concept in science, technology, engineering, and mathematics (STEM). J. Pers. Soc. Psychol. **100**(2), 255 (2011)
23. Townsend, G.C.: People who make a difference: mentors and role models. ACM SIGCSE Bull. **34**(2), 57–61 (2002)
24. Wikberg-Nilsson, Å.: Kvinnor i civilingenjörsprogram: hinder och förutsättningar för ökad rekrytering. Luleå tekniska universitet (2008). (in Swedish)
25. Zirkel, S.: Is there a place for me? Role models and academic identity among white students and students of color. Teach. Coll. Rec. **104**(2), 357–376 (2002)

Alenta: A Practitioner's Case of Technology Usage to Support Special Needs of Populations with Cognitive Disabilities

Guadalupe Montero de Espinosa[1] and Juan C. Torrado[2]([✉]) [iD]

[1] ALENTA, Madrid, Spain
lupemontero@alenta.org
[2] Universidad Autónoma de Madrid, Madrid, Spain
juan.torrado@uam.es

Abstract. Alenta is a special education school in Madrid, Spain that is pioneer on the use of digital technologies to provide solutions for some of the educative issues of individuals with cognitive disabilities. In this paper we describe the trajectory of the center and its approach, which came to be at the vanguard of technological solutions for children, teenagers and adults with cognitive impairment. We also describe the main systems that Alenta has helped validate and provided design assessment, in order to portray an example in which practitioner's role goes beyond pure final testing.

Keywords: Assistive technologies · Collaborative design · Cognitive impairment

1 Introduction

Alenta started its trajectory in 1967 as a special education school for people with intellectual disabilities with the aim to provide support to achieve social inclusion and the fulfillment of their rights. As the school started growing and the number of students increased, Alenta started developing services and creating special centers focused on the particular needs of the adult life. Thus, Alenta has currently a Daycare center for adults with strong support needs, an Occupational center in which they are trained in labor activities and a Service of Housing Entrepreneurship that includes a residence and two supervised apartments where they have developed a pioneer experience in terms of employability of people with cognitive disabilities. Furthermore, they built a Special Employment Center that provides job positions to people with cognitive disabilities in several services such as gardening, maintenance, cleaning or cooking. For this purposes, Alenta has been including several methodologies, programs and innovative experiences sin their activities by means of continuous training of their staff, participation

© IFIP International Federation for Information Processing 2020
Published by Springer Nature Switzerland AG 2020
I. O. Pappas et al. (Eds.): I3E 2019 Workshops, IFIP AICT 573, pp. 17–22, 2020.
https://doi.org/10.1007/978-3-030-39634-3_2

in professional forums and collaborations with other entities, companies and universities. Using technology as a personal support tool has been the central aspect of specialized intervention in Alenta, and their professionals have worked on it from different perspectives: internal endowments, project management, professional formation, research collaboration and software development.

1.1   Most Common Issues and Technological Solutions

The starting point of any technology-based solution that aims to support the activities in the center is always the very individual with cognitive disabilities. Since they are the very target of the intervention, the support they need is designed and built in order to improve their relationship with the environment, their learning capacities and self-awareness. The philosophy of the center relies on the premise that every individual has a great potential that can be developed, so in order to do that, every available tool should be studied, every market niche identified and every possible adapted proposal that might help achieve a certain goal developed. Digital technology offers many answers due to their multimedia and interactive features, which allow adaptation to individual needs, displaying information in a way that can be more accessible and adjusted to several interaction styles. Some usual needs in which digital technology has proven to be helpful for this purposes are:

Communication: There is a considerable number of individuals that have not developed oral communication skills or not at a sufficient level to ensure adequate conversational interaction with their peers nor the exercise of their right to express themselves. Information technologies opened a major way of assistance by means of systems based on Alternative and Augmentative Communication (AAC) [6]. AAC software relies on the use of pictures and adapted text that, unlike Hand Signed Language (HSL), are universal and do not require the interlocutor to learn specific codes. Regarding analog communication systems based on images, AAC software offer a handful of advantages such as the amount of language that can be stored and processed or and the speech synthesizing, which allows more functional, practical uses in several contexts.

Understanding of environment, tasks and time: Cognitive impairment is often invisible in society, but it implies a lack of comprehension of the context and of the expectations that other people put on an individual, that is to say, what are they supposed to do in certain contexts. Compensation strategies for these purposes include anticipation or explanation (signage, visual indications, captions, etc.), which have a predominantly static nature that hinders its application to extended contexts and diverse situations.

Autonomy and self-management: Besides understanding the environment and the activities that are carried out in it, autonomy is another desirable feature. Regarding cognitive disabilities such as intellectual impairment or autism spectrum disorders, there is a clear need of support that help these individuals guessing what to do and which strategies ought to be employed at a certain moment. Some examples of technological support in these matters are alerts, sequences of activities that show the steps that belong to a task or guiding applications to provide wayfinding. Communication facilitators are also included in this category.

Self-regulation: Many individuals in the autism spectrum or with other intellectual disabilities manifest high anxiety levels. Causes such as lack of environment and social situation understanding, high requirements or personal frustration may lead to this inner state. Cognitive challenges related to the executive function are also relevant regarding self-regulation due to the difficulty to inhibit socially inadequate behaviors. Emergent technologies such as wearable devices offer several possibilities to detect anxiety episodes [1]. This devices can also help individuals with cognitive disabilities regain calmness by means of relaxation strategies that are presented in a normalized manner and using similar devices than those used in the mainstream, hence reducing social stigma.

Access to academic learning: The last aspect in which people with cognitive disabilities require significant support is their access to learning. For this purpose, school materials and methods have to be adapted in order to improve their comprehension and management. These adaptations consist of: (a) better presentation to achieve better accessibility, (b) individualization of contents and (c) adjusted time patterns via adapted intervals and repetitions to ensure the acquisition of knowledge. Some existent applications and digital materials allow selection of resources that are adapted to individual need [7]. Additionally, authoring tools allow the generation and customization of didactic materials that include methodological aspects that ease learning processes for these individuals 4.

2 Technology and Cognitive Accessibility

If there is a field in which digital technology has made a positive impact on the lives of people with cognitive disabilities and ASD, that is cognitive accessibility.

Cognitive accessibility can be defined as the right to understand the information available in our own environment, to dominate the communication that is established within it, and to be able to participate and engage with the activities that are carried out in it without discrimination on grounds of age, language, emotional state or cognitive abilities. The concept of *environment* in this context means the space, surrounding objects, services and activities [10].

Technology and cognitive accessibility go hand in hand regarding several scenarios. First, web services can ease the access to information by means of diverse strategies that, in our case, would be centered on the simplification of information, the use of easy reading standards, usable interface design and including visual support.

On the other hand, technology can enhance cognitive accessibility in other environments such as spaces and activities, becoming a paramount support to improve the relationship with the mentioned environment and to increase personal autonomy. This can be achieved through mobile technologies that allow users carry adapted and understandable information that allows them to interpret what happens in their surroundings. Augmented reality and wearable technologies stand as innovative elements that can help to a high extent this sort of accessibility.

3   Alenta and Technologies for Personal Support

Although the usefulness of technology for special intervention and personal support has proven to be significant, it is necessary to emphasize the fact that they cannot be used nor implemented in an arbitrary manner, but included in larger intervention frameworks that involve methodological and functional approaches, as well as technological tools to develop them.

In Alenta, this is not only implemented through specific projects but taking individuals with cognitive disabilities as reference for the creation of apps and tools, and ensuring their participation in the implementation process.

Building on this, Alenta has established collaborations with the Escuela Politécnica Superior of the Universidad Autónoma de Madrid and the Escuela Técnica Superior of the Universidad Rey Juan Carlos, which crystallized in the following actions:

- Show to undergraduate students the impact of their work on society aiming to motivate the development of applications and systems targeting cognitive-disabled populations.
- Spread the concept of 'Universal Design' as an approach to build new environments, products, technologies, information services and communication possibilities that are more accessible, understandable and easy to use. Desirably, this goal is to be achieved in the most natural, general and independent way possible, not having to turn to adapted or specialized solutions [2].
- Collaborate in the testing of apps and systems developed by the students of the aforementioned universities in order to validate the efficacy of their proposals in terms of the existent needs of support.
- Offer ideas of new apps and web services in order to provide solutions to the needs of the individuals with cognitive disabilities that are detected in the daily activity of children, teenagers and adults in the center.
- Participate actively in the development of such apps and technological resources contributing with the professional perspective about people in need of special support in the cognitive area, allowing their very participation in the design, development and testing.
- Contribute actively in research centered on the use of technology on disability with the participation of students, users and professionals in order to provide use evidence and proper practices that are reproducible in other environments and entities.

These are some of the specific collaborations that have been carried out in Alenta with the mentioned universities:

– Universidad Autónoma de Madrid
  - Active participation in the testing of *AssisT-Task* [4], an application for support in daily-life tasks and *AssisT-In* [9], an application for support in indoors wayfinding.
  - Active participation in the validation of *Leo con Lula*, an application for the support of the acquisition of global reading skills for students with autism [3].
  - Participation in the design, implementation, evaluation and testing of *Taimun-Watch* [8], a smartwatch system for the emotional self-regulation of individuals with autism, funded by Fundación Orange.
– Universidad Rey Juan Carlos
  - Active participation in the testing of *Hoy te cuento*, a system developed to ease creative thinking with the creation of stories and comics in tablets [5].
  - Active participation in the testing of *DEDOS*, a system for interactive tables for the creation of digital content for people with special needs.
  - Participation in the design, implementation, evaluation and testing of *Blue Thinking*, a programming environment assessed with cognitive accessibility criteria focused on the development of the executive function of individuals with autism, funded by Fundación Orange.

4   Conclusions

After years of experience and joint collaboration, there is evidence of the need of interdisciplinary collaboration in the design and development of technological resources that allow the integration of several approaches in order to provide personal support for people with cognitive disabilities.

Knowing the cognitive accessibility needs of this population is the fundamental starting point for technology development, since that is the way in which functional and pragmatic designs that respond to their actual needs.

Moreover, the participation of individuals with cognitive impairment in the several project phases has an undeniable value due to the contribution they make and the detailed information they provide in terms of interaction and usability. Developing technology with people instead of for people has proven to be the better way to ensure successful results in our center.

References

1. Chia, G.L.C., Anderson, A., McLean, L.A.: Use of technology to support self-management in individuals with autism: systematic review (2018). https://doi.org/10.1007/s40489-018-0129-5
2. Ginnerup, S.: Hacia la plena participación mediante el diseño universal, p. 106 (2010)
3. Gomez, J., Jaccheri, L., Torrado, J.C., Montoro, G.: Leo con Lula, introducing global reading methods to children with ASD. In: Proceedings of the 17th ACM Conference on Interaction Design and Children - IDC 2018, pp. 420–426. ACM Press, New York (2018). https://doi.org/10.1145/3202185.3202765. http://dl.acm.org/citation.cfm?doid=3202185.3202765

4. Gomez, J., Torrado, J.C., Montoro, G.: Using smartphones to assist people with down syndrome in their labour training and integration: a case study. Wirel. Commun. Mob. Comput. **2017**, 1–15 (2017). https://doi.org/10.1155/2017/5062371. https://www.hindawi.com/journals/wcmc/2017/5062371/abs/

5. Martin, E., Cupeiro, C., Pizarro, L., Roldán-Álvarez, D., Montero-de Espinosa, G.: "Today i tell" a comics and story creation app for people with autism spectrum condition (2018). https://doi.org/10.1080/10447318.2018.1550178. https://www.tandfonline.com/doi/full/10.1080/10447318.2018.1550178

6. Mirenda, P., Beukelman, D.R.: Augmentative & Alternative Communication: Supporting Children & Adults with Complex Communication Needs. Paul H. Brookes, Baltimore (2005)

7. Montero, G., Gomez, J.: Serious games in special education. A practitioner's experience review. In: Clua, E., Roque, L., Lugmayr, A., Tuomi, P. (eds.) ICEC 2018. LNCS, vol. 11112, pp. 397–401. Springer, Cham (2018). https://doi.org/10.1007/978-3-319-99426-0_50

8. Torrado, J.C., Gomez, J., Montoro, G.: Emotional self-regulation of individuals with autism spectrum disorders: smartwatches for monitoring and interaction. Sensors (Switzerland) **17**(6) (2017). https://doi.org/10.3390/s17061359. https://www.mdpi.com/1424-8220/17/6/1359

9. Torrado, J.C., Montoro, G., Gomez, J.: Easing the integration: a feasible indoor wayfinding system for cognitive impaired people. Pervasive Mob. Comput. **31**, 137–146 (2016). https://doi.org/10.1016/j.pmcj.2016.02.003. https://www.sciencedirect.com/science/article/pii/S1574119216000390

10. WC: Web Content Accessibility Guidelines (WCAG) 2.0 (2008)

Evaluating Digitalization of Social Services from the Viewpoint of the Citizen

Anne-Marie Tuikka(✉) ⓘ

University of Turku, 20014 Turku, Finland
anne-marie.tuikka@utu.fi

Abstract. Finland is known as a welfare state, which has small income gap and good ICT infrastructure. In recent decades, Finnish society has aimed to transfer public administration through digital services. They are nowadays available for different purposes including the social services such as unemployment benefits or housing allowance. However, digitalization have not yet expanded to all types of social services and one area of development is the services for people with disabilities. People with disabilities cannot be seen homogenous group of citizens; instead it includes people in different ages, and having different diagnoses. This study focuses only on one age group, the children, and on one type of diagnosis, the autism spectrum. While the children are the prime beneficiaries of the social services, their parents (or other care givers) are the ones responsible for applying and transferring these services to them. Hence, the unit of analysis in this study is the parents of children on the autism spectrum. Interviews with them represent the citizens' viewpoint through which the digitalization of social services is evaluated.

Keywords: Digitalization · Digital services · Social services · Social sector · e-Government

1 Introduction

Finland is one of the North European welfare states, where digitalization had advanced in private and in public sector. Digital services have expanded to social sector, where they cover different purposes such as applying accommodation support, unemployment benefits or child care services. However, all spheres of social sector have not advanced at the same rhythm and local differences exists. One example is the services for people with disabilities which are going through digital transformation. In this study, digitalization of social services for people with disabilities is evaluated from the viewpoint of the citizens. Citizens' viewpoint is represented by the parents of children with disabilities.

International studies have revealed that being a parent for children with disabilities is a challenging responsibility for multiple reasons. For example, caring for a child with disabilities requires more physical, emotional, social, and financial resources than caring for a child without disabilities [18]. In addition, parents must coordinate medical, developmental, and educational interventions of their child [23], and they are responsible for carrying out exercises with their child as part of these interventions

© IFIP International Federation for Information Processing 2020
Published by Springer Nature Switzerland AG 2020
I. O. Pappas et al. (Eds.): I3E 2019 Workshops, IFIP AICT 573, pp. 23–30, 2020.
https://doi.org/10.1007/978-3-030-39634-3_3

[21]. They also experience lack of information and they sometimes need to struggle for achieving suitable public services for themselves and for their child [2, 17].

Research about the parents of children with disabilities living in the Nordic welfare states show that similar types of challenges also apply to Nordic context. According to Gundersen [5], parents of children with disabilities face different or greater challenges than other parents to give their children a dignified life. Studies in Finland demonstrate that situation varies greatly in families, where at least one child has disabilities. Some families have found successful ways of coping [26] while others have problems with applying services [22] and caring for their child [28].

As these examples reflect, parents of children with disabilities face problems related to the social services they or their children need. Thus, this study aims to investigate further social services to support children with disabilities and their parents and their digitalization in Finland. While the social services have already been studied from the viewpoint of families, where at least one child has disabilities, the role of information systems within this service structure has got little attention from academia. Hence, the research question is: how parents of children with disabilities have experienced digitalization of social services? The answer to this question derives from qualitative study among the parents. Preliminary findings show that parents of children with disabilities are willing to use digital services for different purposes but the selection of digital services in the field of social sector is very limited.

2   Citizen's Perspective on e-Government

As a research topic, digitalization of social services fits in the field of e-government. e-Government is interested in the use of ICT to enhance the access and the delivery of public services for the benefit of citizens, business, governmental agencies and other stakeholders [1, 25]. Common theme for e-government research has been to study the intention to use and the utilization of e-government services and websites [1] while future re-search should place citizens at the center of e-government [24]. Helbig et al. [6] encourage researchers to ask, who benefits from e-government and how different groups are influenced.

Citizens' access to e-government relies heavily on their ability to access internet. In countries such as Philippines, citizens' access to e-government is hindered by the disparities to access ICT [29]. It is also important to study the accessibility of the available e-government services. Because e-government services are meant for the whole population, they should be designed according to the principles of universal access. The experiences citizens have for using e-government affect, how they interpret the behavior of public sector agencies [24]. Another aspect is the availability of e-government services. Fisher et al. [4] analyzed governmental websites targeted for people with intellectual and developmental disabilities. In these websites, some states did not include information on certain services, which were probably available. If these services were available in these states, people needing them would not be able to find information on them through governmental websites.

Parents are one group of citizens whose use of e-government have been of interest to researchers. Especially new parents represent a group of citizens who are in the middle of life transition; hence, their need for governmental services is changing. Orzech et al. [19] have studied the use e-services offered by governmental institutions in the UK. They found out that new parents are willing to use these services, but governmental officials may underestimate their willingness to use them. In addition, governmental officials may overestimate the problems that citizens face while using digital services. Madsen and Kraemmergaard [14] have studied how single parents use different channels to access public service in Denmark. They noticed that citizens may change channels offered by a single authority which may lead to unanticipated problems in interaction between citizens and officials. Less research has been done on the use of e-government services among parents of children with disabilities. However, Zeng and Cheatham [31] have studied how Chinese-American parents, whose children have special needs, use internet to find information related to their child. They found out that the age of the parent was related to the frequency of searching information online.

To create useful and accessible e-government services, there is a need to engage citizens in designing e-government solutions. Millard [16] emphasizes that governments need to collaborate closely with non-government actors to take full advantage of e-government in combating challenges of the future. All e-government initiatives should be rigorously evaluated to ensure that they do not reinforce the exclusion of any marginalized group of citizens [13]. To prevent this, Wihlborg, Hedstrom, and Larsson [30] suggest to find out about users demands without being biased by specific interest or certain norms. However, the willingness of citizens to participate in the development of e-government services is an under researched area [7].

3   Digitalization of Social Services

Digitalization of social services have been studied to some extent in prior e-government literature – usually from the perspective of professionals and policy makers. There are hopes that harnessing big data would transfer social sector more transparent, effective and accountable [3]. However, there are many challenges that needs to be solved. Social workers as well as beneficiaries do not always have sufficient digital skills [15]. Citizens might also face barriers of accessing social services through digital mediums while digitalization changes the modes of interaction between professionals and beneficiaries [20].

In Finland, responsibility for different social services is dispersed between municipalities and the Social Insurance Institution of Finland called Kela. Municipalities organize social care for citizens and certain service can be produced by public or by private organization. Social services for people with disabilities include e.g. assistive technologies for children, home adjustments, supported living and sheltered work. Kela has vast funding responsibilities in different spheres of wellbeing among citizens. For people with disabilities, Kela pays e.g. disability allowance, medical rehabilitation, and assistive technologies for education.

Digitalization of social services is ongoing process that have advanced at different pace in Kela and in the municipalities. Most of the allowances offered by Kela can be applied electronically but municipalities vary in their digital service structure. In 2014, the most common online service offered by the social service providers, was an informative website and possibility to give feedback online [8]. Although, the amount of online services offered by the social service providers have increased between years 2014 and 2017, only one out of five organizations offered online application services [12]. Hyppönen et al. [9] studied the use of digital services among citizens. In the case of social services, they found out that 54% of respondents experience some kind of barriers of using digital services and 15% do not have internet and computer to access the services. Despite the challenges, one third of the respondents have experienced benefits such as saving money and time.

One of the biggest e-government projects in Finland is Kanta services, which produce digital services for the healthcare and which is currently expanding to social care. In the first phase, social service providers can participate by transferring their client information to national archive. This archive will facilitate the integration of client information from the social sector to the Kanta services [27].

4   Research Setting

4.1   Research Methods

This study employed participatory approach to evaluate digitalization of social services through the experiences of parents of children on the autism spectrum. The study was conducted by one researcher, the author, who first presented the research plan in the parental peer groups (n = 2) to give parents opportunity to share their views on the importance of the research topic. Participants in the peer groups found the research topic important and some of them were willing to join the study. Later more participants were found through recommendations of other participants or through parental peer groups in Facebook.

The main research method is semi-structured interviews, which were conducted among 13 parents living around Finland during 2016–2018. All interviewees were women. Most of them had good IT skills and were under 45 years old. Each interview lasted 40 to 90 min and most of them were recorded (n = 12). In addition, author organized a focus group which had five participants (four of them were also interviewed personally) all living in the same municipality. One of the participants was a man who joined the focus group with his wife. Focus group lasted 116 min and it was recorded.

4.2   Research Context

In Finland, children with disabilities are entitled to universal health care and social services. Health care includes care for acute health problems and rehabilitation, which aims to improve and maintain patient's abilities to function. In the case of children with disabilities, social services focus on funding their medical rehabilitation and their daily care. Social services are organized by Kela and the municipalities, where the child is living.

Kela offers disability allowances for the children under 16 years to cover the cost and the effort of their care. There are three levels of disability allowances: basic, heighten, and highest. Basic level is suitable for children who have continued health problems such as allergy for dairy products. Heighten level is suitable for children whose daily care is demanding due to their illness or their impairment, while highest level is meant for children who need to be cared round-the-clock due to their illness or their impairment. The decision about the allowance is usually made for certain period of time even if the disability is not assumed to disappear. This is justified according to the possible changes in the need of care, while the child grows [10]. If the child receives heighten or highest level of disability allowance, the cost of their medical rehabilitation is covered by Kela. Otherwise the municipality needs to pay for the child's medical rehabilitation.

Parents, who care for their children with disabilities at home, may be eligible for care allowance. The municipality, where the child with disabilities lives, is responsible for deciding and paying the care allowance. The decision is based on the parent's abilities to care for their child. If a parent is found suitable for caring their child at home, a contract can be made between the municipality and the parent. This contract resembles work contract and the parent is seen more as an employee than a client. The parent receives care allowance and they have a right for two monthly vacation days. During the vacation days municipality has to organize another care option for the child. Social services also supervise parent's abilities to care for their child. If the child is transferred to a long-term care outside home (e.g. in hospital), the payment of the care allowance is cancelled.

5 Preliminary Findings Related to Digitalization of Social Services in Finland

Thematic analysis of the research data indicates that parents of children with disabilities cannot access most of the social services they or their children need through digital platforms. Instead, many service providers, such as municipalities, have webpages where one can download an application form to apply their services. Some of the interviewees have used these websites to download the application forms to apply needed services. In some cases, they have first printed the form and then filled it instead of filling it on their computer. Some parents told they did not use the computer, because they preferred writing by hand. After printing and filling the form, parents sent the application through regular mail, because there was no option to send it digitally.

All interviewees have applied disability allowance from Kela and they have been able to receive heighten disability allowance, even if this had sometimes required sending an official complaint about the initial decision. Some parents had received very good guidance for making the application from the social care workers who worked in their local hospital. As one of the parents said[1]: 'The hospital had social care worker

---

[1] Translated from Finnish to English by the author.

who told everything that could be applied. Great service. Otherwise we probably haven't had energy at that time.'

Conversely, parents were not able to use the digital platform offered by Kela to apply different type of allowances for their child because they "cannot use the e-service to handle their child's affairs" [11]. Hence, the parents needed to send the applications by post. However, one of the parents remembered that she had applied allowance for her child's therapy through it. She recalled that she had used her own credentials to complete the application. 'In that point, I think I did it electronically. During past years I have applied electronically'. It is unsure, why her experience differs from the ones related to applying disability allowances. Perhaps, procedures are different for different type of allowances, although such exceptions are not mentioned in the context of disability services in the website of Kela [11]. Another possibility is that she did not recall all the details correctly.

Most of the interviewees had also applied for care allowance, and received it for their child on the autism spectrum. None of the interviewees reported about any digital platform, which they could use to apply care allowance.

In addition to disability allowance and care allowance, children with disabilities are entitled for short-term care and personal assistance offered by the municipalities. Such services could include assistance for a child with disabilities to play outside home or to visit shops without their parents. To apply these services, one municipality had first introduced service vouchers which parents were able to use for receiving the required services from their preferred service provider. Later this municipality implemented a digital platform, which parents ought to use for spending the vouchers and choosing the service provider.

One of the interviewees had experiences of the vouchers and the digital platform. She explained that her child have had personal assistant before the introduction of the digital platform. However, she found the digital platform difficult to use and stopped applying personal assistance for her child. She said: 'They became electronic. I didn't have energy for it.' Other interviewees who lived in the same municipality have not used the vouchers nor the digital platform. Hence, they were not able to agree or to disagree with her experience.

6   Discussion

This study found out avenues for improvement in the digitalization of social services in Finland. However, these problems represents only part of the challenges faced by the parents of children on the autism spectrum. For example, many interviewees experience fatigue, because they feel overloaded in their daily lives where they were the main carer for their children. In addition, some interviewees were single parents or did not have relatives who would help them by caring for their child on the autism spectrum.

One reason, why parents feel overloaded, is the negative experiences they have for applying social services for their child. The first problem is to know about suitable services. Parents do not always learn about suitable services from professionals who work in social care, health care or education. Instead, they might have learned about the suitable services from other parents either through direct communication or through online discussion groups in Facebook. When a parent knows that certain service exists, they have to apply this. Some parents feel that applying for services takes a lot of their energy, but parents are usually content with any service they have received after applying. Understandably, they are unsatisfied when certain service is declined. Those parents, who have decided to complain about the negative decision(s), feel exhausted by this process.

Although, digital services cannot solve all problems that parents of children with disabilities experience, they have opportunity to be helpful. Many interviewees hoped that allowances offered by Kela could be applied online. Some of them suggested that new services would be created for mobile environment. At the time of the study, the opportunities promised by e-government were not fully realized – instead digital services were sometimes part of the challenges parents of children on the autism spectrum need to cope.

Improving the existing digital services would be technically possible but it would require collaboration with social service providers and IT developers. Future research on this topic would benefit from finding partner who is ready to change it practices and invest in digital transformation to complete the improvements suggested in this study.

References

1. Bélanger, F., Carter, L.: Digitizing government interactions with constituents: an historical review of e-government research in information systems. J. Assoc. Inf. Syst. **13**, 363–394 (2012)
2. Berg, B.: Immigration and disability: minority families with disabled children. In: NNDR 2013 - 12th Research Conference Nordic Network of Disability Research (2013)
3. Coulton, C.J., Goerge, R., Putnam-Hornstein, E., de Haan, B.: Harnessing big data for social good: a grand challenge for social work. Grand Challenges for Social Work Initiative, Working Paper No. 11 (2015)
4. Fisher, K.M., Peterson, J.D., Albert, J.D.: Identifying state resources and support programs on e-government websites for persons with intellectual and developmental disabilities. Nursing Nurs. Res. Pract. (2015). https://doi.org/10.1155/2015/127638
5. Gundersen, T.: Human dignity at stake – how parents of disabled children experience the welfare system. Scand. J. Disabil. Res. **14**(4), 375–390 (2012)
6. Helbig, N., Gil-García, J.R., Ferro, E.: Understanding the complexity of electronic government: implications from the digital divide literature. Gov. Inf. Q. **26**, 89–97 (2009)
7. Holgersson, J., Karlsson, F.: Public e-service development: understanding citizens' conditions. Gov. Inf. Q. **31**, 396–410 (2014)
8. Hyppönen, H., Hämäläinen, P., Reponen, J.: E-health and e-welfare of Finland: check point 2015. THL – Report 18/2015. Juvenes Print Oy – Tampereen yliopistopaino Oy, Tampere (2015)
9. Hyppönen, H., Aalto, A.-M., Reponen, J., Kangas, M., Kuusisto-Niemi, S., Heponiemi, T.: Kansalainen – pystyn itse? Kokemuksia sosiaali- ja terveydenhuollon sähköisistä palveluista kan-salaisille. THL – Tutkimuksesta tiiviisti 2/2018 (2018)
10. Kela: Alle 16-vuotiaan vammaistuki (2017). https://www.kela.fi/vammaistuki-lapselle. Updated 13 Dec 2017. Accessed 22 Apr 2019
11. Kela: Taking care of Kela-matters on behalf of another person (2012). https://www.kela.fi/web/en/authorization?inheritRedirect=true. Updated 22 Oct 2012. Accessed 15 June 2019

12. Kuusisto-Niemi, S., Ryhänen, M., Hyppönen, H.: Tieto- ja viestintäteknologian käyttö sosiaalihuollossa vuonna 2017. THL – Raportti 1/2018. Juvenes Print – Suomen Yliopistopaino Oy, Helsinki (2018)

13. Letch, N., Carroll, J.: Integrated e-government systems: unintended impacts for those at the margins. In: 15th European Conference on Information Systems (2007)

14. Madsen, C.Ø., Kræmmergaard, P.: The efficiency of freedom: single parents' domestication of mandatory e-government channels. Gov. Inf. Q. **32**, 380–388 (2015)

15. Mihai, A., Rentea, G.-C., Gaba, D., Lazăr, F., Munch, S.: Connectivity and discontinuity in social work practice: challenges and opportunities of the implementation of an e-social work system in Romania. J. Comp. Res. Anthropol. Sociol. **7**(2), 21 (2016)

16. Millard, J.: Open governance systems: doing more with more. Gov. Inf. Q. **35**, S77–S87 (2018)

17. Morris, J.: Impairment and disability: constructing an ethics of care that promotes human rights. Hypatia **16**, 1–16 (2001)

18. Murphy, N.A., Christian, B., Young, P.C.: The health of caregivers for children with disabilities: caregiver perspectives. Child Care Health Dev. **33**, 180–187 (2007)

19. Orzech, K.M., Moncur, W., Durrant, A., Trujillo-Pisanty, D.: Opportunities and challenges of the digital lifespan: views of service providers and citizens in the UK. Inf. Commun. Soc. **21**(1), 14–29 (2018)

20. O'Sullivan, S., Walker, C.: From the interpersonal to the internet: social service digitisation and the implications for vulnerable individuals and communities. Aust. J. Polit. Sci. (2018). https://doi.org/10.1080/10361146.2018.1519064. Published online 11 September 2018

21. Rix, J., Paige-Smith, A.: A different head? Parental agency and early intervention. Disabil. Soc. **23**, 211–221 (2008)

22. Sandberg, E.: ADHD perheessä - Opetus-, sosiaali- ja terveystoimen tukimuodot ja niiden koettu vaikutus. Yliopistopaino Unigrafia, Helsinki (2016)

23. Silver, E.J., Westbrook, L.E., Stein, R.E.K.: Relationship of parental psychological distress to consequences of chronic health conditions in children. J. Pediatr. Psychol. **23**(1), 5–15 (1998)

24. Smith, M.L.: Building institutional trust through e-government trustworthiness cues. Inf. Technol. People **23**(3), 222–246 (2010)

25. Srivastava, S.C., Thompson, S.H.T., Devaraj, S.: You can't bribe a computer: dealing with the societal challenge of corruption through ICT. MIS Q. **40**(2), 511–526 (2016)

26. Taanila, A., Syrjälä, L., Kokkonen, J., Järvelin, M.-R.: Coping of parents with physically and/or intellectually disabled children. Child Care Health Dev. **28**, 73–86 (2002)

27. The National Institute for Health and Welfare (THL). Sosiaalihuollon Kanta-palvelut (2018). https://thl.fi/fi/web/tiedonhallinta-sosiaali-ja-terveysalalla/kanta-palvelut/sosiaalihuollon-kanta-palvelut. Update 29 Oct 2018. Accessed 24 Apr 2019

28. Tonttila, T.: Vammaisen lapsen äidin vanhemmuuden kokemus sekä lähiympäristön ja kasvatuskumppanuuden merkitys. Yliopistopaino, Helsinki (2006)

29. Urbina, A.U., Abe, N.: Citizen-centric perspective on the adoption of e-government in the Philippines. Electron. J. E-Gov. **15**(2), 63 (2017)

30. Wihlborg, E., Hedstrom, K., Larsson, H.: e-Government for all – norm-critical perspectives and public values in digitalization. In: Proceedings of the 50th Hawaii International Conference on System Sciences (2017)

31. Zeng, S., Cheatham, G.A.: Chinese-American parents' perspectives about using the Internet to access information for children with special needs. Br. J. Spec. Educ. **44**, 3 (2017)

eHealth Approach for Motivating Physical Activities of People with Intellectual Disabilities

Valter Berg[1], Vebjørn Haugland[1], Marius Foshaug Wiik[1],
Henriette Michalsen[1,2], Audny Anke[1,2], Miroslav Muzny[2],
Javier Gomez[3,4], Santiago Gil Martinez[5], Antonio Martinez-Millana[6],
Andre Henriksen[1], Keiichi Sato[7], and Gunnar Hartvigsen[1(✉)]

[1] University of Tromsø – The Arctic University of Norway,
9037 Tromsø, Norway
gunnar.hartvigsen@uit.no
[2] University Hospital of North Norway, 9038 Tromsø, Norway
[3] Universidad Autónoma de Madrid, 28049 Madrid, Spain
[4] NTNU, 7491 Trondheim, Norway
[5] University of Agder, 4879 Grimstad, Norway
[6] ITACA, Universitat Politècnica de València, 46022 Valencia, Spain
[7] Illinois Institute of Technology, Chicago, IL 60616, USA

Abstract. Compared with the general population, people with intellectual disabilities have worse health, lower levels of activity, and greater barriers to participating in fitness activities. Regular physical activity has positive effects on cardiovascular and psychosocial health and thus it is important to identify effective interventions for people with intellectual disabilities in everyday settings. In this position paper we present the design and development of prototypes of game-based eHealth solutions for behaviour change and health promotion by influencing physical activity. Participatory design and agile development have been applied in this project to deliver a system based on three solutions to promote, motivate and maintain physical activity in people with intellectual disabilities: Guided in-door bicycle exercise, guided out-door exercise and guided mild workouts. All the solutions provide virtual environments and motivation features adapted to people with intellectual disabilities for better engagement.

Keywords: Intellectual disability · eHealth · mHealth · Physical activity · Gamification

1 Introduction

Intellectual disabilities (IDs) are intellectual and functional impairments caused by a neurodevelopment disorder [1]. The prevalence of IDs ranges from 2 to more than 30 per 1,000 children [2], and the classification of IDs depends on the severity of the deficits in the adaptive behaviour (measured by the Intelligence Quotient – IQ). People with IDs are on an increased risk of health-related problems and their health needs are often unrecognized or unmet.

© IFIP International Federation for Information Processing 2020
Published by Springer Nature Switzerland AG 2020
I. O. Pappas et al. (Eds.): I3E 2019 Workshops, IFIP AICT 573, pp. 31–41, 2020.
https://doi.org/10.1007/978-3-030-39634-3_4

Among the comorbidities of people with IDs, metabolic related diseases are the most prevalent [3], caused mainly by a significant lower physical activity and higher weight decompensations [4, 5]. Approximately 50% of people with IDs perform a sedentary life style and 40% has been found to do low physical activity [6]. A recent review found that only 9% of people with IDs worldwide achieved the WHO's minimum physical activity guidelines [7], despite meeting the physical activity guidelines was positively correlated with male gender, younger age, milder IDs, and living without supervised care. In the general population, a more sedentary lifestyle has be-come a pronounced problem in younger people [8], and it is a greater problem in youth with ID [9]. Low levels of physical activity could be due to barriers, such as scarcity of available resources and opportunities or a lack of motivation [10].

Physical activity is a modifiable risk factor for chronic diseases and an important way to improve health and prevent diseases [11]. Several studies have reported on the effects of physical activity interventions for people with ID on physical fit-ness indicators, such as balance, muscle strength, and quality of life [12]. Furthermore, a review found a moderate level of evidence that sport-related activities seem to contribute to well-being and perception of social competence [13]. A multi-component intervention in Sweden to improve diet and physical activity in individuals with ID in community residences showed positive effects on levels of physical activity and work routines [14]. However, only adults with mild to moderate IDs were included, and effect sizes were small. A recent theory-based randomised con-trolled study of adults with all types of ID did not find any significant increases in levels of physical activity (steps per day) [15]. Furthermore, the results of a recent cluster-randomised study of older adults in the Netherlands showed marginal effects and substantial missing data, despite being well prepared with a published protocol and using day-activity centres for the intervention [16].

Studies often include people with mild to moderate ID only, but the benefits for people with severe ID tend to be at least as good [14]. Motivational issues have been challenging, particularly for approaches oriented to sustain the effect after the intervention [13]. The main objective of the project *"Effects of physical activity with e-health support in people with intellectual disabilities"* is to enhance physical activity in youths and adults with IDs by means of motivational technology-based tools. As low physical activity is a determinant of health, and as increasing activity has positive effects on cardiovascular and psychosocial health, identifying effective interventions for use in everyday settings is of utmost importance. Studies conducted to increase physical activity in people with IDs are often non-randomised, in non-natural settings, and not theory-based and often exclude people with more severe IDs. Recent well-designed studies in this field have failed to demonstrate improved levels of physical activity in intervention groups. This paper describes the rationale and characteristics of three prototypes to support and motivate people with IDs to increase their physical activity.

2 Materials and Methods

The study will involve individuals with all types of ID who perform low activity levels, as this target group has been previously identified to have the greatest chances of improving the fitness condition [16]. A person-centred physical activity (PA) programme is expected to increase level of fitness, mental well-being and social support, and improve health conditions such as blood pressure and functional strength [17].

Although previous studies have been theory-based, the person-centred focus could improve with the use of individual goalsetting [18] and we have designed the intervention in a natural setting to enhance the effect [19]. Staff involvement will be central. We also expect the systematic use of e-health with rewards and gamification to be beneficial [20]. In Norway, many individuals with IDs have a smartphone they can use for tailored physical activity games, which has not been tested previously. Accelerometers have been used to examine physical activity and sedentary time patterns in related populations [21].

The project to which this position paper belongs defines three sub-objectives. First: to integrate theory with users' needs to design a motivational e-health support in natural settings. Second: to investigate the effects of this physical activity programme in youth and adults with ID in a randomised controlled trial. Third: to increase research activity and national and international cooperation in this little investigated field.

2.1 Technology-Based Motivation

The technical contribution of the research project *"Effects of physical activity with e-health support in people with intellectual disabilities"* shall be the development of tools that can contribute to increased physical activity. Given the user-centred approach, we aim to take advantages of that many people with IDs enjoy the use of new technologies and multimedia and thus give them access to virtual and real environment through recorded physical activity. We plan to develop several applications that are able to record physical activity and provide real-time motivational feedback. Recorded activity will then be swapped into time to watch movies and TV. We aim at studying different reward and motivation mechanisms from computer games and tailor them to people with IDs.

2.2 User Involvement from Early Stages

Users and user-organisations are involved in all parts of the project. To understand the users' needs and to design effective health behavioural support tools, we will gather data from focus groups and individual interviews. Participants will be selected strategically.

Two focus groups will consist of six to nine participants who will be asked to discuss their opinion regarding the role of technology and behaviour change support. Users, relatives, staff and professionals will be involved to design an optimal enjoyable programme for increasing physical activity [19]. We will use thematic analysis to summarize the results and extract user needs and perceptions.

We wish in the current project to go a step further than just gather user input at the start of the project, and use Participatory design (PD). More specifically, we will use workshops and think-aloud-protocols in our lab and out in the participants daily environment. We will conduct individual interviews with participants after the focus group discussion. Later, these participants will be invited to think aloud while interacting with our prototypes and reflecting its ability to meet their needs.

2.3 Mobile Technologies and Gamification for Motivating Behaviour Change

Despite the promise of mobile health (mHealth) and the explosion of fitness-related apps in markets, the vast majority of solutions are yet focused to a routine care basis and to record health and fitness-related data. Several studies have evaluated the effectiveness of mHealth interventions in specific clinical endpoints related to health promotion and disease worsening preventing [21]. Gamification and coaching techniques are also a promising feature of mobile health apps Sannino et al. [22] introduced the concept of a constant follow-up of the patient's performance along with continuous feedback and reward system according to the user behaviour and disease control.

In the scientific literature, there is a lack of work to create a rigorous process for design of mobile-based solutions for people with IDs targeting a behavioural shift. Giunti proposed a model based on User-Centred Design (UCD) [23] for the design of mHealth solutions for chronic patients using a compromise between medical knowledge, Behaviour Change Technologies and gamification. Schnall et al. explored the use of Information Systems Research (ISR) framework as guide for the design of mHealth apps [24] as a way to promote a change in the users. Jia et al. defined a design framework for self-management mHealth solutions employing the quantitative Fogg Behaviour Model to enhance user's execution ability [25]. Those work used several participatory researching techniques but both including adults and children. Although authors identified the participatory techniques used in their work, no information regarding what type of technology was determinant for promoting a behaviour change, which limits its reproducibility in the context of IDs. To the best of our knowledge, no study has proposed a methodological framework to design context-aware and personalised mHealth solutions to support and motivate people with IDs to increase physical activity habits.

3 Results

This innovative project results in a system composed of three different solutions which can co-exist and motivate people with IDs to increase physical activity on daily basis with the use of mobile phones, wearables and gamification strategies.

3.1   Used-Centred Design Requirements

The thematic workshops with experts, parents and institution staff leaded us to define the baseline requirements of the system. This information was exchanged on meetings and contact through emails in the start phase of the project, but also during implementation to discuss features and decisions. This cooperation has provided valuable information on how to develop a system for this kind of users when it comes to design, content, and layout. At the meeting, the ideas for this project were presented through illustrations of the design and explanations from the authors. The attendants of the meeting were then allowed to give their opinion on what they thought about the ideas. The meeting resulted in constructive input to the project and new features that could be included in the application. It was also motivating to see that the user representants were positive and interested in the project.

Table 1. Summary of the system requirements based on experts opinions.

Scope area	Requirement
Physical activity in people with ID	Critical factors for being physically active are the support from parents and care-takers, to be able to show someone what is achieved, predictability, coping ability of activity, amusing and fun, medals and rewards. It is necessary with a clear correlation between reward and activity
Intervention studies in people with ID	Few intervention studies with ID and E-health and struggles with dropouts and missing data in studies. However, the presenter is favourable to that mobile health apps interventions can provide a significant effect on improving PA levels
Motivation in people with ID	Inner (joyful, meaningful, coping, etc.) should be preferred over external motivation (praise, money, threats, etc.) to get a long-term effect. To achieve a behavioural change takes a structured plan, support from caregivers and much effort
User-friendly environment	It is important to achieve predictability and how the application should be able to express what is about to happen for an individual with ID or at least be helpful to do so. Use figures and icons to explain different activities and support audio

Table 1 summarizes the main requirements of the system based on the opinions of experts. Some of the critical remarks were that e-health should provide amusement, be a tool that can show others the achievements performed and provide rewards that are related to the performance in an activity. An e-health tool should be easy to use, but not childish as it can appear stereotypical and insult some users.

3.2   eHealth Based Proposed Solutions to Increase Physical Activity

Physical activity will be measured using the mobile phones in-built accelerometers, wristbands and a bike-roller for in-door static physical activity. This input will be the basis for the game. Our approach provides primary rewards mechanisms including fun and achievement elements. Social interaction has been identified as a powerful reward, so opportunities for collaborative missions are included.

The game needs to offer progressive mastery experiences, which again means that it will have to be tailored to the user. Care workers involved in the project helped to tailor the physical activity game to the individual' goals and resources and specifics of the intervention will be developed iteratively in close collaboration with users.

The system provides three main solutions: Guided in-door bicycle exercise for aerobic mild intensity exercise, which makes use of a tricycle and a bike-roller connected through Bluetooth to a tablet; an augmented-reality based game for out-door moderate exercising and a coaching app for promoting in-door workouts for moderate to hard exercises.

Proposed Solution #1: Guided In-Door Bicycle Exercise. The first solution comprises hardware and software modules to track and record the amount (intensity and time) of physical activity on indoor bikes. To this end, the solution can use two different bikes: (1) an outdoor bike mounted on a Tacx roller, and (2) an indoor, stationary exercise bicycle/ergometer bike. The goal is to detect the activity performed on the bike and transfer the activity measurement to a tablet-based entertainment system, which will react to the performance of the user in the bike and will show different multimedia records (real routes, virtual routes or media).

This solution will provide continuous feedback during realization of the physical activity. Therefore, the designed setup will monitor parameters such as speed, cadence and power. The setup is capable of transmitting data wirelessly (in the current prototype is Bluetooth LE) and in a real-time to a control unit (e.g. smartphone/tablet). The user is rewarded when selecting heavy load on the bike and for cycling for longer periods of time, proportionally. The graphical user interface contains computer game features connected to the hardware of the bicycle, so for example, by cycling through a landscape with computer game elements, receiving rewards in the form of symbols, animations, sounds, etc., during the exercise.

The first prototype uses a Tacx Flow Smart trainer (Upside left corner in Fig. 1) that support Bluetooth Low Energy and Ant+ connection. This trainer measures speed, cadence, and resistance; and it is possible to adjust the resistance on the power wheel. A cadence is a standard unit of measurement for bike trainers, and it means the frequency of the pedal turns when cycling. This trainer suits most type of bikes with a power wheel with a size between 26″ and 30″. For testing of the first solution during development, we borrowed a three-wheel bike from NAV, a welfare institution in Norway among other services provide equipment for those who have special needs (https://nav.no). Using a three-wheel bike is that it will appear steady and stable to ride.

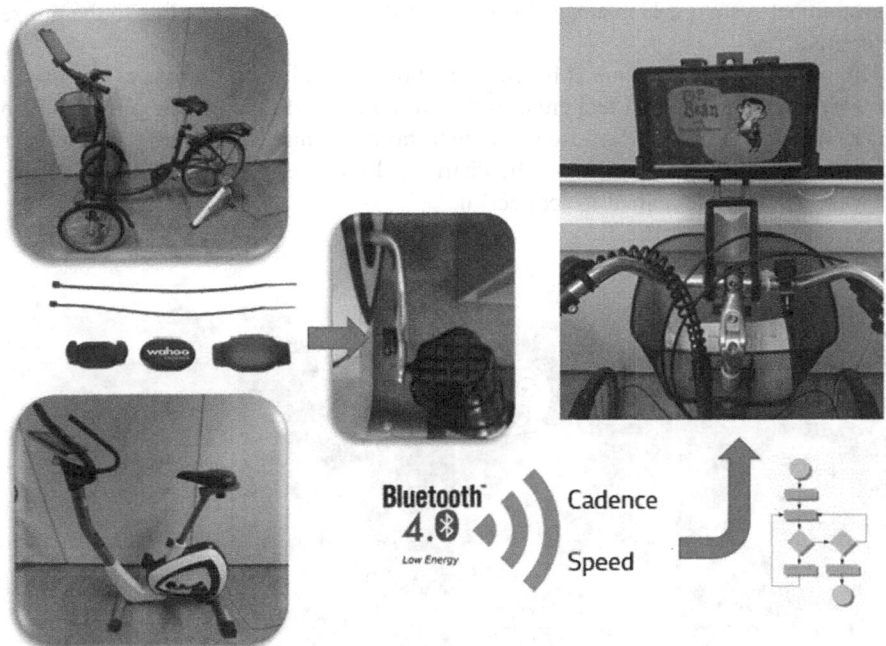

Fig. 1. Set up of the in-door bicycle based activity monitor.

The second prototype is mounted on an U.N.O. Fitness ET1000 (https://www.fitshop.no) ergometer bike (Down-left corner in Fig. 1). The bike comes with an embed computer that measures speed, resistance, and distance during a training session. To make the setup of the system more straightforward and scalable we decided to use a separate Wahoo cadence sensor which supports Bluetooth Low Energy (BLE) connectivity (central part in Fig. 1). The Wahoo sensor uses the FTMS protocol through BLE, the same as the Tacx Smart Flow trainer which makes the connection implementation simpler as it can be used in both solutions.

When the application starts (Upside-right corner in Fig. 1), a display showing the status of the current week activity time performed. From the start page, there is a navigation option to settings, video mode, game mode and history of activity. Video mode and game mode are the two options for activity sessions this system provides. After an activity session is finished, the activity time is added to the total activity time of the current week.

Proposed Solution #2: Guided Out-Door Exercise. The second solution provides a tool for people with intellectual disability to make them more physically active in mild to moderate intensities (walking and hiking). The technical solution is a mobile application that can be used anywhere and is tailored for a user group that previously have had no specially tailored solution with the same objective.

The app tacks the amount of physical activity in outdoor walking, hiking, etc. by means of step counters and GPS-tracking. This information is then transmitted to the entertainment system, which adapts the environment and reacts according to the pre-set preferences.

The gamification technique is based on augmented reality and proposes the user to chase virtual animals into a real environment (recorded with the mobile phone built-in camera). The user can select four different farm animals displayed through user-friendly avatars (Fig. 2), which will be distributed into the user surroundings, so they can walk towards the animal to 'collect' it.

Fig. 2. Graphical user interface of the guided out-door exercise app.

Once the animal is collected, they will be prompted with a supportive message on the screen, and a voice recording encouraging and recognizing success. In addition, the screen has confetti bouncing on it, and a medal will be displayed containing the animal they reached. The setup is able to monitor parameters such as intensity, type of activity and time, and in future extensions it will transmit recorded data to a control unit/cloud-based application.

Proposed Solution #3: Guided Mild Workouts. The third solution provides a coach-based mobile application to promote physical activity in people with ID by means of a three-dimension avatar. This virtual character is customizable so that each user can make it look like he/she wants, so that connection between the user and the character may lead to higher levels of engagement and them wanting to use and interact with it. Once the avatar is created and customized, the app provides a set of basic workouts and pre-set combinations of them, so the user can choose to perform specific or complete routines.

When selecting an activity, the user interface shows the activity animation to make it clear to the user what it entails (Fig. 3). This is because it can be difficult to explain an exercise activity without any type of movement. Text To Speech features are also included in the app, to help the users understand context and functionality of the app which can otherwise be hard to convey using only the visual user interface. The app includes reminders by means of notifications to sustain the adherence to work out routines in case of periods of inactivity.

Fig. 3. Screenshots of the guided workouts app and the avatar.

4 Discussion

E-health provides a wide range of possibilities for monitoring and motivating people in the self-management of chronic illnesses. In this position paper we present the design and development of prototypes of game-based eHealth solutions for behaviour change and health promotion by influencing physical activity. Motion sensor games have been explored and found to be promising in people with ID.

Our approach to move out of the lab and into actual use included a first stage for meeting user's needs. Participatory design and agile development have been applied in this project to deliver a system based on three solutions to promote, motivate and maintain physical activity in people with IDs. These solutions may contribute to the physical activity of the user group of individuals with intellectual disability and also act as ring effect their physical and mental health, as well as improving their health and lifestyle situation. Once these applications have been assessed and improved in beta-tests, they will be used into a randomized-control trial to assess the effect of eHealth in direct physical activity indicators and secondary health endpoints.

References

1. van Schrojenstein Lantman-de Valk, H.M.J., Walsh, P.N.: Managing health problems in people with intellectual disabilities. BMJ **337** (2008). https://doi.org/10.1136/bmj.a2507
2. Boat, T., Wu, J.: Clinical characteristics of intellectual disabilities (2015). https://doi.org/10.17226/21780

3. Carey, I.M., et al.: Health characteristics and consultation patterns of people with intellectual disability: a cross-sectional database study in English general practice. Br. J. Gen. Pract. **66**, e264–e270 (2016)
4. Evans, E., Howlett, S., Kremser, T., Simpson, J., Kayess, R., Trollor, J.: Service development for intellectual disability mental health: a human rights approach. J. Intellect. Disabil. Res. **56**, 1098–1109 (2012). https://doi.org/10.1111/j.1365-2788.2012.01636.x
5. Hilgenkamp, T.I., van Wijck, R., Evenhuis, H.M.: Low physical fitness levels in older adults with ID: results of the HA-ID study. Res. Dev. Disabil. **33**, 1048–1058 (2012). https://doi.org/10.1016/j.ridd.2012.01.013
6. Haveman, M., et al.: Ageing and health status in adults with intellectual disabilities: results of the European POMONA II study. J. Intellect. Dev. Disabil. **36**, 49–60 (2011). https://doi.org/10.3109/13668250.2010.549464
7. Dairo, Y.M., Collett, J., Dawes, H., Oskrochi, G.R.: Physical activity levels in adults with intellectual disabilities: a systematic review. Prev. Med. Rep. **4**, 209–219 (2016). https://doi.org/10.1016/j.pmedr.2016.06.008
8. Winther, A., et al.: The Tromso Study: Fit Futures: a study of Norwegian adolescents' lifestyle and bone health. Arch. Osteoporos. **9**, 185 (2014). https://doi.org/10.1007/s11657-014-0185-0
9. Wallen, E.F., Mullersdorf, M., Christensson, K., Malm, G., Ekblom, O., Marcus, C.: High prevalence of cardio-metabolic risk factors among adolescents with intellectual disability. Acta Paediatr. **98**, 853–859 (2009). https://doi.org/10.1111/j.1651-2227.2008.01197.x
10. Howie, E.K., Barnes, T.L., McDermott, S., Mann, J.R., Clarkson, J., Meriwether, R.A.: Availability of physical activity resources in the environment for adults with intellectual disabilities. Disabil. Health J. **5**, 41–48 (2012). https://doi.org/10.1016/j.dhjo.2011.09.004
11. Elinder, L.S., Bergstrom, H., Hagberg, J., Wihlman, U., Hagstromer, M.: Promoting a healthy diet and physical activity in adults with intellectual disabilities living in community residences: design and evaluation of a cluster-randomized intervention. BMC Public Health **10**, 761 (2010). https://doi.org/10.1186/1471-2458-10-761
12. Shields, N., Taylor, N.F., Wee, E., Wollersheim, D., O'Shea, S.D., Fernhall, B.: A community-based strength training programme increases muscle strength and physical activity in young people with Down syndrome: a randomised controlled trial. Res. Dev. Disabil. **34**, 4385–4394 (2013). https://doi.org/10.1016/j.ridd.2013.09.022
13. Hutzler, Y., Korsensky, O.: Motivational correlates of physical activity in persons with an intellectual disability: a systematic literature review. J. Intellect. Disabil. Res. **54**, 767–786 (2010). https://doi.org/10.1111/j.1365-2788.2010.01313.x
14. Bergstrom, H., Hagstromer, M., Hagberg, J., Elinder, L.S.: A multi-component universal intervention to improve diet and physical activity among adults with intellectual disabilities in community residences: a cluster randomised controlled trial. Res. Dev. Disabil. **34**, 3847–3857 (2013). https://doi.org/10.1016/j.ridd.2013.07.019
15. Melville, C.A., et al.: Effectiveness of a walking programme to support adults with intellectual disabilities to increase physical activity: walk well cluster-randomised controlled trial. Int. J. Behav. Nutr. Phys. Act. **12**, 125 (2015). https://doi.org/10.1186/s12966-015-0290-5
16. van Schijndel-Speet, M., Evenhuis, H.M., van Wijck, R., van Montfort, K.C., Echteld, M.A.: A structured physical activity and fitness programme for older adults with intellectual disabilities: results of a cluster-randomised clinical trial. J. Intellect. Disabil. Res. **61**, 16–29 (2017). https://doi.org/10.1111/jir.12267
17. McConkey, R., Collins, S.: Using personal goal setting to promote the social inclusion of people with intellectual disability living in supported accommodation. J. Intellect. Disabil. Res. **54**, 135–143 (2010). https://doi.org/10.1111/j.1365-2788.2009.01224.x

18. Dixon-Ibarra, A., Driver, S., Vanderbom, K., Humphries, K.: Understanding physical activity in the group home setting: a qualitative inquiry. Disabil. Rehabil. **39**, 653–662 (2017)
19. Taylor, M.J., Taylor, D., Gamboa, P., Vlaev, I., Darzi, A.: Using motion-sensor games to encourage physical activity for adults with intellectual disability. Stud. Health Technol. Inform. **220**, 417–423 (2016)
20. Izquierdo-Gomez, R., et al.: Objective assessment of sedentary time and physical activity throughout the week in adolescents with Down syndrome. The UP&DOWN study. Res. Dev. Disabil. **35**, 482–489 (2014)
21. Marcolino, M.S., Oliveira, J.A.Q., D'Agostino, M., Ribeiro, A.L., Alkmim, M.B.M., Novillo-Ortiz, D.: The impact of mHealth interventions: systematic review of systematic reviews. JMIR mHealth uHealth. **6**, e23 (2018). https://doi.org/10.2196/mhcalth.8873
22. Sannino, G., Forastiere, M., De Pietro, G.: A wellness mobile application for smart health: pilot study design and results. Sensors **17**, 611 (2017). https://doi.org/10.3390/s17030611
23. Giunti, G.: 3MD for chronic conditions, a model for motivational mHealth design: embedded case study. JMIR Serious Games **6** (2018). https://doi.org/10.2196/11631
24. Schnall, R., et al.: A user-centered model for designing consumer mobile health (mHealth) applications (apps). J. Biomed. Inform. **60**, 243–251 (2016). https://doi.org/10.1016/j.jbi.2016.02.002
25. Jia, G., et al.: A framework design for the mHealth system for self-management promotion. Bio-Med. Mater. Eng. **26**, 1731–1740 (2015). https://doi.org/10.3233/BME-151473

Trust and Privacy Aspects of Smart Information Environments - TPSIE

TPSIE 2019 Workshop - Message from the Chairs

What can our facial images reveal about us? This was one of the interesting examples presented by the keynote speaker at TPSIE, Eirik Gulbrandsen, a Senior Engineer at The Norwegian Data Protection Authority (Datatilsynet). The First Workshop on Trust and Privacy Aspects of Smart Information Environments (TPSIE 2019) was held in conjunction with the 18th IFIP Conference on e-Business, e-Services, and e-Society (I3E 2019), during September 18–20, 2019, in Trondheim.

This workshop started with a keynote speech given by Eirik Gulbrandsen, who presented privacy and GDPR as a human rights related issue and highlighted new challenges that Machine Learning and AI applications may bring. His presentation had inspirations from Yuval Noah Harari's books and presented some thought-provoking quotes from Harari. He also presented examples from real life that highlighted the relevance of being aware of protecting our privacy to avoid potential undesirable consequences.

With 10 submissions and 5 accepted papers, out of which 2 were short papers, the workshop drew a small, but very engaged audience from Greece, Germany, Spain, and Norway. The 5 papers that were presented spanned different aspects of privacy related research, ranging from softer aspects to more technical and design related issues.

In the first presentation, the 'right not to be deceived' was discussed in the context of news and media personalization as further developed in the paper "Towards a Right Not to Be Deceived? An Interdisciplinary Analysis on Personalization in the light of the GDPR." Afterwards, a framework to facilitate the analysis of privacy implications in the design of ubiquitous computing systems was presented with the paper "Software Assisted Privacy Impact Assessment in Interactive Ubiquitous Computing Systems." The third presentation, on the short paper titled "Facilitating GDPR Compliance: The H2020 BPR4GDPR Approach," outlined the idea and architecture of the H2020 project BPR4GDPR. Work from another H2020 project, HUMAN Manufacturing, was presented with the second short paper "Designing a Privacy Dashboard for a Smart Manufacturing Environment." The paper presentation sessions were concluded with the presentation of "RRTxFM: Probabilistic Counting for Differentially Private Statistics" on differential privacy as one of the methods for sharing data while withholding some information. Interestingly, among the papers there was less focus on the concept of trust in the presentations.

The final part of the TPSIE 2019 workshop was an open discussion among the participants with the aim to pursue the common interests and to explore ideas for a research article and future collaborations. The energy and momentum at TPSIE 2019 workshop was inspiring and very encouraging, which means that the organizers foresee a growing interest in this research area and look forward to organizing TPSIE workshops in the future.

We would like to express our gratitude for the success of the TPSIE 2019 workshop, to all authors, the Program Committee's valuable reviews, as well as the organizers of the I3E 2019 conference for helping with the practicalities of the workshop.

September 2019

Felix Mannhardt
Sobah Abbas Petersen
Agnes Koschmider

TPSIE Organization

Workshop Chairs

Felix Mannhardt	SINTEF, Norway
Sobah Abbas Petersen	Norwegian University of Science and Technology (NTNU), Norway
Agnes Koschmider	Kiel University, Germany

Program Committee

Wil M. P. van der Aalst	RWTH Aachen University, Germany
Anne Adams	Open University, UK
Nathalie Baracaldo	IBM Almaden Research Center, USA
Andrea Burratin	Technical University of Denmark, Denmark
Jörg Cassens	University of Hildesheim, Germany
Anders Kofod-Petersen	Alexandra Institute, Denmark
Renata Medeiros de Carvalho	Eindhoven University of Technology, The Netherlands
Mauro Conti	University of Padua, Italy
Martin Degeling	Ruhr-Universität Bochum, Germany
Judith Michael	RWTH Aachen University, Germany
Ali Sunyaev	Karlsruhe Institute of Technology, Germany
Manuel Oliveira	SINTEF, Norway
Pieter J. Toussaint	NTNU, Norway
Hans Torvatn	SINTEF, Norway
Matthias Weidlich	Humboldt University of Berlin, Germany
Moe Wynn	Queensland University of Technology, Australia

Towards a Right not to Be Deceived?
An Interdisciplinary Analysis of Media
Personalization in the Light of the GDPR

Urbano Reviglio(✉) iD

LAST-JD International Joint Doctorate in Law, Science and Technology,
University of Bologna, Bologna, Italy
urbanoreviglio@hotmail.com

Abstract. Privacy is a pillar of European law and of the new GDPR. Social and
technological developments question its protection and raise the need for more
comprehensive legal analysis. Informational and decisional privacy, in particular, prove to be fundamental rights to tackle the pervasiveness of surveillance
practices and persuasive technologies. Yet, their protection is uncertain. The
paper is a theoretical and interdisciplinary contribution structured as follows. In
the first part, it is reviewed the literature on profiling and online personalization
in order to provide an overview of the socio-technical landscape, with a special
focus on media content and news personalization. In the second part, the consequences of the GDPR on media personalization is analyzed. In the third part,
the interplay between data protection, consumer and media law is discussed. In
particular, the right to receive information and the value of serendipity are
introduced to eventually discuss the idea of a 'right not to be deceived' as a
precondition to properly protect privacy and other human rights as well as to
preserve trust between users and platforms.

Keywords: Privacy · Profiling · Personalization · GDPR · Data protection

1 Introduction

Recently, much attention has been given to the assessment of the legal and social outcomes of the new General Data Protection Regulation (GDPR) as well as the E-privacy
regulation draft. Despite the introduction of new individual rights and a more comprehensive understanding of the data protection landscape, many commentators
observed the limitations of these regulations. GDPR, for example, lacks a precise
language and explicit and well-defined rights and safeguards [1]. There are many
doubts on the existence or even efficacy of novel rights such as a right to explanation –
which is not explicitly mentioned in the GDPR – the right to transparency and the right
to non-discrimination. Thus, many epistemic, technical, and practical challenges must
first be overcome.

The article questions how the phenomenon of online personalization – particularly
media and news personalization – is currently approached in the European legal framework and to what extent privacy is protected. More generally, it questions how the

© IFIP International Federation for Information Processing 2020
Published by Springer Nature Switzerland AG 2020
I. O. Pappas et al. (Eds.): I3E 2019 Workshops, IFIP AICT 573, pp. 47–59, 2020.
https://doi.org/10.1007/978-3-030-39634-3_5

'personalization paradox' – a trade-off between privacy and personalization quality – and the 'privacy paradox' – the users' inconsistent will to protect their privacy could be tempered. In more detail, the following questions are addressed: how can data subjects exercise their rights if the processing itself is opaque, difficult to understand, and unaware consent is usually given? To what extent does the GDPR ensure that profiling is legal, fair and non-discriminatory with regards to media personalization? And how does the European legislation deals with the risks posed by the employment of increasingly sophisticated techniques of persuasion and engagement that may eventually lead to manipulation?

In this paper, we specifically focus on personalization of media content which raises several social concerns and ethical discussions. In Sect. 2, we review the literature on emerging issues surrounding profiling and online personalization. In Sect. 3, an analysis of the new GDPR is done in order to clarify its effectiveness, its ambiguities and its limitations. More generally, we argue that data protection law is insufficient to prevent certain risks posed by media content personalization. Also, the paper advocates for the need to move from a mostly data-centric to a more user-centric view of privacy. Therefore, in Sect. 4 critical principles and human rights engaged in informational privacy are introduced and discussed and, eventually, conclusions are drawn.

2   Profiling and Data-Driven Personalization

Humans constantly categorize, generalize and classify the world around them to reduce complexity. Algorithms can be programmed to automatically process information in similar ways. Profiling practices, thus, create, discover or construct knowledge from large sets of data from a variety of sources that then are used to make or inform decisions [2, 3]. Profiling occurs in a range of contexts and for a variety of purposes. This paper focuses on profiling that makes or informs decisions (presumed preferences) that personalize a user's media environment (e.g. content selection and ordering).

Of course, individuals can be misclassified, misidentified or misjudged, and such errors may disproportionately affect certain groups of people [4]. Profiling technologies, in fact, creates a kind of knowledge that is inherently probabilistic. They cannot produce or detect a sense of self but they can, however, influence a person's sense of self [2, 3]. In the case of media content personalization, individuals may start to want what is recommended to them without even realizing it, in a self-fulfilling prophecy [5]. Algorithms indeed threaten a foundational link in microeconomic theory, that is, preferences' formation [6]. At the same time, mass personalisation can be understood as pursuing the logic of market segmentation until each individual user is reduced to a unique market [7].

Aside from natural human dispositions such as selective exposure, confirmation bias and homophily, personalization of media content - particularly if implicit - can eventually limit information exposure and discovery. As such, filter bubbles [8] and echo chambers [9] are strengthened. In fact, personalization – in particular news personalization – could reduce opportunities to self-determine and negatively affect truth finding by reducing the exposure to alternative points of view and serendipity in the 'marketplace of ideas' [8, 9]. There may be several other consequences on both individual character, mindset and collective moral culture of our societies [7]; from the limitation of personal creativity to a reduction in the ability to build productive social capital. Mass personalization could also weaken media pluralism, solidarity and make people more politically polarized, narcissistic and vulnerable to (self)propaganda [9].

And in a self-reinforcing cycle, this would make people more susceptible to fake news or polarizing messages, help to spread misinformation and, ultimately, erode interpersonal trust. In general, critics argue that these are moral panics, and that personalization might instead foster the cultivation of expert citizens with stronger group identities [10]. It is no more than human nature empowered by the Internet. Yet, another prominent risk remains growing 'epistemic inequality', that is, the richer an individual's social network and the higher the education, the better the benefits of personalization.

In practice, the risks of personalization are very hard to prove and, eventually, to counteract [11]. There is indeed a crisis on the study of algorithms [12]. Their functioning is opaque and 'black-boxed' and their interpretability is not even clear [13]. Also, users consider filtering mechanism as neutral and actually few recognize them or attempt to output [14]. Furthermore, concerns are growing because of the rise of increasingly sophisticated persuasive technologies and the ability of big-data to 'hyper-nudge' individuals and bring them to deception [15] (discussed in Sect. 4.3). Ultimately, key issues remain unsolved: to what extent personalization is detrimental and whether current legislation is sufficient to address these issues. Before problematizing the interplay between different legal fields, it is necessary to analyze the promises and perils of the current European data protection landscape.

3 European Legislation, GDPR and Its Limits

In the last years, the EU has adopted some provisions that give consumers the power to manage their personal data and not to be subject to automated decision-making such as personalization and algorithmic assistants. The right to data portability[1] envisaged in the new GDPR, as well as the e-Privacy regulation[2], and also the "retrieve them all" provision of the proposed Digital Content Directive, are all tools whereby digital consumers will supposedly have the chance to decide who should use their data to offer them the goods and services that they want [16]. These regulatory interventions bring to the fore a reshaping of the traditional landscape of the consumer protection rules providing a more comprehensive vision of "data consumer law". They in fact grant users several rights, such as the right to transfer data from one controller to another and the right to retrieve any data produced or generated through their use of a platform. They are expected to rebalance the relationship between data subjects and data controllers and to encourage competition between companies. These represent a new

---

[1] Data portability refers to the ability to move, copy or transfer data easily from one database, storage or IT environment to another. To make an example, move one's Facebook profile to another social network.

[2] Notice that the E-Privacy Regulation should be treated as *lex specialis* in relation to the GDPR. However, the enforcement mechanisms of GDPR and E-privacy Regulation remain the same.

paradigm that abandons a purely protective and paternalistic regulation focused only on consumers' weaknesses to experiment with a more proactive approach [16].

Yet, critics suggest that the GDPR – one of the most lobbied piece of EU legislation to date [17] – delivers personalisation to companies on a golden plate [5]. Firstly, by shifting the prerequisite for more expansive (re)uses of personal data from anonymisation to 'pseudonymisation' (which still allows for some form of reidentification). In fact, although anonymised data is effective in protecting privacy, much analytical value of the data is lost through anonymisation (which is relevant for personalisation purposes).

Secondly, the GDPR facilitates personalisation by making the collection and processing/use of personal data essentially a matter of informational self-determination. This emphasis suggests to users that all that is at stake in data protection is their own personal interest whereas also fundamental collective public goods are actually at stake, such as deliberative democracy. Moreover, the GDPR lacks a precise language and explicit and well-defined rights and safeguards [1]. A number of provisions may thus lead to confusion, enforcement gaps or asymmetrical interpretations. This is understandable given that the reform of EU data protection is ongoing and need further guidelines.

The focus of the following analysis is specifically on the most relevant GDPR's articles affecting personalization dependent, above all, on 'profiling' which is a relatively novel concept in European data protection regulation (Art 4(4)). It refers to both the creation and the use of profiles. By virtue of deriving, inferring or predicting information, practices of profiling generate personal and sensitive data. The rights to erasure (Art 17) and restriction of processing (Art 18) are then useful forms of redress in the context of unlawful profiling techniques. Further guidance, however, is needed to clearly set out these Articles' scopes of application. This is also true for highly debated articles that we are going now to briefly analyze, namely Articles 13–15 and Article 22.

3.1   The Right to Transparency

Transparency is often assumed to be an ideal for political discourse in democracies and it is generally defined with respect to "the availability of information, the conditions of accessibility and how the information…may pragmatically or epistemically support the user's decision-making process" [18, p. 106]. This is significant regarding decisions – in the case analyzed in this paper, prioritizing personalized media content – that are extremely complex and inevitably black-boxed.

Auditing is one promising mechanism for achieving transparency [19]. For all types of algorithms, auditing is a necessary precondition to verify correct functioning. For platforms that mediate political discourse, auditing can create a procedural record to demonstrate bias against a particular group. Auditing can also help to explain how citizens are profiled and the values prioritized in content displayed to them. It allows for prediction of results from new inputs and explanation of the rationale behind decisions.

Yet, many epistemic, technical, and practical challenges must first be overcome [20]. Firstly, a right to transparency might undermine the privacy of data subjects and the autonomy and competitive advantage of service providers, or even national security. Secondly, the rationale of an algorithm can be epistemically inaccessible, rendering the legitimacy of decisions difficult to challenge. Nevertheless, algorithm auditing may be quickly approaching and the belief that highly complex algorithms are incomprehensible to human observers should not be used as an excuse to surrender high quality political discourse. Developing practical methods for algorithmic auditing is highly needed. For example, Tutt [21] suggests that a regulatory agency for algorithms may be required, and this agency can "classify algorithms into types based on their predictability, explainability, and general intelligence" (p. 15) to determine what must be regulated. Actually, GDPR requires data processors to maintain a relationship with data subjects and explain the logic of automated decision making when questioned (Art 13, 14 and 15). The regulation may indeed prove a much-needed impetus for algorithmic auditing.

However, with opacity, implementing transparency and the right to an explanation in a practically useful form for data subjects will be extremely difficult, necessary yet likely insufficient, as will be argued throughout the paper.

3.2 The Right to an Explanation

Especially relevant to profiling, there are the right to be informed (Art 13) and the right of access (Art 14). In particular, Articles 13(2)(f) and 14(2)(g) require data controllers to provide specific information about automated decision-making, based solely on automated processing, including profiling, that produces legal or similarly significant effects, namely: (1) the existence of automated decision-making, including profiling; (2) meaningful information about the logic involved; and (3) the significance and envisaged consequences of such processing for the data subject.

Article 15(1)(h) uses identical language as of the above articles and provides data subjects with a right of access to information about solely automated decision-making, including profiling. However, some key expressions in Articles 13–14, specifically "meaningful information about the logic involved" as well as "the significance and the envisaged consequences" (Art 13(2)(f)), need to be interpreted to provide data subjects with the information necessary to understand and challenge profiling and automated individual decision-making. As a result, the right to explanation has been interpreted in two drastically different ways: as an exante general explanation about system functionality or as an ex-post explanation of a specific decision (Art 15). Yet, in the interest of strong consumer protection, meaningful information must be sufficient to answer questions that the data subject might have before they consent to the processing (notification) and after a decision has been made (right of access).

A right to explanation is thus not explicitly mentioned in the GDPR. However, relative legal basis have been detected [1]. In particular, Recital 71 states that data subjects have the right 'to obtain an explanation'. Yet, the legal status of recitals is debated as, in general, they only provide guidance to interpret the Articles so they are not considered legally binding. This is a critical gap in transparency and accountability [17].

3.3 The Right to Non-discrimination

Article 22(1) of the GDPR contains additional safeguards against one specific application of profiling, namely the case of automated individual decision-making that fulfils is "based solely on automated processing" and produces "legal effects concerning him or her or similarly significantly affects him or her". Profiling can indeed form the basis of decision-making that is both automated and produces significant effects, in particular discriminatory. A right to non-discrimination is, in fact, deeply embedded in the normative framework that underlies the EU and the use of algorithmic profiling for the allocation of resources is, in a sense, inherently discriminatory [22]. In this sense, Article 22 is set. There are, however, several ambiguities that must be settled.

Firstly, the wording of the "right not to be subject to automated decision-making" can be interpreted as either a prohibition or a right to object. This ambiguity has existed since the Data Protection Directive 1995 [1], but resolving it is nowadays critical [2]. Since profiling and automated decision-making often occur without the awareness of those affected, data subjects may not be able to effectively exercise their right to object. Moreover, Article 22 only applies to decisions that are "based solely" on automated processing, including profiling. Since "based solely" is not further defined in the regulation, the regulation allows for an interpretation that excludes any human involvement whatsoever. This would render the article inapplicable to many current practices of automated decision-making and there is the risk is that the controller may fabricate human involvement. Finally, paragraph 71 and Article 22(4) specifically address discrimination from profiling that makes use of sensitive data. Goodman and Flaxman [22] broadly questioned the interpretation of the wording 'sensitive data' and argued how significant is its clarification.

In summary, GDPR defines novel rights for data subjects and duties for data controller. Along with the e-Privacy regulation draft, it actually strenghtens 'data consumer protection'. Users can indeed decide whether to enter into a contract, be informed, access the data generated, receive information about the logic involved and not to be subject to automated decision-making based solely on automated processing. The data subject, however, waives some of these rights when entering into a contract for which an automated decision is 'necessary'. As a matter of fact, a user does not have any effective agency towards the logics involved in the personalized news provision. While at first sight data-driven personalization may appear to be only a matter of data protection law, the analysis of automated inferences, predictions or decisions more often lies outside of it [5]. In other words, data protection law focuses on 'inputs' rather than 'outputs', that are mostly out of its scope. Eventually, users will still have a limited (and indirect) control over the outcomes of personalization. In the following chapter, we evaluate the extent to which users may exercise such right and be fruitfully empowered.

4   A Comprehensive Approach to Media Personalization

Data protection law shows some limitations when it comes to the actual consumption of information in the context of media personalization. Yet, the application of consumer protection law to data-related commercial practices can certainly add to the protection offered by data protection law [23].[3] The complex interplay between data

---

[3] Yet, applying consumer law to deals regarding personal data should never be construed as a justification for using personal data as a commodity as it would conflict with human rights.

protection and consumer law need to be further analyzed in order to understand whether and how they might complement each other so as to be able to prevent the risks of media personalization. There is indeed a fundamental need for interdisciplinary work, not only across academics and practitioners, but also between different legal jurisdictions and across different disciplines. GDPR, for example, does not impose any responsibility on data controllers as regards the information a data subject might consume. Technically, there are two main dimensions that affect an individual's choice – the decision parameters employed by the algorithm and the level of choice which remains at the hands of the user [4] – GDPR focuses only on the former and ignores the latter. This critical point is particularly relevant in concentrated markets in which players refuse traditional editorial responsibility. As such, not only media law but particularly competition law maintain a significant – if not indispensable – role in setting standards and levelling the playing field [24].

To begin with, we acknowledge that informational and decisional privacy are fundamental for criticizing emerging means of opinion formation and behavioral change arising from personalization [25]. The latter is complementary with the former, and it is broadly intended as the right against unwanted access such as unwanted interference in our decisions and actions.[4] In addition, the right to freedom of expression is also significantly involved, especially because individual privacy has not been traditionally justified in terms of public good or interest of groups [5]. Thus, a reconceptualization of the right to be informed as a 'right to receive information' in order to increase control over data-driven personalization is discussed [26]. Related to this, it is introduced the value of serendipity as a design principle [27]. These, however, may not even be sufficient to tackle the risks that personalization brings to privacy and freedom of expression, especially considering emerging techniques of behavioral modification [14, 15, 28]. In this light, the idea of a 'right not to be deceived' is introduced, as a conceptualization that could enact more effectively other fundamental human rights.

4.1 The Right to Receive Information

The news consumers' fundamental rights to receive information guaranteed by Article 10 ECHR may prove an important point of departure to realize democratic values in the personalized media landscape [26]. Information consumption is indeed deeply changed and needs to be reconceived. Given the vast amount of information produced and consumed, to some extent users are necessarily passive actors who have to delegate information filtering to algorithms and, therefore, to platforms. Thus, the right to information is, in effect, a right to receive information. How this would eventually translate is difficult to argue. Article 10 may nonetheless entail positive obligations for the state, such as ensuring that media users receive balanced news. Yet, it is an undertheorized right, lacking a framework to understand the rights of news consumers or the obligations of states regarding news recipients.

---

[4] Even if decisional privacy does not feature as a concept in the European legal tradition, art.8 of the ECHR does ackowledge the function of privacy as a right to personal development and autonomy as its underlying value.

Media (and in particular news) personalization invites us to reconsider subjective rights to receive information. In traditional one-to-many media, people have a subjective right to receive information that others are willing to impart, but they do not have a right to receive information that the media is not willing to impart. In fact, the media would lose its editorial freedom if people could demand specific news stories and distribute these to them and, at the same time, if these were conflicting, it would be difficult to decide whose right to receive information should prevail. By enabling one-to-one communication, personalization technologies could, in theory, resolve conflicts between subjective rights to receive information and the media's or other parties' freedom of expression. Such a type of subjective right to receive information could help to establish what news consumers legitimately may expect from the news media with respect to the diversity or relevance of personalized recommendations.

Actually, media personalization may enable or hinder the exercise of this largely institutionally protected right. There are many different values and interests at stake especially with news personalization, which may lead to conflicts (prominently truth finding versus social cohesion) that are not likely to end up in court but must be discussed in public. There is a need to discuss what the right to receive information should mean nowadays, how it relates to data protection, and to empirically study how people's information seeking strategies and privacy attitudes influence the exercise of this right.

Harambam et al. [10] identifies four ways in which people so far can actually influence the algorithmically curated information they encounter, and these are: (1) Alternation, that is, switching between different news outlets and media forms, and also by using multiple or different recommenders. Yet, it requires effort, skills, and it does little to work around hidden biases in algorithmic curation. Then, (2) awareness, that is, being aware of algorithms functioning. In this respect, the GDPR, which raises the bar on transparency and user control over personal data processing, may have a positive impact.[5] (3) Adjustment, that is, adjust algorithms according to personal interests and wishes. Most news outlets, however, have not developed formal ways to influence their curating algorithms. And finally, (4) Obfuscation, that is, mobilizing against the data-driven processes through the deliberate addition of ambiguous, confusing, or misleading information to interfere with data collection. Yet, this may run against some of the goals and benefits of personalization.

The above techniques are not particularly effective as well as are difficult to pursue for the average user.[6] Yet, what forms of intervention at the level of data inputs and processing can be achieved in the context of algorithmic news recommenders to guarantee this right must be discussed further. This leads to a related issue which might help to better define strategies to tackle the current limitations of data protection law previously outlined.

---

[5] This is the case with Facebook which is implementing a feature "why I am seeing this" to provide users a better understanding of the reasons why a post has been recommended [29].

[6] Recently, it is even questioned whether the actual 'horizontal approach' based on the notion of 'average consumers' is fit to protect all consumers in a highly personalized digital environment [27].

4.2   The Value of Serendipity

Personalization also affects media law and threatens basic democratic principles such as diversity and pluralism. Generally speaking, media pluralism is achieved when users autonomously enjoy a diverse media diet. Even if media diversity online is shown to be more than in traditional media, such exposure does not always end up in an actual experience of diversity. Cognitive and affective factors that drive Internet users must also be considered [30]. This requires employing a user-centric perspective and extending beyond the assumption that supply diversity equals experience of diversity, and that diversity of sources equals diversity of content. Also, pluralism as a normative principle remains vague and under-theorized, and it is not a reliable indicator of a society's level of freedom, since it may create only the illusion of content diversity [31] In the digital age, it is indeed becoming less clear in which sense it is meaningful to speak of media pluralism if the consumption is characterized by limitless choice [32].

Given such limitations, current debates center on whether designing for more 'serendipity' might sustain diversity and represent an innovative design and ethical principle for information environments [27]. Extensive accounts on how to research serendipity and cultivate it in digital environments provide ground for novel studies. Yet, serendipity is an elusive and nuanced phenomenon; in this context, it is intended as the attempt to design for unexpected and meaningful information encountering that are indeed statistically less likely, thus less accurate, and that intersect users' profiles. As such, it has the potential to prevent the threats of filter bubbles, echo chambers and 'over-personalization'. In practice, it implies a diversification of information and more interactive control over the algorithmic outputs. Sunstein [9] advocated an "architecture of serendipity" as it would sustain 'chance encounters and shared experiences' that he regards as preconditions for well-functioning democracies. Therefore, taking into consideration serendipity in the design process can fruitfully inform designers, users and eventually policy-makers to stimulate what Harambam et al. [10] defined as alternation, awareness, adjustment and obfuscation.

4.3   Towards a "Right not to Be Deceived"?

Human behavior can be manipulated by priming and conditioning, using rewards and punishments. Algorithms can autonomously explore manipulative strategies that can be detrimental to users [13, 25]. Basically, they exploit human biases and vulerabilities to affect self-control, self-esteem and personal beliefs.[7] Therefore, autonomy and democracies are indeed seriously threatened [6, 28, 33, 36].

Such Big Data-driven nudging is defined by Yeung [15] as a technique of "hyper-nudging", that is, a "nimble, unobtrusive and highly potent, providing the data subject with a highly personalised choice environment". Hyper-nudging operates through the

---

[7] For example, Facebook is especially committed to maintain friends' relationships. Its "NewsFeed" is thus moderated by homophily [33] which is, however, the primary driver of content diffusion, especially misinformation and conspiracy theories, with a frequent result of homogeneous, polarized clusters that tend to lead to emotionally charged and divisive content [9].

technique of 'priming', dynamically configuring the user's informational choice context to influence their decisions. Thus, it concerns the entire design process, not only algorithmic decision-making [34, 36]. This introduces a new form of power, a new 'invisible hand' in which power is identified with ownership of behavioral modification (i.e. artificial emotional intelligence) [37]. In this sense, social media already act as addictive machines [33]. As such, users are tempted to give up their rights to benefit from such hyper-nudging personalization. In theory, using such techniques goes against the 'fairness' and 'transparency' provisions of the GDPR [28]. In this sense, GDPR proves to be a necessary yet insufficient step. In fact, as smart environments will permeate societies, users (especially young people [35]) will be automatically plugged in and guided through life along algorithmically determined pathways, and the boundary between legitimate persuasion and deception will become increasingly blurred.

The right most clearly implicated by big data-driven hyper-nudging is the right to informational privacy. As such, data controllers are obliged to follow the principle of data protection by design and by default. This might go beyond the individual to focus a priori on the creation of better algorithms [17]. For example, privacy might be fundamental also to enable what Hildebrandt [3] defines as 'agonistic machine learning', that is, demanding companies or governments that base decisions on machine learning to 'explore and enable alternative ways of datafying and modelling the same event, person or action'. In this sense, the value of serendipity is also understood.

Of course, also consumer law could actually help to protect consumers against unfair profiling and persuasion practices [23]. However, the extensive uncertainty and context dependence imply that people cannot be counted on to navigate the complex trade-offs involving terms of services and privacy self-management [38]. There is overwhelming evidence that most people neither read nor understand online privacy policies. According to behavioral sciences as well, existing notice and consent model cannot be relied upon to protect the right to informational privacy [15].

In addition to privacy, online digital users could have a separate and distinct right not to be deceived, rooted in a moral agent's basic right to be treated with dignity and respect given that deception violates the autonomy of the person deceived, involving the control of another without that person's consent. Appropriate information and specific consent to the use of techniques of deception ought to be given. Unfolding the preconditions of such a right may help tech companies to regain and preserve trust. Online platforms should in fact routinely disclose to its users and the public any experiment that the users were subjected to with the purpose of promoting engagement. Yet, given the complexity and subtleness of online deception the choice may not even be sufficiently informed and conscious even with consent. Independent and external review boards need to be established to review and approve experiments in advance. The current massive power asymmetry between global digital service providers and individual users in fact cannot be ignored [24, 37]. As it is currently set, the EU legal framework seem to be insufficient to prevent users' potential deception.

5 Conclusions

GDPR defines novel rights for data subjects and duties for data controllers. However, GDPR's rights to an explanation, transparency and non-discrimination may actually prove ineffective in practice when users consume information filtered by proprietary algorithms, and even nurture a new kind of "transparency fallacy". Developments in personalization can actually narrow privacy conceptions and make data protection insufficient to protect fundamental human rights. Data protection actually relies too much on individual rights for what are too often group harms. There is indeed high need for user-centric as well as group-centric approaches to critically govern emerging issues of data-driven media personalization. Also, users cannot be fully relied to manage all the complexities of data protection. On the contrary, personalized persuasive techniques are likely to be employed on a mass scale and, therefore, contrary to recent trends in policy, it is also advocated a more paternalistic approach.

Even if conceptualizing alternative privacy strategies for the online media context has proven to be difficult, two intertwined human rights have been introduced to enrich discussion on privacy in relation to profiling and media personalization. Firstly, we argued that data protection law should complement with media and consumer law in order to guarantee individuals a right to receive information. In general, such right could empower users to bypass and adjust algorithmic filters and receive more serendipitous information outside one's predetermined algorithmic path. Secondly, given the increasingly sophisticated techniques of behavioral modification and the characteristics of personalized persuasive technologies, a right not to be deceived in the online context has been introduced. Above all, any experiment that the users may be subjected to with the purpose of promoting engagement ought to be disclosed by platforms and approved by an independent agency. By discussing the above perspectives, the article provided a more comprehensive legal understanding on personalized online services in the light of the GDPR and offered an argumentative basis for further contextualisation and reflection.

References

1. Wachter, S., Mittelstadt, B., Floridi, L.: Why a right to explanation of automated decision-making does not exist in the general data protection regulation. Int. Data Priv. Law **7**(2), 76–99 (2017)
2. Kaltheuner, F., Bietti, E.: Data is power: towards additional guidance on profiling and automated decision-making in the GDPR. J. Inf. Rights Policy Pract. **2**(2) (2018)
3. Hildebrandt, M.: Privacy as protection of the incomputable self: from agnostic to agonistic machine learning. Theor. Inq. Law **19**(1), 83–121 (2019, forthcoming)
4. Rannenberg, K., Royer, D., Deuker, A. (eds.): The Future of Identity in the Information Society: Challenges and Opportunities. Springer, Heidelberg (2009). https://doi.org/10.1007/978-3-642-01820-6
5. Kohl, U., Davey, J., Eisler, J.: Data-driven personalisation and the law-a primer: collective interests engaged by personalisation in markets, politics and law (2019)
6. Gal, M.S.: Algorithmic challenges to autonomous choice. Mich. Telecommun. Technol. Law Rev. **25**, 59–104 (2017)

7. Yeung, K.: Five fears about mass predictive personalisation in an age of surveillance capitalism. Int. Data Priv. Law **8**, 3 (2018, forthcoming)
8. Pariser, E.: The Filter Bubble: How the New Personalized Web is Changing What We Read and How We Think. Penguin, New York (2011)
9. Sunstein, C.R.: #Republic: Divided Democracy in the Age of Social Media. Princeton University Press, Princeton (2017)
10. Harambam, J., Helberger, N., van Hoboken, J.: Democratizing algorithmic news recommenders: how to materialize voice in a technologically saturated media ecosystem. Phil. Trans. R. Soc. A **376**(2133) (2018)
11. Zuiderveen Borgesius, F.J., Trilling, D., Moeller, J., Bodó, B., De Vreese, C.H., Helberger, N.: Should we worry about filter bubbles? Internet policy review. J. Internet Regul. **5**(1), 1–16 (2016)
12. Bodo, B., et al.: Tackling the algorithmic control crisis - the technical, legal, and ethical challenges of research into algorithmic agents. Yale JL Tech. **19**, 133 (2017)
13. Albanie, S., Shakespeare, H., Gunter, T.: Unknowable manipulators: social network curator algorithms. arXiv preprint arXiv:1701.04895 (2017)
14. Gillespie, T.: The relevance of algorithms. In: Media Technologies: Essays on Communication, Materiality, and Society, p. 167 (2014)
15. Yeung, K.: 'Hypernudge': big data as a mode of regulation by design. Inf. Commun. Soc. **20**(1), 118–136 (2017)
16. Colangelo, G., Maggiolino, M.: From fragile to smart consumers: shifting paradigm for the digital era. Comput. Law Secur. Rev. **35**(2), 173–181 (2019)
17. Edwards, L., Veale, M.: Slave to the algorithm: why a right to an explanation is probably not the remedy you are looking for. Duke L. Tech. Rev. **16**, 18 (2017)
18. Turilli, M., Floridi, L.: The ethics of information transparency. Ethics Inf. Technol. **11**(2), 105–112 (2009)
19. Mittelstadt, B.: Automation, algorithms, and politics| auditing for transparency in content personalization systems. Int. J. Commun. **10**, 12 (2016)
20. Burrell, J.: How the machine 'thinks': understanding opacity in machine learning algorithms. Big Data Soc. **3**(1), 1–12 (2016)
21. Tutt, A.: An FDA for algorithms. Social Science Research Network (2016)
22. Goodman, B., Flaxman, S.: European union regulations on algorithmic decision-making and a "right to explanation". arXiv preprint arXiv:1606.08813 (2016)
23. Helberger, N., Borgesius, F.Z., Reyna, A.: The perfect match? A closer look at the relationship between EU consumer law and data protection law. Common Market Law Rev. **54**(5), 1427–1465 (2017)
24. Lynskey, O.: Grappling with "data power": normative nudges from data protection and privacy. Theor. Inq. Law **20**(1), 189–220 (2019)
25. Lanzing, M.: "Strongly recommended" revisiting decisional privacy to judge hypernudging in self-tracking technologies. Philos. Technol. **32**, 549–568 (2018)
26. Eskens, S., Helberger, N., Moeller, J.: Challenged by news personalisation: five perspectives on the right to receive information. J. Media Law **9**(2), 259–284 (2017)
27. Reviglio, U.: Serendipity as an emerging design principle of the infosphere: challenges and opportunities. Ethics Inf. Technol. **21**, 151–166 (2019)
28. Zarsky, T.Z.: Privacy and manipulation in the digital age. Theor. Inq. Law **20**(1), 157–188 (2019)
29. Facebook Newsroom. https://newsroom.fb.com/news/2019/03/why-am-i-seeing-this/. Accessed 07 June 2019
30. Hoffmann, C.P., Lutz, C., Meckel, M., Ranzini, G.: Diversity by choice: applying a social cognitive perspective to the role of public service media in the digital age. Int. J. Commun. **9**(1), 1360–1381 (2015)

31. Karppinen, K.: Media and the paradoxes of pluralism. In: The Media and Social Theory, pp. 27–42 (2008)
32. Helberger, N., Karppinen, K., D'Acunto, L.: Exposure diversity as a design principle for recommender systems. Inf. Commun. Soc. **21**(2), 191–207 (2016)
33. Deibert, R.J.: The road to digital unfreedom: three painful truths about social media. J. Democr. **30**(1), 25–39 (2019)
34. Calo, R.: Digital market manipulation. Geo. Wash. L. Rev. **82**, 995 (2013)
35. Kidron, B., et al.: Disrupted Childhood: The Cost of Persuasive Design. 5rights, London (2018)
36. Fogg, B.J., Lee, E., Marshall, J.: Interactive technology and persuasion. In: The Handbook of Persuasion: Theory and Practice. Sage, Thousand Oaks (2002)
37. Zuboff, S.: Big other: surveillance capitalism and the prospects of an information civilization. J. Inf. Technol. **30**(1), 75–89 (2015)
38. Acquisti, A., Brandimarte, L., Loewenstein, G.: Privacy and human behavior in the age of information. Science **347**(6221), 509–514 (2015)

Software Assisted Privacy Impact Assessment in Interactive Ubiquitous Computing Systems

Alfredo Pérez Fernández[✉] and Guttorm Sindre

Norwegian University of Science and Technology, 7491 Trondheim, NO, Norway
{alfredo.perez.fernandez,guttorm.sindre}@ntnu.no
http://www.perezfer.com/

Abstract. Developing ubiquitous computing systems in compliance with the data protection regulation is a difficult task. The European General Data Protection Regulation requests system developers to apply a privacy-by-design methodology and perform privacy impact assessments throughout the whole development life-cycle. Our proposal is a software assisted process framework that facilitates the analysis of privacy implications in ubiquitous computing systems. This software has been evaluated with students and ubicomp experts.

Keywords: Privacy · Privacy-by-design · Privacy-impact-assessment · Internet-of-Things

1 Introduction

Through history, different advances in technology have tended to facilitate the flow of information of any kind, including personal information. Probably, one of the first and most cited references that confirm this idea is the law review article written by Warren and Brandeis in 1890, *The Right to Privacy*, where they say: "Instantaneous photographs and newspaper enterprise have invaded the sacred precincts of private and domestic life" [32]. Personal computing and the advent of the Internet also supposed a threat to personal privacy since the beginning, as David and Fano mention: "If every significant action is recorded in the mass memory of a community computer system, and programs are available for analyzing them, the daily activities of each individual could become open to scrutiny" [6]. The last great revolution of technology we are witnessing is the Internet of Things (IoT) and it is also raising the concern among the population [4]. The public administration is aiming at maintaining the situation under control by hardening privacy regulations. The new European General Data Protection Regulation (GDPR) (https://www.eugdpr.org/) is applicable from May 25th 2018 and it requires system developers and engineers to acquire a privacy-by-design (PbD) approach during the development and conduct privacy impact assessments (PIA). However, engineers are not given concrete indications of which steps, operations or methods should be used to accomplish that

© IFIP International Federation for Information Processing 2020
Published by Springer Nature Switzerland AG 2020
I. O. Pappas et al. (Eds.): I3E 2019 Workshops, IFIP AICT 573, pp. 60–71, 2020.
https://doi.org/10.1007/978-3-030-39634-3_6

[3, 20, 28]. The focus now is to find strategies to operationalize PbD but there is still a gap between the set of principles and the specific tasks that need to be performed [15]. This gap is even more pronounced if we look at IoT and ubiquitous computing scenarios, since most of the proposed frameworks are developed with PC-based applications in mind, not necessarily suitable for a situation where much of the user's interaction with information systems will be through surrounding *smart things*. Even though there are a large number of methods, models and frameworks designed to guide developers in the analysis of privacy threats in many different scenarios, we find that not many of these tools have been implemented in software to automate the process. Our contribution is a software implementation of the Privacy Aware Transmission Highway (PATH) [25] process framework. This assistant facilitates the evaluation of privacy risks in interactive ubiquitous computing scenarios. This software has been evaluated with students and experts in ubiquitous computing systems.

In Sect. 2 of this paper, we analyze the related work on frameworks for supporting privacy-by-design in HCI and ubiquitous computing. Section 3 gives a brief description of our research methodology. We describe our proposed framework and the adaptation to the software platform in Sect. 4. Section 5 shows the scenarios used for the evaluation of our framework. In Sect. 6 we show the result of the evaluation. Finally, Sect. 7 provides some concluding remarks.

2   Related Work

Iachello [11] identified existing privacy frameworks and methods in the field of HCI, grouped as *guidelines* [8, 9, 17], *process frameworks* [7, 12, 31] and *model frameworks* [13, 18, 30]. STRAP [12] and PriFs [31] focus specifically in requirements elicitation combined with goal oriented analysis methods [5, 16]. Spiekermann [29] proposes a framework specific to *RFID* to identify privacy vulnerabilities based on previously defined privacy targets. Inah Omoronyia [21] developed PSatAnalyser a software tool to assist the analysis of smart objects based architectures from a privacy-by-design perspective. The Software Assurance Technology Center (SATC) developed a software tool [33] that made use of natural language processing techniques to analyze the quality of the requirements document based on the structure of the sentences that described the requirements. They compiled a list of quality attributes that could be measured following this approach. Natural language processing has been proposed, as well, to analyze the privacy policies [1] with respect to *vagueness* with the objective of estimating the perception of privacy risks by the users of the system. In February 2018, the Commission Nationale de l'Informatique et des Libertés (CNIL) released a template to conduct a PIA on an IoT based scenario assisting the evaluator through a multiplatform application (https://www.cnil.fr/en/privacy-impact-assessment-pia). Even thought the templates system provides guidance with respect to the type of information that is needed in order to conduct the PIA, the system does not perform any type of automated verification or validation of the entered information, other than checking that there are no empty fields and providing guidance to the user on how this information should be elaborated. There are a number of limitations in the existing solutions, including, lack of evaluation in real-case scenarios, focus outside of ubiquitous computing scenarios and limited process automation.

3   Research Method

The Design Science Research Methodology (DSRM) [22] has been used to conduct our research, since our motivation was not limited to gaining understanding of privacy-by-design as phenomena, but also to generate an asset that could be used by system engineers to ease the development and analysis of privacy aware ubiquitous computing systems. Our approach is to conduct the six activities of DSRM following the nominal sequential order: *problem identification and motivation, specifying the objective of the solution, design and development, demonstration, evaluation* and *communication*.

- **Problem identification and motivation:** Our initial experience, the analysis of the literature and the findings after iterating over the research process indicate that operationalizing PbD cannot be considered a straightforward process and needs to be assisted in some form.
- **Specifying the objective of the solution:** The overall objective of our research is to develop an asset that can be used by system engineers in the analysis and implementation of ubiquitous computing systems. This objective is divided into two, describing a process framework to guide the engineers and implementing a software that facilitates following such a process.
- **Design and development:** The requirements of the process and the software tool are elicited taking real case scenarios as examples. To do that, we contacted a group of experts and system engineers. The requirement for selecting the candidates was that they needed to be involved on the development of a ubiquitous computing project, excluding system engineers and developers of classical computer based applications. The feedback obtained from the evaluations is used to improve the design of the PATH framework.
- **Demonstration:** To demonstrate the usability of the PATH framework and the PATH assistant, we apply it to a case study application of our own, a prototype implementation of a body coupled communication (BCC) [35] device.
- **Evaluation:** The evaluation of the PATH assistant takes place in the form of empirical experiments where experts apply it to their own projects. The PATH framework is also evaluated in comparison with other benchmark frameworks (the results of this study are pending publication).

During the different iterations, we have constrained our research with two main assumptions. First, we consider the reference model proposed by Ziegeldorf [34] as a starting point, if there is a privacy incidence in a ubiquitous computing scenario it has to take place as the result of the interaction between the user and the surrounding *smart things* (which we prefer to call *interaction mechanisms*). And second, the reason why that privacy incidence is caused by an *interaction mechanism* is because of one or more of its attributes.

4   The Software Assistant

As a proof of concept, a software assistant has been implemented following the guidelines of the *Privacy Aware Transmission Highway* (PATH) framework [25]. The PATH framework consists of four phases that are applied iteratively during design and development: goal-oriented analysis (GOA), elaboration and incorporation of the Privacy Related Interaction Vocabulary (PRIV), PRIV based evaluation and iteration.

4.1   Goal-Oriented Analysis

The PATH assistant starts by requesting the participant to introduce a textual description of the project with the objective of identifying implicit over specifications of the interaction mechanism [26]. The text of the description is compared against a reduced database with preselected interaction mechanisms. This description is compared against the database of interaction mechanisms to identify potential over specifications (Fig. 1). If the PATH assistant detects that the description includes an implicit over specification a warning is displayed with the corresponding term highlighted (In the example given, the expert is introducing an over specification that the application needs to use GPS signals to detect the user's location). The interaction mechanisms are selected separately from a list (or included if they are not present) (Fig. 2).

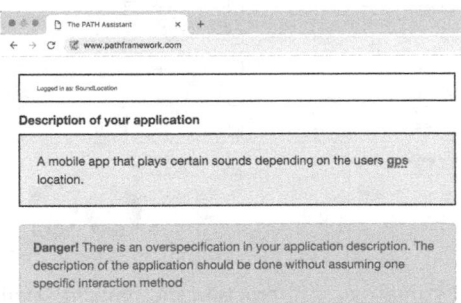

Fig. 1. Screen capture of the automated goa for the high level description of the application

Fig. 2. Selection of the alternative interaction mechanisms

4.2 Privacy Related Interaction Vocabulary

After the GOA phase, a list of attributes for each interaction mechanism are presented to the user (Fig. 3). The user selects those that are applicable to the scenario that was described during the GOA phase. If an attribute of an interaction mechanism is identified, it can be added to the list at this point and it will be considered for the rest of interaction mechanisms. The attributes of the interaction mechanisms can be ranked from 1 (very low) to 5 (very high) depending on how they are estimated by the user.

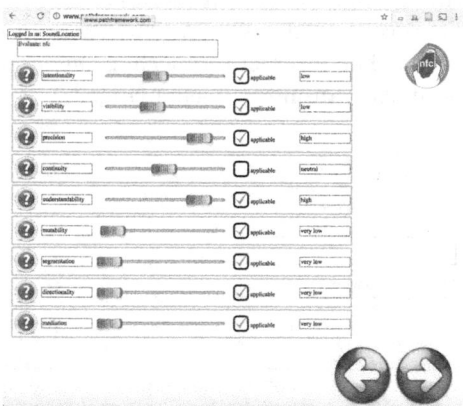

Fig. 3. Estimation of interaction mechanism attributes

4.3 Privacy Impact Assessment

After the value of the attributes have been estimated for each interaction mechanism, another estimation is given for the likelihood of that attribute impacting negatively on users' privacy. The PATH assistant summarizes a chart with the given values and calculated uncertainties that can lead to privacy threats (Fig. 4). Those controversial attributes that present more disagreements and uncertainty are more relevant candidates to be investigated in a user evaluation with a prototype.

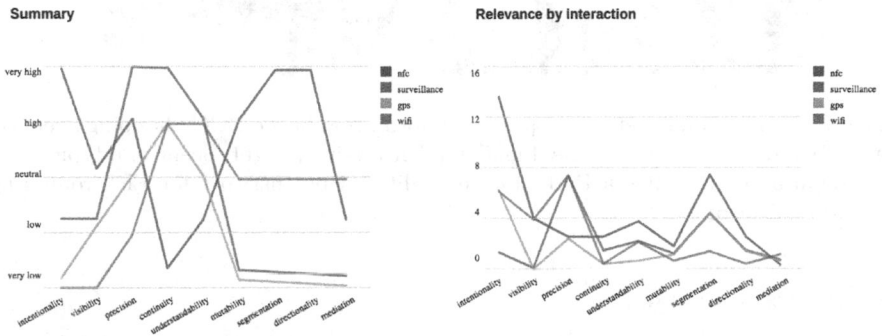

Fig. 4. Overview of attributes estimation (summary) and uncertain attributes that have an impact on privacy (relevance)

4.4 Iteration

Based on the findings from the PIA, it should be possible to replace or modify the interaction mechanisms or their implementations so that the impact on user's privacy is minimized. After any change is made in the design or the implementation of the system, a new iteration needs to be done to evaluate the new changes.

5 Framework Evaluation Scenarios

The PATH assistant has been evaluated with eight experts in four different scenarios, the Body Coupled Communication Based Shopping, the Adressapark, the Museums Visitor Tracker and the Location Based Sound Player.

5.1 Body Coupled Communication Based Shopping Scenario

The Body Coupled Communication (BCC) [23, 35] Based Shopping [14] is a user scenario utilized at Linköping University (LiU) to frame their research. In this scenario, a retail store customer holds a BCC enabled wearable or mobile device that receives random product information when she touches a smart tag situated in the shelf next to the product label (Fig. 5, left).

Fig. 5. Left, A customer retrieving product information in the BCC Shopping Scenario (Image facilitated by Acreo, Ri.Se, Linköping University), Right: Scene of a typical use case scenario of the Adressa Park (Image facilitated by Institutt for Elektronikk og Telekommunikasjon, IET)

5.2   Adressaparken

Adressaparken [19] is an interactive media space developed as a collaboration between the municipality of Trondheim (Trondheim kommune), the regional newspaper Adressa (Adresseavisen), and the Norwegian University of Science and Technology (NTNU). An audiovisual storytelling content is projected on the ground while the user walks near the area (Fig. 5, right). A set of 12 boxes contains different sensors (temperature, air, light, sun, noise and pollution) and each box holds a Raspberry Pi v2 with an attached night vision infrared camera.

5.3   Museum Visitors Tracker

The Museum Visitors Tracker project was originated as a collaboration between the Technology Transfer Office (TTO) at NTNU and the Science Museum in Trondheim (Vitensenteret). Vitensenteret had already implemented a computer vision system to track visitors and estimate their engagement based on their facial expression (Fig. 6). The goal was to implement a privacy-friendly tracking system to obtain statistical information about visitors (age range, gender and preference group) linked to the engagement metrics (time spent) for each exhibition. To achieve this goal, it was planned to evaluate the use of BCC as an interaction mechanism in a similar way as proposed by [24].

5.4   Location Based Sound Player

A *do-it-yourself* (DIY) practitioner started a personal project to conceptualize an augmented noise application [10] similar to the echoes app (https://www. echoes.xyz). The idea of the project was to create a collection of geographically tagged sounds that could be played when the user had visited the associated locations. Since the project was at an early stage only a few high level decisions were specified. Whether the sounds had to be played immediately without supervision of the user or not was to be decided in later stages of development.

Fig. 6. Example of visitors tracking based on computer vision and facial expression

6 Evaluation Results

In our evaluation of the GOA phase with the PATH assistant, two of the eight experts introduced a high level description of an application that was detected by the system as over specified, one for the BCC Shopping (for the term BCC) and one for the Location Based Sound Player (for the term GPS). A total of 24 interaction mechanisms were selected by the experts, an average of three each. For the attributes estimations a total of 216 attributes estimations were given by the eight experts. Each estimation ranged from 1 (very low) to 5 (very high). They gave an average estimation of 3.59 with a standard deviation of 1.27 for customer related attributes (CA), intentionality, visibility, precision and understandability, and an average estimation of 2.57 with a standard deviation of 1.63 for non customer related attributes (NCA), continuity, mutability, segmentation, directionality and mediation (Fig. 7). From the given attribute estimations, 38 (18%) were accounted as a strong disagreement. We consider a strong disagreement in the estimation of two attributes when two team members give opposed values (high or very high against low or very low). If the team members participate in the same project, the disagreements are considered internal and, if the project is different, the disagreements are considered external. In the Adressa Park four experts participated in the evaluation. Three of them, selected video recording as interaction mechanism, since that was already specified as a requirement for the project. From the nine estimations they assigned to the attributes, five were in disagreement with the estimations provided by the rest of the team (internal disagreements) (Fig. 8).

The experts gave a total of 24 estimations for the impact on privacy. The average for the CAs was 3.6 with standard deviation 1.27. The average for the NCAs was 2.57 with a standard deviation of 1.63 (Fig. 9). As can be observed from the difference in the standard deviation, experts tend to disagree more when estimating attributes or impact on privacy for NCAs. Another observation is that estimated impact on privacy on CAs is lower than the estimated corresponding

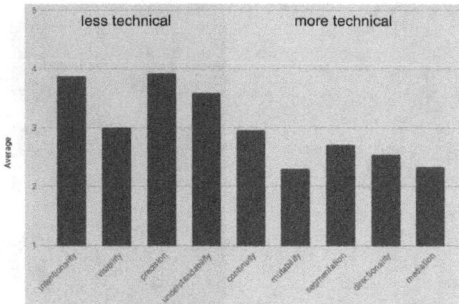

Fig. 7. Overall 216 attribute estimations provided by the experts

Attribute	Expert (W)	Expert (J)	Expert (A)	Expert (Z)
intentionality	4	1	4	0
visibility	1	4	3	0
precision	5	4	4	0
continuity	5	4	3	0
understandability	4	4	5	0
mutability	5	1	1	0
segmentation	5	1	5	0
directionality	1	1	3	0
mediation	5	1	1	0

Fig. 8. Attribute estimations for the video recording interaction mechanism provided by the Addressaparken team.

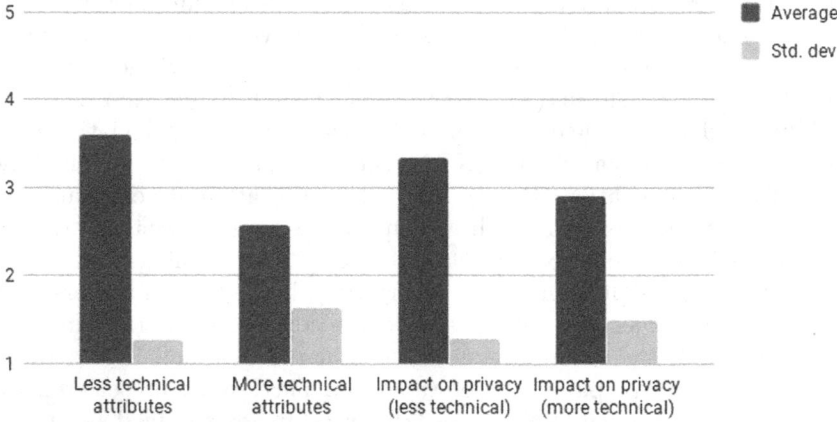

Fig. 9. Average estimated attributes and average estimated privacy impact

attribute, while the behaviour is the opposite for NCAs, where estimated impact on privacy is higher than the corresponding estimated value of the corresponding attribute. Our interpretation of this phenomena is that the practitioners tend to give lower values to attributes that are more difficult to understand. We also conclude that terms they understand less are associated with higher risks.

7   Conclusions and Future Work

In this paper we have demonstrated our approach to automate the PIA of ubiquitous computing systems. We have observed that it is possible to assist the process of over specification detection based on the analysis of high level system descriptions. Disagreements in the estimation of interaction mechanisms attributes can be used, as well, as indicators of uncertainties in the PIA of a system. Our prototype, the PATH assistant, only includes a basic search through a small database to identify names of interaction mechanisms. A much better performance in the automated detection of over specified requirements could be achieved by incorporating a more thorough natural language processing [27]. Elaborating new terms that can be incorporated to the PRIV is a difficult task since the attributes of the interaction mechanisms are not easily perceived and some are not so applicable to the privacy domain. We are considering the incorporation of two new terms in the initial PRIV, *wearability* (when the interaction mechanism is being carried by the user and this could expose the location of the user, i.e. *RFIDs* used in clothes) [2] and *personability* (when the interaction mechanism is tightly associated with a person or group of people, their identities or personal information, i.e. mobile devices are innocuous when bought new but, as they are used, they absorb more and more personal information after the user logs in with different accounts, synchronizes the device with other previous devices or take some pictures) [18]. The current implementation of the PATH assistant is in the process of being adapted as an Asana (https://www.asana.com/) plugin. It makes use of the project description to detect potential over specifications and generates a report based on identified risks for user's privacy caused by different interaction mechanisms. This implementation will be used for future empirical evaluations with experts and students.

References

1. Bhatia, J., Breaux, T.D., Reidenberg, J.R., Norton, T.B.: A theory of vagueness and privacy risk perception. In: 2016 IEEE 24th International Requirements Engineering Conference (RE), pp. 26–35. IEEE (2016)
2. Bylund, M., Höök, K., Pommeranz, A.: Pieces of identity. In: Proceedings of the 5th Nordic Conference on Human-Computer Interaction: Building Bridges, NordiCHI 2008, pp. 427–430. ACM, New York (2008)
3. Cavoukian, A., Staff, C.: Operationalizing privacy by design. Commun. ACM 55(9), 7–7 (2012)
4. Chellappan, V., Sivalingam, K.M.: Security and privacy in the Internet of Things. In: Buyya, R., Vahid Dastjerdi, A. (eds.) Internet of Things, pp. 183–200. Morgan Kaufmann, January 2016
5. Darimont, R., Delor, E., Massonet, P., van Lamsweerde, A.: GRAIL/KAOS: an environment for goal-driven requirements engineering. In: Proceedings of the 19th International Conference on Software Engineering, pp. 612–613. ACM (1997)
6. David, Jr., E.E., Fano, R.M.: Some thoughts about the social implications of accessible computing. In: Proceedings of the Fall Joint Computer Conference, Part I, AFIPS 1965 (Fall, Part I), Las Vegas, Nevada, 30-November–1 December 1965, pp. 243–247. ACM, New York (1965)

7. ElShekeil, S.A., Laoyookhong, S.: GDPR Privacy by Design (2017)
8. Garfinkel, S.: Adopting fair information practices to low cost RFID systems. In: Privacy in Ubiquitous Computing Workshop (2002)
9. Gellman, R.: Fair information practices: a basic history (2017)
10. Hastrup, S.: Augmented noise - exploring mobile technology design as an enabler of social interaction and spatial awareness (2017)
11. Iachello, G., Abowd, G.D.: Privacy and proportionality: adapting legal evaluation techniques to inform design in ubiquitous computing. In: Proceedings of the SIGCHI conference on Human factors in computing systems, pp. 91–100. ACM (2005)
12. Jensen, C., Tullio, J., Potts, C., Mynatt, E.D.: STRAP: a structured analysis framework for privacy (2005)
13. Jiang, X., Landay, J.A.: Modeling privacy control in context-aware systems. IEEE Pervasive Comput. **1**(3), 59–63 (2002)
14. Kazim, M.I.: Variation-aware system design simulation methodology for capacitive BCC transceivers. Ph.D. thesis, Linköping University Electronic Press (2015)
15. Kroener, I., Wright, D.: A strategy for operationalizing privacy by design. Inf. Soc. **30**(5), 355–365 (2014)
16. Kung, A., et al.: A privacy engineering framework for the Internet of Things. In: Leenes, R., van Brakel, R., Gutwirth, S., De Hert, P. (eds.) Data Protection and Privacy: (In)visibilities and Infrastructures. LGTS, vol. 36, pp. 163–202. Springer, Cham (2017). https://doi.org/10.1007/978-3-319-50796-5_7
17. Langheinrich, M.: Privacy by design—principles of privacy-aware ubiquitous systems. In: Abowd, G.D., Brumitt, B., Shafer, S. (eds.) UbiComp 2001. LNCS, vol. 2201, pp. 273–291. Springer, Heidelberg (2001). https://doi.org/10.1007/3-540-45427-6_23
18. Lehikoinen, J.T., Lehikoinen, J., Huuskonen, P.: Understanding privacy regulation in ubicomp interactions. Pers. Ubiquitous Comput. **12**(8), 543–553 (2008)
19. Mansilla, W.A., Perkis, A.: Multiuse playspaces: mediating expressive community places. IEEE MultiMedia **24**(1), 12–16 (2017)
20. Martín, Y.S., Alamo, J.Md., Yelmo, J.C.: Engineering privacy requirements valuable lessons from another realm. In: 2014 IEEE 1st International Workshop on Evolving Security and Privacy Requirements Engineering (ESPRE), pp. 19–24, August 2014
21. Omoronyia, I.: Privacy engineering in dynamic settings. In: 2017 IEEE/ACM 39th International Conference on Software Engineering Companion (ICSE-C), pp. 297–299. IEEE (2017)
22. Peffers, K., Tuunanen, T., Rothenberger, M.A., Chatterjee, S.: A design science research methodology for information systems research. J. Manag. Inf. Syst. **24**(3), 45–77 (2007)
23. Pérez Fernández, A.: Towards the tangible hyperlink. In: The Seventh International Conference on Advances in Computer-Human Interactions, ACHI 2014, pp. 17–20 (2014)
24. Pérez Fernández, A., Sindre, G.: Protecting user privacy when sharing mobile devices: research in progress. In: Norsk informasjonssikkerhetskonferanse (NISK), vol. 7, November 2014
25. Pérez Fernández, A., Sindre, G.: The privacy aware transmission highway framework. Int. J. Inf. Priv. Secur. Integrity **3**(4), 327–350 (2018)
26. Pérez Fernández, A., Sindre, G.: Mitigating the impact on users' privacy caused by over specifications in the design of IoT applications. Sens. Spec. Issue Secur. Priv. Trustworthiness Sens. Netw. Internet Things **19**(19), 4318 (2019). (1–20)

27. Sizov, G.: Automating Problem Analysis Using Knowledge Extracted from Text (2017)
28. Spiekermann, S.: The challenges of privacy by design. Commun. ACM **55**(7), 38–40 (2012)
29. Spiekermann, S.: The RFID PIA - developed by industry, endorsed by regulators. In: Wright, D., De Hert, P. (eds.) Privacy Impact Assessment. Law, Governance and Technology Series, vol. 6, pp. 323–346. Springer, Dordrecht (2012). https://doi.org/10.1007/978-94-007-2543-0_15
30. Spiekermann, S., Cranor, L.F.: Engineering privacy. IEEE Trans. Softw. Eng. **35**(1), 67–82 (2009)
31. Thomas, K., Bandara, A.K., Price, B.A., Nuseibeh, B.: Distilling privacy requirements for mobile applications. In: Proceedings of the 36th International Conference on Software Engineering, pp. 871–882. ACM (2014)
32. Warren, S.D., Brandeis, L.D.: The right to privacy. Harvard law review, pp. 193–220 (1890)
33. Wilson, W.M., Rosenberg, L.H., Hyatt, L.E.: Automated analysis of requirement specifications. In: Proceedings of the 19th International Conference on Software Engineering, pp. 161–171. ACM (1997)
34. Ziegeldorf, J.H., Morchon, O.G., Wehrle, K.: Privacy in the Internet of Things: threats and challenges. Secur. Commun. Netw. **7**(12), 2728–2742 (2014)
35. Zimmerman, T.G.: Personal area networks: near-field intrabody communication. IBM Syst. J. **35**(3.4), 609–617 (1996)

Facilitating GDPR Compliance: The H2020 BPR4GDPR Approach

Georgios V. Lioudakis[1($\boxtimes$)], Maria N. Koukovini[1],
Eugenia I. Papagiannakopoulou[1], Nikolaos Dellas[2], Kostas Kalaboukas[2],
Renata Medeiros de Carvalho[3], Marwan Hassani[3], Lorenzo Bracciale[4],
Giuseppe Bianchi[4], Adrian Juan-Verdejo[5], Spiros Alexakis[5],
Francesca Gaudino[6], Davide Cascone[6], and Paolo Barracano[7]

[1] ICT abovo P.C., Iridanou 20, 11528 Athens, Greece
{georgios.lioudakis,mariza.koukovini,
eugenia.papagiannakopoulou}@ict-abovo.gr
[2] SingularLogic S.A., Achaias 3 & Trizinias, 14564 Kifisia, Greece
nikolaos.dellas@gmail.com,kkalaboukas@singularlogic.eu
[3] Eindhoven University of Technology,
De Groene Loper 5, Eindhoven, The Netherlands
{R.Medeiros.de.Carvalho,M.Hassani}@tue.nl
[4] University of Rome "Tor Vergata", Via del Politecnico 1, 00133 Rome, Italy
{lorenzo.bracciale,giuseppe.bianchi}@uniroma2.it
[5] CAS Software AG, CAS Weg 1-5, 76131 Karlsruhe, Germany
{adrian.juan,Spiros.Alexakis}@cas.de
[6] Baker McKenzie, Piazza Filippo Meda 3, 20121 Milano, Italy
{Francesca.Gaudino,Davide.Cascone}@bakermckenzie.com
[7] Innovazioni Tecnologiche SRL, Via Arcidiacono Giovanni 43, 70124 Bari, Italy
P.Barracano@intempra.com

Abstract. This paper outlines the approach followed by the H2020 BPR4GDPR project to facilitate GDPR compliance. Its goal is to provide a holistic framework able to support end-to-end GDPR-compliant intra- and inter-organisational ICT-enabled processes at various scales, while also being generic enough, fulfilling operational requirements covering diverse application domains. To this end, solutions proposed by BPR4GDPR cover the full process lifecycle addressing major challenges and priorities posed by the Regulation.

Keywords: GDPR compliance · Data protection · Process management · Privacy-aware access and usage control · Process mining

1 Introduction

The General Data Protection Regulation (GDPR) [1] comprises a milestone in data protection, creating an environment able to cope with the technological and business reality, and provide for the protection of privacy. However, organisations declare difficulties in GDPR implementation, despite the resources and

© IFIP International Federation for Information Processing 2020
Published by Springer Nature Switzerland AG 2020
I. O. Pappas et al. (Eds.): I3E 2019 Workshops, IFIP AICT 573, pp. 72–78, 2020.
https://doi.org/10.1007/978-3-030-39634-3_7

money spent, The challenges, either technical or organisational, include, among others: interpretation of GDPR requirements; operational adaptation towards compliant business practices; holistic data views and processing actions inventory; enforcement of security means; management of the relations with third parties and the data subjects, and enforcement of rights thereof; last but not least, significant resources are required and, whereas big companies may have resources to invest, this does not necessarily apply for SMEs.

This paper presents the approach followed by the H2020 BPR4GDPR project[1], towards a new GDPR compliance paradigm. BPR4GDPR is building tools for facilitating the implementation of the appropriate measures, particularly by SMEs, to ensure that data collection and processing is performed in accordance with the GDPR. The BPR4GDPR compliance approach consists in automatically re-engineering workflows, being business processes or low-level service compositions, so that they become compliant *by design*, whereas enforcement is supported by an easy to deploy "compliance toolkit", providing the fundamental common functions for cryptography, access management, and enforcement of data subjects' rights. In the following, Sect. 2 outlines the operational phases towards an holistic approach to GDPR compliance, whereas Sect. 3 provides an overview of the technical architecture of the project.

2   BPR4GDPR Operational Phases

The BPR4GDPR process lifecycle (Fig. 1) consists of six main stages, numbered 1 6, dealing with process design or discovery, its analysis and re-design, implementation, execution and monitoring. Two additional phases, vertical to the process lifecycle, are devised for the initial "set-up" actions (Phase 0) and for the operations that are either horizontal, or process-independent (Phase 7). The eight phases are summarised in the following.

Phase 0: Set-Up. This consists in setting up the base elements for system operation. These include the specification of the information models, the classification of data and other resources, the assignment of roles and attributes, the definition of purposes behind data collection and processing, and the specification of policies and rules that should govern the system operation.

Phase 1: Process Identification. This concerns the definition of process models, by: (i) process discovery mechanisms, based on process logs; (ii) definition of procedures using the appropriate graphical tool. Either way, the outcome will be process model specifications providing for the incorporation, by later phases, of sophisticated constraints enforceable at run-time.

Phase 2: Process Analysis. This concerns the policy-based analysis of a process model in order to identify the risks, flaws and points of non-compliance. This

[1] H2020 BPR4GDPR: Business Process Re-engineering and functional toolkit for GDPR compliance, contract number 787149 (01/05/2018 – 30/04/2021) http://www.bpr4gdpr.eu/.

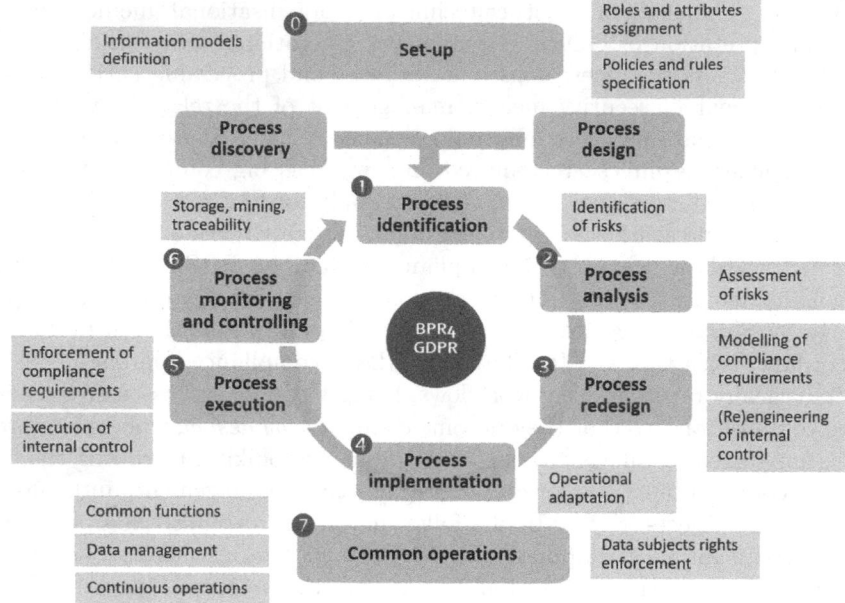

Fig. 1. BPR4GDPR operational phases.

way, process models shall be evaluated and verified as regards their compliance with the GDPR. This phase entails a highly expressive policy framework, considering a variety of aspects, such as attributes, context, dependencies between actions and participating entities therein.

Phase 3: Process Redesign. This phase complements process analysis, by providing for the automatic transformation of non-compliant process models, so that they are rendered inherently privacy-aware before being deployed for execution. It is supported by a Compliance Metamodel, a comprehensive process modelling technology able to capture advanced privacy provisions.

Phase 4: Process Implementation. This concerns the effective enactment of GDPR-compliant processes, mainly as regards two aspects. The first entails a comprehensive set of tools able to support the requirements arising from GDPR (data handling, data subjects' involvement, etc.). The second is related to the alignment of modelled processes with the actual infrastructure of the organisation; grounded primarily on the BPR4GDPR semantic foundations, it will enable refinement and adaptation of the models to each organisation's reality.

Phase 5: Process Execution. This extends Phase 4 by ensuring compliant process execution, following the configuration set forth. That is, it is mainly during this phase when the mechanisms towards real-time privacy protection are applied and respective provisions are enforced.

Phase 6: Process Monitoring and Controlling. This concerns the use of process mining for process ex post analysis, in order to ensure that specified policies are indeed enforced, fostering accountability. Furthermore, such techniques will enable automatically improving process models over time.

Phase 7: Common Operations. This refers to operations that are not (necessarily) part of a process lifecycle, but are executed asynchronously to processes or are independent thereof. They fall in different categories, including: (i) functions that are supportive to all phases (e.g., authorisation mechanisms); (ii) enforcement of data subject rights; (iii) data management functions; (iv) continuous operations, such as risk estimation, logging, etc.

3   Architecture

In order to cover its functional needs towards GDPR compliance and cope with the operational phases described in Sect. 2, BPR4GDPR has specified the system architecture highlighted in Fig. 2. As illustrated, the BPR4GDPR architecture is divided in four "quadrants", reflecting different groups of functionalities. In the following, the main principles and technical ideas are summarised.

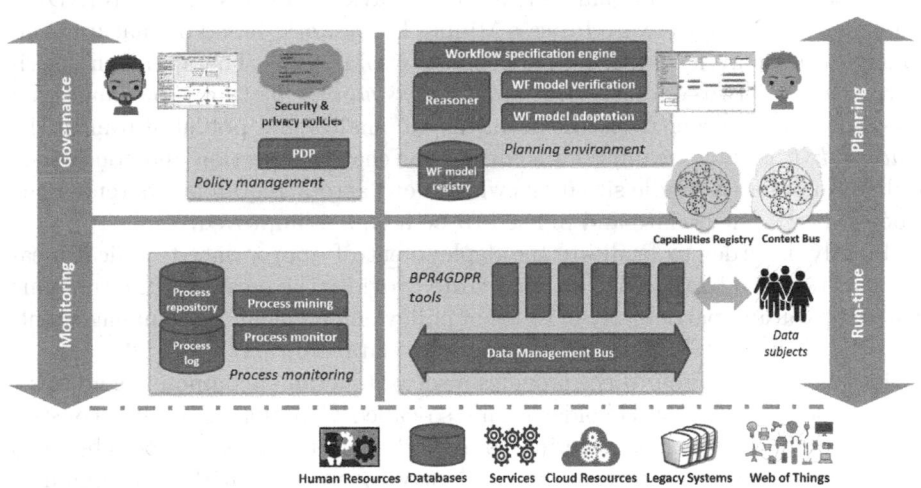

Fig. 2. BPR4GDPR architecture.

Governance provides all functions related to policy management, representing the Policy Decision Point (PDP) of the system. In BPR4GDPR, policies hold a dual role: (i) they provide the means for system governance, in the sense that they set the rules that regulate the operation of BPR4GDPR components; (ii) they comprise the knowledge base that feeds the procedure of process re-engineering, towards *by design* compliant process models.

To this end, BPR4GDPR develops a comprehensive Policy-based Access and Usage Control framework, tailored for the needs of highly distributed environments, involving multiple stakeholders, even in cross-border scenarios. The ground technology is the academic work described in [8], along with the respective software prototype, whereas policies are grounded on the Compliance Ontology, providing a high-level codification of GDPR into concepts that need to be taken into consideration by the policy framework.

Planning concerns the specification of workflow models and their verification as regards compliance with the GDPR, and their subsequent transformation, if needed, so that they become compliant *by design*. The first step in this direction is facilitated by tools allowing their description in a way that effectively guides their execution, while also being expressive enough to capture associated provisions; these tools are grounded upon prior academic work of BPR4GDPR researchers [7]. Further, in order to automatically incorporate policies as part of workflow design, the BPR4GDPR approach involves sophisticated means for the evaluation of process specifications against a number of compliance aspects. Their main aim is to control access to, usage of, and flow of information and prevent illegitimate activity, as well as to determine whether critical tasks are properly included and, if not, impose their execution.

Monitoring deals with process mining and monitoring with the aim to identify discrepancies between compliant and actual behaviour. To this end, BPR4GDPR implements a Privacy-Aware Process Mining Framework, based on mature technology brought by its partners, particularly ProM[2] [2,6]. The approach is primarily based on two concepts: *streaming process mining* [5], that allows analysing real-time data in order to detect problems, anomalies and potential frauds; the *concept drift* issue [4], calling for solutions for change detection and continuous update, in order to handle situations where new factors/requirements render the process model out-of-date and in need to be adapted/improved.

Finally, in order to facilitate the deployment of appropriate technical measures, as required by the GDPR, **Run-time** provides the means for the run-time system operation, particularly in terms of policy enforcement, data management, privacy-enhancing tools, and interaction with data subjects.

In this context, the project provides a set of functional components addressing common needs of stakeholders. This so-called Compliance Toolkit consists of modular functions that, fostering "plug and play" to the extent possible, will be easy to deploy, easy to configure and easy to integrate within an organisation's ICT environment, while they will be automatically incorporated to process chains, as a result of re-engineering. The toolkit's modules fall into three families:

- Privacy-enhancing technologies, particularly cryptographic tools, devised for data and communications confidentiality, anonymisation and pseudonymisation, as well as enforcement of access rights by cryptographic means [3].
- Data management tools that, by means of data access and usage management, provide for controlling data handling, including retention and storage,

---

[2] http://www.promtools.org/.

pre- and post-processing, etc. A core position is held by the Data Management Bus (Fig. 2), comprising the main Policy Enforcement Point (PEP).
– User-centered tools, providing for the enforcement of the data subjects' rights, including information and notification, consent, and consideration of own preferences as regards data handling.

4   Conclusion

In the rapidly maturing privacy market, currently available solutions do not appear to sufficiently cover important GDPR aspects, while process orientation has not been extensively incorporated either. In order to address such shortcomings, BPR4GDPR aims to offer *privacy-by-design* throughout the entire process lifecycle, based on a broad spectrum of innovations. These will concern, at a first stage, process analysis and redesign, i.e., automatic verification of process models according to GDPR provisions but also transformation of non-conformant ones. Further, a compliance toolkit will be devised encompassing sophisticated functionalities, such as cryptography, data handling and notification mechanisms, as well as user-centered tools ensuring consent, but also the exercise of other data subjects' rights. From another perspective, process mining will be used for process discovery, process monitoring and controlling, enabling a posteriori analysis and compliance check of running processes. BPR4GDPR will thus provide a user-friendly environment for the definition of inherently GDPR-compliant processes and the automatic inclusion of necessary measures, relieving end-users from the considerable operational burden of continuous compliance assessment, and preventing business and other risks associated with potential violations.

Acknowledgment. This research is being supported by the European Commission, in the frame of the H2020 BPR4GDPR project (Grant No. 787149). The authors would like to express their gratitude to the Consortium for the fruitful discussions.

References

1. Regulation (EU) 2016/679 of the European Parliament and of the Council of 27 April 2016 on the protection of natural persons with regard to the processing of personal data and on the free movement of such data, and repealing Directive 95/46/EC (General Data Protection Regulation) (May 2016)
2. van der Aalst, W.M.P., et al.: ProM: the process mining toolkit. Proc. BPM Demos. **489**(31), 2 (2009)
3. Bethencourt, J., Sahai, A., Waters, B.: Ciphertext-policy attribute-based encryption. In: 2007 IEEE Symposium on Security and Privacy (SP 2007) (May 2007)
4. Hassani, M.: Concept drift detection of event streams using an adaptive window. In: ECMS 2019 Proceedings of the 33rd European Council for Modeling and Simulation (to appear) (June 2019)
5. Hassani, M., et al.: Efficient process discovery from event streams using sequential pattern mining. In: IEEE Symposium Series on Computational Intelligence, SSCI 2015, Cape Town, South Africa, December 7–10, 2015, pp. 1366–1373 (2015)

6. Kalenkova, A.A., de Leoni, M., van der Aalst, W.M.P.: Discovering, analyzing and enhancing BPMN models using ProM. In: Proceedings of the BPM Demo (2014)
7. Koukovini, M.N.: Inherent privacy awareness in service-oriented architectures. Ph. D. thesis, National Technical University of Athens (2014)
8. Papagiannakopoulou, E.I.: Semantic access control model for distributed environments. Ph. D. thesis, National Technical University of Athens (2014)

Designing a Privacy Dashboard
for a Smart Manufacturing Environment

Felix Mannhardt[1,2(✉)], Manuel Oliveira[1,2], and Sobah Abbas Petersen[2]

[1] KIT-AR, London, UK
{felix.mannhardt,manuel.oliveira}@kit-ar.com
[2] SINTEF Digital, Trondheim, Norway
sobah.petersen@sintef.no

Abstract. In smart manufacturing environments sensors are collecting data about work processes. This data likely also contains references to actions of a single worker, which can be considered personal data. Privacy dashboards convey information on what personal data is stored by a system and provide means for users of a system to control what personal data is shared according to their needs. Dashboards put the control over their personal data in the hands of the users. However, to act as a trust building component, the dashboard needs to convey or mediate the trade-off between the user's privacy and the benefits of data sharing. This work describes the design process and an elicitation of preliminary requirements for a privacy dashboard that is developed in the context of the H2020 project HUMAN Manufacturing.

Keywords: Privacy · Dashboard · Smart manufacturing · Industry 4.0

1 Introduction

Smart manufacturing environments make use of data collected through smart sensor technologies (e.g., wearables, IoT) in the context of the Industry 4.0 paradigm [5,10]. Such technologies promise to increase productivity and support operators in their increasingly complex work as simple routine tasks are being automated. Much of the success of these new technologies depends on the availability of data related to the worker and the workplace. However, collecting data from and about workers in organisations is not a trivial task. Ensuring the safe, secure and correct use of the data by authorized people is one of the difficult challenges faced by many organisation in our increasingly data-centric world. Organisations need to build trust among their workers and trust in the organisation as well as making the services beneficial enough to convince workers

---

This research has received funding from the European Union's H2020 research and innovation programme under grant agreement no. 723737 (HUMAN).

© IFIP International Federation for Information Processing 2020
Published by Springer Nature Switzerland AG 2020

I. O. Pappas et al. (Eds.): I3E 2019 Workshops, IFIP AICT 573, pp. 79–85, 2020.
https://doi.org/10.1007/978-3-030-39634-3_8

of the value in sharing their data. Consequently, a value and trust-based app-roach to data collection and use of data is necessary to achieve the purpose of facilitating trust between workers and their organisation.

This may require looking at trust and privacy from different perspectives, in particular, from the perspectives of the different stakeholders, when designing the various systems and technologies that are used by the workers. Privacy and trust in the workplace and in a working context not only require trust in a specific technology, but also in the organisation itself [2]. EU's General Data Protection Regulation (GDRP) [1] advocates privacy by design and privacy by default, which require considering privacy from the initial design stages and throughout the complete development process of new products, processes or services that involve gathering and processing personal data. It also means that when a system or service includes choices for the individual on how much personal data he or she shares with others, the default settings should be the most privacy friendly ones.

When considering productivity tools in the workplace, a particular tool that could be used to foster trust and accommodate regulatory pressure is a Privacy Dashboard[1], which put emphasis not only on the technological perspective (i.e., the ability to review/change one's own privacy), but also on the organisational and social perspectives. Privacy dashboards have been previously extensively researched, e.g. as a mechanism to enhance user control in the Privacy Bridges project [4], in the context of GDPR [9], or referred to as Privacy Mirrors in [7].

The main aim of this paper is to report our experience in designing a privacy dashboard for workers in the manufacturing industry, driven by the trust and privacy framework [6] developed within the context of the H2020 research project HUman MANufacturing[2]. The project researched the use of digital technologies (e.g., augmented reality and exoskeletons) to physically and cognitively enhance the workers on the shopfloor, which implied the use of wearable devices to collate information on the worker and their work context. Clearly, the gathering of personal data raises serious privacy concerns and hard challenges on workers' trust in both the digital solution and the organisation. So far, less attention has been paid to such an application area compared to the use of services in a private context (e.g. social networks).

The remainder of this paper is structured as follows. In the next Sect. 2, the smart manufacturing environment in HUMAN is described. In Sect. 3, we present the initial design process of the Privacy Dashboard and Sect. 4 concludes the paper.

2   Smart Manufacturing in HUMAN

The HUMAN project aims to digitally enhance the worker on the shopfloor to support them in their work, assisting them in mitigating any productivity losses resulting from either physical or cognitive fatigue whilst contributing to

---

[1] https://www.privacypatterns.org/patterns/Privacy-dashboard.
[2] http://humanmanufacturing.eu/.

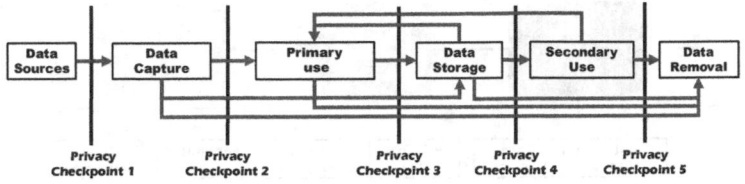

Fig. 1. Overview of data life-cycle transitions of the HTPF. Figure adapted from [6].

the worker's greater well-being. This is achieved by collating physiological data from the worker through wearable sensors and combining the production context (e.g. tasks, workplace) in which the worker is embedded. The primary use of the captured data is to reason, via different machine learning techniques, on how best to support the worker. However, the captured and processed data can also be re-used after being stored for analysis purposes, which may be an example for secondary use of the data. An example for such indirect usage is the improvement of workplaces or work processes by identifying bottlenecks in the production process when analysing aggregated historical data.

The underlying premise in HUMAN is to gather as much data as possible from the worker, their behavior and activities, to determine the best contextual support. However, this raises serious concerns over privacy and trust that may undermine the acceptance of the HUMAN system by the workers. As such, the HUMAN Trust and Privacy Framework (HTPF) was developed to support the dialogue amongst the different stakeholders in smart manufacturing work environments [6]. The HTPF (Fig. 1) is based on existing work on privacy in information systems (e.g. the design strategies in [3]) but puts emphasis on the lifecycle and transitions of data and a set of privacy checkpoints.

For each checkpoint, the HTPF provides guidelines for designers and developers of digital solutions to take the necessary precautions and actions for ensuring that the privacy of individuals and organisations are safeguarded, which will contribute to foster trust among the workers and within the organisation. The checkpoints serve as gateways, where the processing of the data may be different after that point. The main users of this framework will be designers and developers of IT systems and services and the individuals, groups or organisational units that will use and/or deploy these systems and services. From an end user's perspective, the HTPF illustrated in Fig. 1 can help to increase users' awareness about privacy and increase their knowledge of their rights to privacy and when and what they should expect of the services they use.

3   Design of the Privacy Dashboard

A key design principle adopted in the HUMAN project was the co-creation methodology, involving the different stakeholders from inception of ideas to the deployment of the prototypes for field evaluation. A strong requirement, driven by the users and supported by management, was the idea of a Privacy Dashboard

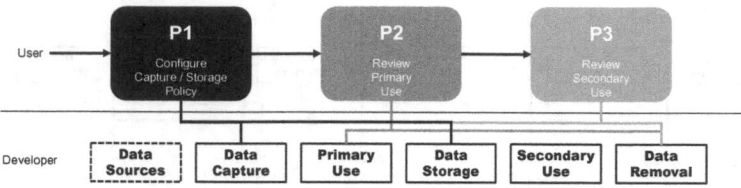

Fig. 2. Three main touch-points (P1-P3) with the Privacy Dashboard and their link to the HTPF.

that first emerged during a workshop on Opportunities and Threats with use case partners in a user study with the HUMAN consortium [8]. The potential threats related to organisations collecting significant amounts of personal data were clear, which would invalidate the potential benefits. The main reason for this was related to the potential risk of privacy violations and breach of trust. While they could appreciate the value of data collection and the potential benefits that could lead to, the representatives of the end-user organisations expressed the need for the workers to have control of their privacy settings and the need for transparency. Given these needs from the workers, and the requirement to be GDPR compliant, the idea of a privacy dashboard emerged. In the case of the HUMAN Knowledge In Time service, which uses AR to support the operator on the shop-floor, the aim of the Privacy Dashboard is to provide data owners, (e.g. workers), transparency about how their data is used as well as the option to limit the future usage of their data or delete previously stored data here and now.

3.1 Design Process

After the initial workshop, and aligned with the co-creation methodology, several workshops were conducted involving all the relevant stakeholders with privacy being a prominent feature continuously addressed in the development of the KIT service. The initial phase of the design was the identification and sketching of use cases, based on the analysis of the needs and requirements that emerged from the co-creation workshops conducted with the HUMAN consortium partners. Then, we used the HTPF to review each use case sketch based on the framework and its guidelines. Where relevant, we refined the existing use case sketches to ensure privacy by design, in the light of the framework; or defined new use case sketches to clarify and add detail to the original use cases.

The use of HTPF supported both the design of the dashboard and the dialogue with end-users. However, our studies within the HUMAN project show that the users found the framework useful in understanding their needs for privacy and consequences related to sharing their data. However, the user or worker is not likely interested in the subtle details of the privacy of the system, but rather in the privacy threat vs. benefits trade-off. Consequently, to facilitate the dialogue further with the users, the decision was made to simplify the HTPF for end users of the KIT solution, resulting in the diagram depicted in Fig. 2, where we identified three main touch-points through which workers would inter-act with the Privacy Dashboard. Nonetheless, each of the touch-points can be associated with one or more stages of the HTPF, which can help a developer in realising a concrete instance of the proposed dashboard. Each of the touch-points addresses one or more use cases of the privacy dashboard and, next to revealing already stored information or allowing to configure the applicable policies, also highlights the advantages as well as the threats of sharing one's personal data. In our preliminary analysis, we identified 9 use cases along with requirements for the Privacy Dashboard, which we group as follows to the three touch-points: Touch-point P1 (Configure Capture/Storage Policy) with use cases:

- Configure data capture policy (P1-1),
- Configure primary usage policy (P1-2),
- Configure data storage policy (P1-3),
- Configure secondary usage policy (P1-4), and
- Configure data removal policy (P1-5);

touch-point P2 (Review Primary Use) with use cases:

- Review/monitor data capture (P2-1) and
- Review/monitor primary data usage (P2-2);

and touch-point P3 (Review Secondary Use) with use cases:

- Review/monitor data storage (P3-1) and
- Review/monitor secondary data usage (P3-2).

As the design of the dashboard is ongoing, we envision that additional use cases may be identified. We now exemplify the envisioned design by describing functional requirements for two of the identified use cases.

Configure Data Capture Policy (P1-1). A primary use case of the touch-point P1 is to adjust the policy regarding the Data Capture phase of the life-cycle in the HTPF. From a developer's point of view, this policy corresponds to setting up what personal data may pass Privacy Checkpoint 2 in Fig. 1. From a user's perspective, the main question addressed by this use case is: *What do I want to share with only the system or other users of the system or the organisation?* We gathered the following requirements for the design from a user's perspective.

- Get information on why data needs to be captured.
- Configure what can be captured.
- Configure access rights to captured data (e.g., only the system or also other users).

Following this, there are the following requirements from a developer's perspective:

- Ensure user is informed of the implications of capturing data.
- Ensure user is informed of needs and benefits of capturing data.

In fact, from an organisations point of view the last requirement is essential when certain services can only be offered with access to the data. For example, when using the wearable sensors on the worker for activity recognition, then this can enable convenience services supporting the worker with just-in-time information. However, this could also be a privacy risk when being used for profiling an individual worker's performance.

Review/Monitor Secondary Data Usage (P3-2). The second use case that we want to highlight is related to touch-point P3. It is about reviewing how data was re-used for secondary purposes. Here, the main questions answered for the users is: *Who had access to the data capture/stored about me in the HUMAN system?* This corresponds to reviewing what data was transferred beyond Privacy Checkpoint 4 in Fig. 1 as well as to get insights on how it was used. Again, we gathered requirements from the user's perspective:

- Review who accessed my data and when;
- Review who could have accessed my data;
- Review for which purpose my data was accessed;
- Review which data was exported from the system;

and the developer's perspective:

- Provide transparency/notification of access rights and actual access;
- Provide transparency on the kind of use either based on individual features or application/services.
- Provide transparency on the outcomes, i.e., was it used for an intervention or caused changes in the work process.

Our goal for the design of the privacy dashboard is to put emphasis on providing transparency on the outcomes of the secondary data usage rather than just providing details on data usage which are difficult to interpret for users of the system.

4   Conclusion

This paper describes the design process and initial requirements identified in several use cases of a privacy dashboard to be used in a smart manufacturing environment. We used a recently proposed trust and privacy framework [6], which was developed in the same project, to guide the design process. We acknowledge that the design of the dashboard is at an early stage of requirements elicitation. In the future, we plan to implement a prototype and compare our design to existing privacy dashboards based on the specific requirements of work environments such as manufacturing plants.

References

1. European Union: Regulation (EU) 2016/679 of the European parliament and of the council of 27 April 2016 on the protection of natural persons with regard to the processing of personal data and on the free movement of such data, and repealing directive 95/46/EC (general data protection regulation). Off. J. Eur. Union **L119**, 1–88 (2016)
2. Galford, R., Seibold Drapeau, A.: The enemies of trust. Harv. Bus. Rev. **81**, 88–95 (2003)
3. Hoepman, J.-H.: Privacy design strategies. In: Cuppens-Boulahia, N., Cuppens, F., Jajodia, S., Abou El Kalam, A., Sans, T. (eds.) SEC 2014. IAICT, vol. 428, pp. 446–459. Springer, Heidelberg (2014). https://doi.org/10.1007/978-3-642-55415-5_38
4. Irion, K., Yakovleva, S., Hoboken, J.V., Thompson, M.: A roadmap to enhancing user control via privacy dashboards. Tech. rep., IViR (2017)
5. Lasi, H., Fettke, P., Kemper, H.G., Feld, T., Hoffmann, M.: Industry 4.0. Bus. Inf. Syst. Eng. **6**(4), 239–242 (2014)
6. Mannhardt, F., Petersen, S.A., Oliveira, M.F.: A trust and privacy framework for smart manufacturing environments. J. Ambient Intell. Smart Environ. **11**(3), 201–219 (2019)
7. Nguyen, D.H., Mynatt, E.D.: Privacy mirrors: understanding and shaping socio-technical ubiquitous computing systems. Tech. rep., Georgia Institute of Technology (2002)
8. Petersen, S.A., Mannhardt, F., Oliveira, M., Torvatn, H.: A framework to navigate the privacy trade-offs for human-centred manufacturing. In: Camarinha-Matos, L.M., Afsarmanesh, H., Rezgui, Y. (eds.) PRO-VE 2018. IAICT, vol. 534, pp. 85–97. Springer, Cham (2018). https://doi.org/10.1007/978-3-319-99127-6_8
9. Raschke, P., Küpper, A., Drozd, O., Kirrane, S.: Designing a GDPR-compliant and usable privacy dashboard. In: Hansen, M., Kosta, E., Nai-Fovino, I., Fischer-Hübner, S. (eds.) Privacy and Identity 2017. IAICT, vol. 526, pp. 221–236. Springer, Cham (2018). https://doi.org/10.1007/978-3-319-92925-5_14
10. Thoben, K.D., Wiesner, S., Wuest, T.: "Industrie 4.0" and smart manufacturing – a review of research issues and application examples. Int. J. Autom. Technol. **11**(1), 4–16 (2017)

RRTxFM: Probabilistic Counting for Differentially Private Statistics

Saskia Nuñez von Voigt$^{(\boxtimes)}$ and Florian Tschorsch

Distributed Security Infrastructure Group, Technical University of Berlin,
Straße des 17. Juni 135, 10623 Berlin, Germany
{saskia.nunezvonvoigt,florian.tschorsch}@tu-berlin.de
https://www.dsi.tu-berlin.de

Abstract. Data minimization has become a paradigm to address privacy concerns when collecting and storing personal data. In this paper we present two new approaches, RSTxFM and RRTxFM, to estimate the cardinality of a dataset while ensuring differential privacy. We argue that privacy-preserving cardinality estimators are able to realize strong privacy requirements. Both approaches are based on a probabilistic counting algorithm which has a logarithmic space complexity. We combine this with a randomization technique to provide differential privacy. In our analysis, we detail the privacy and utility guarantees and expose the impact of the various parameters. Moreover, we discuss workforce analytics as application area where strong privacy is paramount.

Keywords: Probabilistic counting · Differential privacy · Randomized response

1 Introduction

For data analytics, one of the fundamental operations is to determine the number of distinct elements in a data stream. Due to their small memory footprint and low computational overhead, probabilistic counting algorithms like FM sketches [14], Count-Min sketches [7], and Bloom filters [5] are widely used to estimate the set cardinality efficiently. In fact, they are suitable to record and derive statistics for any categorical data.

Probabilistic counting algorithms can also be used as privacy-enhancing technology, for example, to count Tor users [23], to collect browser statistics [11], or to track users moving from one area to another [3]. In our work, we consider workforce analytics as running example to illustrate a setting, where privacy is crucial and where we have to deal with data integration and data collection at the same time.

Example 1. In recent years, workforce or human resource (HR) analytics is growing rapidly [1]. Workforce analytics combines data from different HR systems and collects additional HR data to understand interrelationships, to predict trends,

© IFIP International Federation for Information Processing 2020

Published by Springer Nature Switzerland AG 2020
I. O. Pappas et al. (Eds.): I3E 2019 Workshops, IFIP AICT 573, pp. 86–98, 2020.
https://doi.org/10.1007/978-3-030-39634-3_9

and to give advice for future developments. The prime example is to predict employee turnover and to infer its reasons by using workforce analytics [13].

For simplicity, assume we are interested in determining the number of employees who work overtime. We use a counting sketch, e.g. , an FM sketch, to record the IDs of employees who work overtime on a monthly basis. By merging the corresponding sketches a data analyst should be able to estimate the number of employees who work overtime over arbitrary time ranges but unable to identify individual employees in the sketch.

In Europe, processing HR data requires special protection and is allowed only under certain circumstances, which is even more strictly regulated since the introduction of the General Data Protection Regulation (GDPR). One way to mitigate the risk of data misuse is to anonymize the data. However, incidents in the past have shown that supposedly anonymized data can be deanoymized. In 2006, Netflix published an anonymous dataset of film reviews for research purposes. By linking the dataset to auxiliary information, e.g. , the Internet Movie Database, it was possible to identify the majority of users [18]. This result shows that pseudonymity is not sufficient to protect privacy.

In this paper, we propose two new approaches, RSTxFM and RRTxFM, for differentially private statistics by using privacy-enhanced FM sketches. To this end, we collect and aggregate data in sketches at a central point after performing our algorithms. We generally consider the counted data to be ephemeral and only RSTxFM and RRTxFM sketches to be persistent. Moreover, we assume that an (hones-but-curious) adversary knows the probabilistic counting algorithm, the IDs of all users in the dataset, and has access to the sketches. Even when using additional means of protection as in [23], the *absence* of an ID, i.e., the ID has not been recorded, reveals sensitive information. That is, in our example the adversary could reveal that an employee does *not* work overtime, which might be used to identify "unmotivated" personnel. We tackle this problem by employing a randomization step before recording IDs in a sketch. We mitigate the risk of being identified, independently of whether the user is in the dataset or not, by guaranteeing ϵ-differential privacy [9].

In the privacy analysis and the empirical evaluation, we expose the impact of the various system parameters. In particular, we show that our approaches provide strong differential privacy guarantees ($\epsilon < 1$), while still being able to produce accurate estimations (error $< 10\%$). We also discuss the merits of our two approaches: While RSTxFM is able to provide accurate results for very small ϵ, it strictly requires adding additional perturbation. In contrast, RRTxFM also provides differential privacy without this perturbation, which makes it the preferred solution when aggregating sketches. Accordingly, the main contributions of our paper can be summarized as follows:

- We identify probabilistic counting as basis for differentially private cardinality estimation in Sect. 3.
- We quantify the privacy level and prove that our algorithms satisfy differential privacy in Sect. 4.

– We analyse the accuracy of RSTxFM and RRTxFM in Sect. 5. We compare it to
related approaches and show that appropriate parameters can be found to
adjust the trade-off between the privacy and accuracy.

2   Related Work

Privacy-preserving statistics often consider a centralized architecture. The data
is stored at a central place and noise is added to the output according to a
Laplace or exponential distribution to reduce the risk for an individual to be
identified [10,12]. This approach however does not protect from data breaches
performed by external or internal adversaries. Our approach is based on so-called
FM sketches [14], which already aggregate data to some extent and therefore
reduce the risks of a data breach.

Probabilistic data structures are generally suitable for privacy-enhanced data
analytics [4,15] as they reduce the amount of personal data and inherently follow
the privacy principle of data minimization. Obfuscation by hashing IDs and
relying on the probabilistic nature of the data structures alone is not sufficient
to guarantee the privacy of all users [8]. Additional means of protection are
necessary. However, even by adding additional noise [21,23], it may become
evident that an ID is not present in the dataset. While in some scenarios this
might be a reasonable assumption, in our example (see Example 1), we consider
that the absence of an ID also leaks sensitive information.

A multitude of approaches address the issue by combining the randomized
response technique (RRT) [24] with Bloom filters to conceal a user ID's
absence [2,3,11,17,19,22]. For example, with RAPPOR [11] Google collects data
about the startpage of Chrome users. The response (i.e., the user's startpage)
is mapped to a Bloom filter. By employing a two-step RRT, RAPPOR flips
each bit with a given probability and provides privacy, even if an attacker links
several reports from a single user. In general, the accuracy of a Bloom filter
depends on the number of utilized hash functions and the size of the Bloom
filter, which increases linearly with the expected number of IDs. On the other
hand, cardinality estimators and FM sketches in particular, require significantly
less space (growing logarithmically with the number of IDs), which makes them
more suitable if the number of distinct IDs is unknown in advance.

Because of the output perturbation, RAPPOR needs a high sample size
for accurate estimations [20]. In contrast, PRIVAPPROX [20] perturbs the
input and therefore requires a smaller sample size when compared to RAP-
POR. Regarding the perturbation technique the approach is very similar to our
approaches. However, PRIVAPPROX is designed for stream analytics and does
not fit well with existing data like in workforce analytics. Therefore we use FM
sketches which can be used to further combine and aggregate individual datasets.

3   Differentially Private Cardinality Estimators

We use Probabilistic Counting with Stochastic Averaging (PCSA) [14] as basis to
estimate the number of distinct user IDs in a dataset. Accordingly, the family of

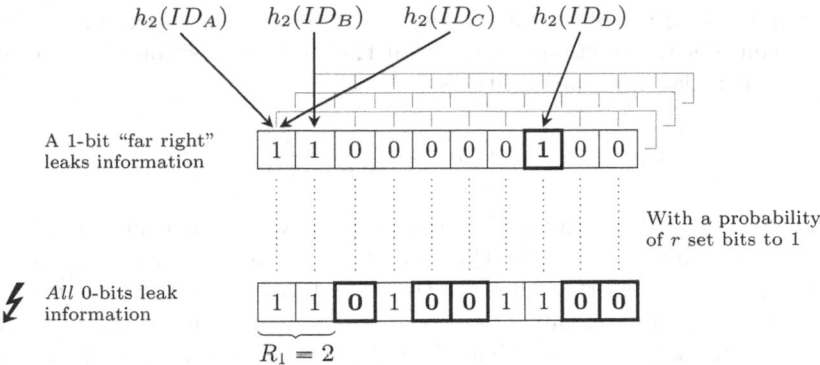

Fig. 1. Illustrating PCSA(r) as in [23] and revealing a privacy issue with 0-bits.

probabilistic counting algorithms also became known as cardinality estimators. To some extent, our findings are applicable to cardinality estimators in general.

PCSA uses m FM sketches (with $m \geq 1$) in parallel and two hash functions h_1 and h_2. A single FM sketch is a bit array $B = b_1, ...b_L$, of length $L \geq 1$, which is initialized to zero. We count a user by hashing the ID and using the result to determine a bit position in one of the FM sketches that we set 1. More specifically, hash function h_1 is used to determine an FM sketch and h_2 to map the IDs to an index in the bit array. While h_1 is a uniformly distributed hash function, h_2 is a geometrically distributed hash function, which yields the probability $P(h_2(ID) = i) = 2^{-i}$ that a specific bit at index i is set. In practice, we also use a uniformly distributed hash function, inspect the binary representation of the hash value, and consider the least significant set bit's index as output. Assume for example that the binary representation of $h_2(ID_A) = [1001]_2$. The least significant set bit is $i = 1$ and therefore maps A's ID to the respective bit. We illustrate counting different IDs in Fig. 1, where four distinct IDs (ID_A, ID_B, ID_C, and ID_D) are mapped on the first FM sketch.

Given the fact that h_2 is geometrically distributed, fewer IDs are mapped to higher indexes (right-hand side). In the worst case, only a single ID maps to a specific bit and an adversary can be sure that this ID was counted. To guarantee the privacy for all counted IDs, the authors of [23] introduce a perturbation technique. Each bit will be set with an additional probability r, which makes 1-bits "ambiguous" (cf. Fig. 1). In the following, we will call this approach PCSA(r). Note that if $r = 0$, the approach is identical to vanilla PCSA.

PCSA(r) also uses the number of consecutive 1-bits R_j to estimate the cardinality, but adapts the correction factor φ depending on r. The estimate C_{PCSA} is calculated with m FM sketches accordingly as

$$C_{\text{PCSA}} = \frac{m \cdot 2^{\sum_{j=1}^{m} R_j / m}}{\varphi(r)}. \tag{1}$$

When R_j is small, the estimation leads to inaccuracies. These can be mitigated to some extent by using a different estimation method based on "hit counting" [16] as long as the fraction of set bits (taking false positives into account) is below 30%, we consider the fraction k of 0-bits at the first bit position ($i = 1$) of each sketch and calculate the cardinality as:

$$C_{\mathrm{PCSA}} = (-2.0 \cdot m) \cdot \log \left(\frac{k}{m \cdot (1.0 - r)} \right).$$

While PCSA is generally well suited to estimate the cardinality, PCSA(r) also protects counted users/IDs. Unfortunately, the approach still leaks information: all 0-bits reveal that all respective user IDs have *not* been counted (cf. Fig. 1). In our running example, we are interested to estimate the cardinality of all employees who work overtime. The absence of an employee ID indicates that this employee has not worked overtime, which reveals sensitive information. Accordingly, the privacy is not fully guaranteed.

In the following, we will present two approaches which tackle this privacy issue. Our general solution strategy is to induce "uncertainty" to the counting procedure with the goal to ensure privacy even if an adversary knows all user IDs in the dataset. To this end, we apply two randomization techniques to perturb the input. Our first algorithm RSTxFM uses *random sampling* to count only a sample of all IDs. Our second algorithm RRTxFM adopts the *randomized response technique* (RRT) to scramble the input in such a way that it contains true and false information. In both approaches, *each* bit in a sketch (0 *and* 1) yields plausible deniability as it remains unclear whether the answer is a result of randomization or truly corresponds to an ID. Later we will formalize this property and show that both approaches achieve differential privacy.

3.1   RSTxFM

In this approach, we randomly count a fraction p_1 of all IDs only. Let us assume we want to estimate the number of employees who work overtime as in Example 1. Moreover, assume that $\hat{p}$ is the fraction of employees who indeed work overtime, i.e., the set of IDs we are interested in. As shown in Fig. 2, an employee working overtime is counted with a probability p_1. For counting user IDs, we use PCSA(r). As a consequence, an adversary does not know which employees have been selected. A 0-bit can indicate that the corresponding employees did not work overtime or simply were not selected. We can still estimate the total cardinality C by evaluating the sketches according to Eq. (1) and setting the result in proportion to p_1, which yields

$$C = \frac{C_{PCSA}}{p_1}. \tag{2}$$

3.2   RRTxFM

Our second approach follows the general idea of RRT [24], a method used in surveys to guarantee privacy. The data is perturbed in a way that a data collector

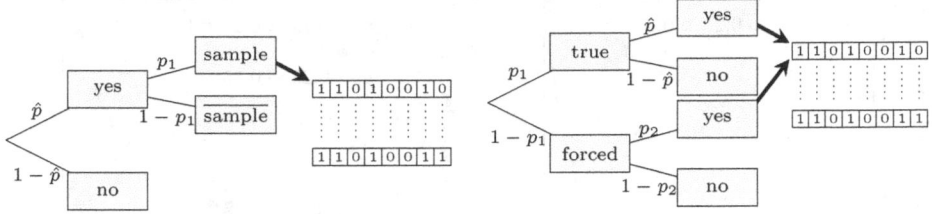

Fig. 2. Procedure of `RSTxFM`.   **Fig. 3.** Procedure of `RRTxFM`.

cannot tell whether the answer contains true or false information. In recent years this method has been modified. We adopt the Forced Response Model [6]. The method can be best described by an example: Before answering a question an employee flips a coin. If the coin comes head the employee answers truthfully whether he works overtime. If the coin comes tail the employee's answer is forced by flipping another coin. For head the answer is "yes" (i.e., working overtime) and for tails "no" (i.e., not working overtime). In Fig. 3, we sketch the procedure.

In order to control the impact of true and forced answers, we leave the parameters flexible and do not use a static coin flipping mechanism. With a probability p_1, we count the true fraction $\hat{p}$ of IDs we are interested in, e.g. , employees working overtime. These IDs are mapped to a `PCSA(r)` sketch. With a probability $1 - p_1$ we use a forced answer. The forced answer is counted as well (i.e., "yes") with probability of p_2. With probabilities $p_1 = p_2 = 0.5$, `RRTxFM` is identical to the example using a coin flip to determine the input data.

With the probability tree in Fig. 3 we can estimate the true fraction $\hat{p}$. Basically, there are two ways a bit can be set: by answering truthful and by a forced answer. The probability of getting a "yes" answer is $p_1 \cdot \hat{p} + (1 - p_1) \cdot p_2$. Setting the total number of "yes" responses C_{PCSA} equal to this probability and solving for $\hat{p}$, we can estimate the true cardinality C by calculating

$$C = \frac{\frac{C_{PCSA}}{N} - p_2 + p_1 \cdot p_2}{p_1} \cdot N. \tag{3}$$

4   Privacy Analysis

With our approaches we aim for satisfying the strict concept of ϵ-differential privacy introduced by Dwork et al. [9]. It guarantees privacy regardless of the amount of background knowledge of an adversary. Accordingly, a function f provides ϵ-differential privacy if all pairs of answers a_1 and a_2 and all $S \subseteq$ Range(f) satisfy

$$P[f(a_1) \in S] \leq e^\epsilon P[f(a_2) \in S]. \tag{4}$$

A smaller ϵ generally yields a stronger privacy. For $\epsilon = 0$, the output of function f is the same independent of the input, i.e., it is irrelevant whether a_1 or a_2 is in the dataset. While $\epsilon = 0$ leads to the strongest privacy guarantees, it obviously

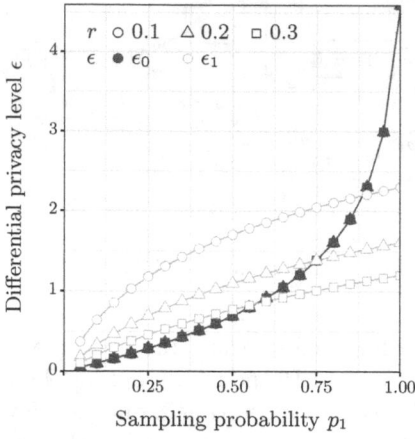

Fig. 4. Privacy level of RSTxFM.   **Fig. 5.** Privacy level of RRTxFM.

cannot be used to obtain meaningful results. Finding a balance between the privacy level ϵ and the accuracy of results is necessary.

Differential privacy expects the worst case [10]. For this reason we assume that an adversary knows all IDs and all algorithmic details, particularly the hash functions to map IDs to a sketch. The worst case is, as elaborated intuitively in the previous section, a bit where only a single ID is mapped to.

In the following, we show that our approaches are differentially private and satisfy Eq. (4). Since IDs are mapped to a single bit only, the privacy level ϵ is independent of the number of sketches and we only need to derive ϵ-differential privacy for one sketch. Therefore, we have to distinguish two possible answers, 1 for a positive and 0 for a negative answer. Accordingly, we have to show

$$\epsilon_0 \geq \ln\left(\frac{P[f(0) = 0]}{P[f(1) = 0]}\right) \quad \text{and} \quad \epsilon_1 \geq \ln\left(\frac{P[f(1) = 1]}{P[f(0) = 1]}\right),$$

where ϵ_0 describes the privacy level for the absence and ϵ_1 for the presence of an ID. The differential privacy level ϵ is then given by the maximum of ϵ_0 and ϵ_1, i.e., $\epsilon = \max(\epsilon_0, \epsilon_1)$.

4.1   Privacy Level of RSTxFM

With RSTxFM, there are two reasons for setting a bit: either an ID has a certain property and is sampled with a probability p_1, or the bit is set by the perturbation technique of PCSA(r) with a probability r. We can use this observation to calculate the conditional probabilities $P[f(0) = 0]$, $P[f(1) = 0]$, $P[f(1) = 1]$ and $P[f(0) = 1]$ and derive ϵ_0 and ϵ_1 accordingly. That is,

$$\epsilon_0 = ln\left(\frac{1}{1 - p_1}\right) \quad \text{and} \quad \epsilon_1 = ln\left(\frac{p_1 + (1 - p_1) \cdot r}{r}\right).$$

First of all, please note that the privacy level depends on p_1 and r. Only for $r > 0$ and $p_1 \neq 1$, RSTxFM satisfies the definition of differential privacy. In Fig. 4, we plotted ϵ_0 and ϵ_1 with p_1 on the x-axis and varying values for r. The influence of p_1 and r is as expected. The probability r has no impact on ϵ_0. For high values of p_1, ϵ_0 increases quickly so that for $p_1 \rightarrow 1 : \epsilon_0 = \infty$. In contrast, ϵ_1 depends on both probabilities p_1 and r. Overall, for a decreasing p_1 and an increasing r, $\max(\epsilon_0, \epsilon_1)$ decreases and provides stronger privacy, respectively.

4.2 Privacy Level of RRTxFM

Proving ϵ-differential privacy for RRTxFM is equivalent to RSTxFM. First, we have to calculate the conditional probabilities, which now not only depend on p_1 and r but also on p_2, before we can derive ϵ_0 and ϵ_1. We obtain

$$\epsilon_0 = \ln \left(\frac{p_1 + (1 - p_1) \cdot (1 - p_2)}{(1 - p_1) \cdot (1 - p_2)} \right) \quad \text{and}$$

$$\epsilon_1 = \ln \left(\frac{p_1 + (1 - p_1) \cdot p_2 + (1 - p_1) \cdot (1 - p_2) \cdot r}{p_1 \cdot r + (1 - p_1) \cdot p_2 + (1 - p_1) \cdot (1 - p_2) \cdot r} \right).$$

The privacy level depends on p_1, p_2 and r. For $p_1 \neq 1$ and $p_2 \neq 1$, RRTxFM satisfies the definition of differential privacy. That is, r is not strictly required to guarantee differential privacy.

In Fig. 5, we show ϵ_0 and ϵ_1 (absence and presence of an ID) in relation to p_2. The influence of r and p_1 are represented by the different lines. As for RSTxFM, r has no influence on ϵ_0. For high values of p_2, ϵ_0 increases quickly. We observe that for an increasing p_1 (i.e., truthful answers), ϵ_0 and ϵ_1 increase.

With rising p_1 the privacy level ϵ_1 becomes flatter. While r is not strictly required to gain differential privacy, it still has an influence on ϵ_1. The privacy level decreases with increasing p_2. Higher values of r have a positive effect on the privacy and make the curve's slope smaller, effectively decreasing ϵ_1 and thus ϵ.

5 Evaluation

In this section, we examine the accuracy of our approaches with respect to the privacy level ϵ. In particular, besides comparing the accuracy of RSTxFM and RRTxFM, we evaluate the cost of privacy. To this end, we implemented a simulation and generated synthetic datasets with different cardinalities. Each dataset consists of N unique random numbers, which serve the purpose of IDs. Since we know the true cardinalities, we can calculate the error of our cardinality estimations and directly compare the different approaches.

From PCSA it is known that it has a standard error of $0.78/\sqrt{m}$ [14]. A higher number of sketches consequentially results in a better accuracy. Since the number of sketches has no impact on the privacy level, though, we set $m = 64$ and the length of each sketch to 64 bit, large enough to count $\approx 7 \cdot 10^{19}$ elements. Please note that this is one of the benefits of building upon PCSA instead of Bloom filters, because we can set these parameters independently of N.

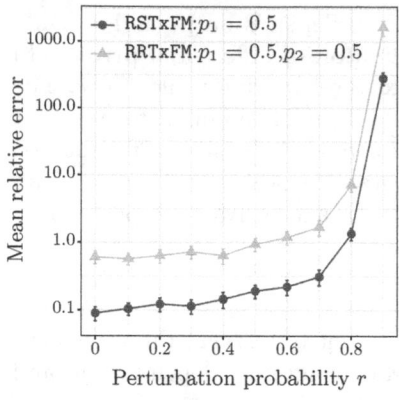

Fig. 6. Impact of r ($N = 10^4$).

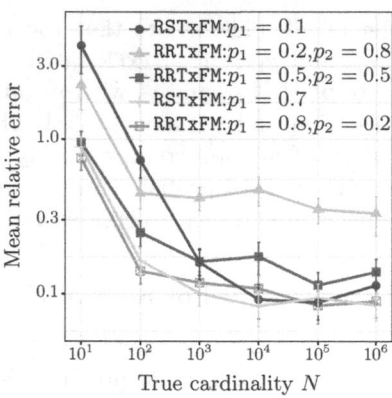

Fig. 7. Impact of p_1, p_2, and N.

The perturbation and randomization in our approaches can lead to negative estimations. As this makes no sense, we set negative estimations to zero. In order to obtain statistically sound results, we repeat each experiment 50 times with varying random seeds. For all results, we show the arithmetic mean; error bars indicate 95% confidence intervals.

5.1   Impact of Parameters

We first investigate the accuracy of estimating the cardinality with varying perturbation probability r. In Fig. 6, we show the relative error for RSTxFM and RRTxFM. For clarity, we set $p_1 = p_2 = 0.5$. For an increasing r, the relative error also increases. In line with the results of [23], the error remains at reasonable levels for $m = 64$ and $r < 0.4$. In the following experiments, we set $r = 0.2$, because we believe it provides a good trade-off between accuracy and privacy.

We also analyzed how the randomization parameters p_1 and p_2 and the cardinality size N influence the relative error. Probabilities were chosen to satisfy $\epsilon < 2$. Figure 7 generally indicates that the error decreases with higher cardinalities and stabilizes at some point. As expected, low cardinalities yield a high error. Also as expected, increasing p_1 decreases the error of both RSTxFM and RRTxFM. For RRTxFM, the probability p_2 (forced answers) also influences the accuracy. Increasing p_2 also increases the relative error. For high cardinalities, however, we observed that p_1 has the strongest impact on the loss of accuracy.

5.2   Cost of Privacy

Privacy comes at a cost. In order to quantify these costs, we compare our algorithms with vanilla PCSA (i.e., $r = 0$) and PCSA(r) with a perturbation probability $r = 0.2$. Please note that both, PCSA and PCSA(r), do not satisfy the definition of differential privacy. Figure 8 shows that the relative error is less

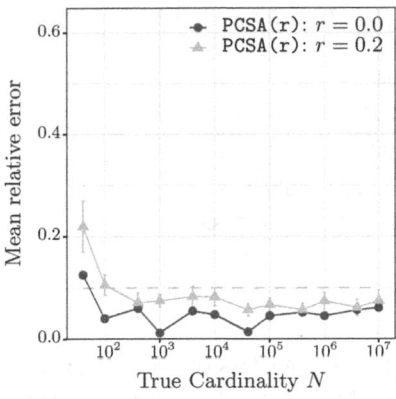

Fig. 8. Accuracy of PCSA.

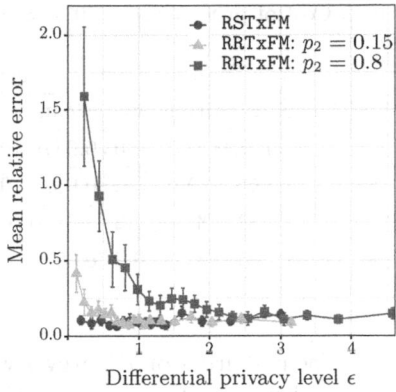

Fig. 9. Accuracy vs. privacy ($N = 10^4$).

than 10%, even for small cardinalities. Figure 9 shows a trade-off between accuracy and privacy for RSTxFM and RRTxFM. As expected, more privacy guarantees (i.e., a smaller ϵ) yields a higher accuracy loss (particularly when compared to Fig. 8). For a very small differential privacy level ($\epsilon = 0.23$), RRTxFM shows a high accuracy loss (error ≈ 1.6). RSTxFM, in contrast, is able to provide accurate results (error < 0.1) also for very small ϵ. Notably, the same privacy level does not lead to the same relative error. In particular, RRTxFM has a higher error for a higher probability p_2, even though the overall privacy guarantees are the same. This observation can also be made for higher cardinalities, where the error becomes even smaller. Lower cardinalities result in a higher error even with optimal parameters.

Table 1 summarizes the cost of privacy for appropriate parameters. As we mentioned above, stronger privacy comes at the cost of an increased loss of accuracy. However, the accuracy loss remains at a reasonable level for large cardinality sizes and an appropriate choice of parameters.

5.3 Discussion

In terms of the privacy level our approaches can be compared to RAPPOR [11] as it also uses RRT. The basic one-time RAPPOR guarantees differential privacy with $\epsilon \leq ln(3)$. With $\epsilon < 1$, we guarantee stronger privacy and an average error of less than 10%. According to [8], an error of less than 10% is classified as a precise cardinality estimator. To identify trends and reasons for employee turnover (as outlined in Example 1) this accuracy seems reasonable.

For the sake of clarity, we have envisioned our algorithms in a centralized setting so far only. That is, collecting data at a central point, which manages the sketches and performs the randomization. RSTxFM and RRTxFM however can also be used in a local mode and therefore provide *local differential privacy*. In this mode, each employee will manage the sketches and perform the described algorithm locally. The perturbed sketches will then be transmitted to the data

Table 1. Cost of privacy ($N = 10^4$; RSTxFM: $p_1 = 0.3$; RRTxFM: $p_1 = 0.4$, $p_2 = 0.15$).

Algorithm	r	Relative error			Privacy
		Mean	Median	SD	
PCSA(r)	0.0	0.0476	0.0476	0.0	–
PCSA(r)	0.2	0.0820	0.0698	0.0624	only 1-bits
RSTxFM	0.2	0.0880	0.0658	0.0695	$\epsilon = 0.7885$
RRTxFM	0.2	0.0996	0.0659	0.0897	$\epsilon = 0.7777$

collector. The perturbation r however will lead to a higher loss of accuracy when aggregating sketches. We therefore suggest to prefer RRTxFM for data collection and integration as it provides differential privacy even for $r = 0$.

When collecting data over time, the time series can leak information and eventually reveal the true value. In case of static already existing data, this is not relevant. However, it becomes relevant for employee satisfaction surveys, for example. RAPPOR provides protection against this type of information leakage by employing so-called memoization [11]. The memoization part "remembers" the result of RRT instead of recalculating it for a new query. This method is also applicable to RRTxFM. In the future, we will extend our evaluation and compare the results to various related approaches, including RAPPOR.

6 Conclusion

In this paper, we have shown that probabilistic counting can be used for differentially private statistics. We combined counting sketches with an additional randomization step to prevent personal data leakage. By comparing our developed algorithms, RSTxFM and RRTxFM, we exposed various parameter dependencies and found that the same privacy level does not necessarily result in the same accuracy. We however also showed that appropriate parameters can be found to gain privacy and accuracy.

In summary, our approaches provide strong differential privacy guarantees ($\epsilon < 1$) with a loss of accuracy below 10% and therefore balance the trade-off between privacy and accuracy.

References

1. Abbatiello, A., Agarwal, D., Bersin, J., et al.: The rise of the social enterprise. In: 2018 Deloitte Global Human Capital Trends. Deloitte (2018)
2. Alaggan, M., Cunche, M., Gambs, S.: Privacy-preserving Wi-Fi analytics. Proc. Priv. Enhancing Technol. **2018**(2), 4–26 (2018)
3. Alaggan, M., Gambs, S., Matwin, S., Tuhin, M.: Sanitization of call detail records via differentially-private bloom filters. In: Samarati, P. (ed.) DBSec 2015. LNCS, vol. 9149, pp. 223–230. Springer, Cham (2015). https://doi.org/10.1007/978-3-319-20810-7_15

4. Bianchi, G., Bracciale, L., Loreti, P.: "Better than nothing" privacy with bloom filters: to what extent? In: Domingo-Ferrer, J., Tinnirello, I. (eds.) PSD 2012. LNCS, vol. 7556, pp. 348–363. Springer, Heidelberg (2012). https://doi.org/10.1007/978-3-642-33627-0_27

5. Bloom, B.H.: Space/time trade-offs in hash coding with allowable errors. Commun. ACM **13**(7), 422–426 (1970)

6. Boruch, R.F.: Assuring confidentiality of responses in social research: a note on strategies. Am. Sociol. **6**, 308–311 (1971)

7. Cormode, G.: Count-min sketch. In: Encyclopedia of Database Systems, pp. 511–516 (2009)

8. Desfontaines, D., Lochbihler, A., Basin, D.A.: Cardinality estimators do not preserve privacy. CoRR (2018)

9. Dwork, C., McSherry, F., Nissim, K., Smith, A.: Calibrating noise to sensitivity in private data analysis. In: Halevi, S., Rabin, T. (eds.) TCC 2006. LNCS, vol. 3876, pp. 265–284. Springer, Heidelberg (2006). https://doi.org/10.1007/11681878_14

10. Dwork, C., Roth, A.: The algorithmic foundations of differential privacy. Found. Trends Theor. Comput. Sci. **9**(3–4), 211–407 (2014). https://doi.org/10.1561/0400000042

11. Erlingsson, Ú., Pihur, V., Korolova, A.: Rappor: randomized aggregatable privacy-preserving ordinal response. In: Proceedings of the 2014 ACM SIGSAC Conference on Computer and Communications Security, pp. 1054–1067. ACM (2014)

12. Fan, L., Jin, H.: A practical framework for privacy-preserving data analytics. In: Proceedings of the 24th International Conference on World Wide Web, pp. 311–321 (2015). https://doi.org/10.1145/2736277.2741122

13. Fitz-Enz, J.: THE NEW HR ANALYTIC Predicting the Economic Value of Your Company's Human Capital Investments (2010)

14. Flajolet, P., Martin, G.N.: Probabilistic counting algorithms for data base applications. J. Comput. Syst. Sci. **31**(2), 182–209 (1985)

15. Kamp, M., Kopp, C., Mock, M., Boley, M., May, M.: Privacy-preserving mobility monitoring using sketches of stationary sensor readings. In: Blockeel, H., Kersting, K., Nijssen, S., Železný, F. (eds.) ECML PKDD 2013. LNCS (LNAI), vol. 8190, pp. 370–386. Springer, Heidelberg (2013). https://doi.org/10.1007/978-3-642-40994-3_24

16. Lieven, P., Scheuermann, B.: High-speed per-flow traffic measurement with probabilistic multiplicity counting. In: INFOCOM, pp. 1253–1261 (2010)

17. Lin, B., Wu, S., Tsou, Y., Huang, Y.: PPDCA: privacy-preserving crowdsensing data collection and analysis with randomized response. In: 2018 IEEE Wireless Communications and Networking Conference (WCNC), pp. 1–6 (2018). https://doi.org/10.1109/WCNC.2018.8377050

18. Narayanan, A., Shmatikov, V.: Robust de-anonymization of large sparse datasets. In: 2008 IEEE Symposium on Security and Privacy, SP 2008, pp. 111–125. IEEE (2008)

19. Qin, Z., Yang, Y., Yu, T., Khalil, I., Xiao, X., Ren, K.: Heavy hitter estimation over set-valued data with local differential privacy. In: Proceedings of the 2016 ACM SIGSAC Conference on Computer and Communications Security, pp. 192–203. ACM (2016)

20. Quoc, D.L., Beck, M., Bhatotia, P., Chen, R., Fetzer, C., Strufe, T.: PrivApprox: privacy-preserving stream analytics. In: 2017 USENIX Annual Technical Conference, pp. 659–672 (2017)

21. Sparka, H., Tschorsch, F., Scheuermann, B.: P2KMV: a privacy-preserving counting sketch for efficient and accurate set intersection cardinality estimations. Technical report 234 (2018)
22. Stanojevic, R., Nabeel, M., Yu, T.: Distributed cardinality estimation of set operations with differential privacy. In: 2017 IEEE Symposium on Privacy-Aware Computing (PAC), pp. 37–48 (2017)
23. Tschorsch, F., Scheuermann, B.: An algorithm for privacy-preserving distributed user statistics. Comput. Netw. **57**(14), 2775–2787 (2013)
24. Warner, S.L.: Randomized response: a survey technique for eliminating evasive answer bias. J. Am. Stat. Assoc. **60**(309), 63–69 (1965)

Innovative Teaching of Introductory Topics in Information Technology - 3(IT)

3(IT) 2019 Workshop - Message
from the Chairs

The Workshop on Innovative Teaching of Introductory Topics in Information Technology (3(IT) 2019) was arranged for the very first time as part of the I3E 2019 conference in Trondheim, during September 2019.

The 3(IT) workshop, as its name indicates, focuses on the challenges of teaching introductory topics in IT, and on innovative approaches for improving the students' learning in such courses. Introductory programming has long been seen as a challenging topic to teach, with high failure rates in many such courses. Classes in introductory IT topics tend to be big, and increasing, as more and more students want to have some competencies in IT. Moreover, there tends to be huge variation in students' previous knowledge.

3(IT) 2019 received eight submissions. Each paper was evaluated by 3 independent members of the Program Committee – which in total had 12 highly competent members from 8 different countries. Three papers were accepted for publication based on reviews and subsequent consensus discussion. In addition, two more submissions were invited for short presentations, although not having their full papers accepted in the proceedings. All in all, the five presented works were from three different countries (Greece, Norway, and Spain) and represented a nice mixture of issues related to the workshop topic.

The paper "Empowering Female Students to Seek Careers in Game Development and Creative IT Studies" by Helga Dis Isfold Sigurdardottir looks especially at challenges with recruitment and gender balance, as many IT studies tend to have very few girls, and studies focusing on game development, such as those of the Nord University, are no exception.

The paper "ATMF: A Student-Centered Framework for the Effective Implementation of Alternative Teaching Methods for CSEd" by Anastasios Theodoropoulos, Costas Vassilakis, Angeliki Antoniou, Manolis Wallace, and George Lepouras presents a framework to help teachers select alternative and more active learning methods for their courses, rather than having students as passive consumers in monologue lectures.

The paper "Framework for Pupil-To-Student Transition, Learning Environment and Semester Start for First-Year Students" by Omid Mirmotahari, Gunnar Rye Bergersen, Yngvar Berg, Kristin Bråthen, and Kristin Broch Eliassen presents the approach for onboarding first year informatics students at the University of Oslo.

The two short presentations by Clara Benac Earle and Majid Rouhani et al. both concentrated on introductory programming courses. The former discussed an approach to such a course for "normal" students, the latter looking at a continuing education course for teachers.

After the conference, the authors of the three full papers prepared the final versions of their articles, being able to take into account both reviewer comments and feedback at the workshop. The revised versions passed a second stage of editorial reviewing before being included in the I3E 2019 workshops proceedings.

We would like to thank the authors of submitted papers, the members of the Program Committee, and last but not least the organizers of the main conference, I3E 2019, for their great effort in making the 3(IT) 2019 workshop happen.

September 2019

Line Kolås
Guttorm Sindre

3(IT) Organization

Workshop Chairs

Guttorm Sindre   Norwegian University of Science
and Technology (NTNU), Norway

Line Kolås   Nord University, Norway

Program Committee

Roy Andersson	Lund University, Sweden
Andrew Cain	Deakin University, Australia
Monica Divitini	NTNU, Norway
Rune Hjelsvold	NTNU, Norway
Madeleine Lorås	NTNU, Norway
Andrew Luxton-Reilly	The University of Auckland, New Zealand
Anders Malthe-Sørenssen	University of Oslo, Norway
Linda Mannila	Åbo Akademi University, Finland
Simon McCallum	Victoria University Wellington, New Zealand
Omid Mirmotahari	University of Oslo, Norway
Andreas Muehling	Kiel University, Germany
Robin Munkvold	Nord University, Norway
Anne-Kathrin Peters	Uppsala University, Sweden

Empowering Women to Seek Careers in Game Development and Creative IT Studies

Helga Dís Ísfold Sigurðardóttir[(✉)] [iD]

NORD University, 7716 Steinkjer, Norway
helga.d.sigurdardottir@nord.no

Abstract. The purpose of this paper is to investigate what may increase the interest of young women in considering studies and careers within game development and creative IT studies in Nordic countries. The study is based on data gathered through a Nordplus project in 2017–2018, in Iceland and Norway, through surveys and group interviews with 16–19 year old female secondary school students and one of their teachers.

The findings reveal that young women appreciate chances to try out some creative IT tools and the participants also expressed generally positive attitude towards creative IT. They regret not having received more information about creative IT as well as insight into creative IT fields, study and job opportunities throughout their schooling, and they appreciate visible female role models within technology.

Keywords: Young women in creative IT · Recruitment of women to creative IT · Role models

1 Introduction

Gender aspects in digital games industry have become increasingly acknowledged and discussed in recent years [1, 2][1]. This study is based on data gathered through a Nordplus preparation project in 2017–2018. The project was a cooperation project between Nord University (Norway), Reykjavik University (Iceland) and Aalborg University (Denmark) and several other supporting institutions and organizations. It resulted in another 3-year project where the focus on this topic is further developed. The involved university departments offer programs within a variety of areas such as Games and Entertainment Technology, 3D art, animation & visual effects and Film & TV production (Nord University) and Computer Science (Reykjavik University). To try to group all the relevant subject areas under one concept I use the common label "creative IT" – sometimes adding "media technology" as well.

In all the respective university departments, female students are a minority, in some cases not present at all [3]. The Nordplus project aspires to find solutions to such

---

[1] A quick clarification of how I refer to "gender" in this paper: The data is limited to the traditional binary division genders; male and female. This is not to say that I am not aware of the complex nature of gender, sex and sexual identity, not necessarily bound to physically assigned sex. The non-exclusionary group of participants who identified as female may have included trans-non-binary students but the act of identifying as female was the only requirement.

© IFIP International Federation for Information Processing 2020
Published by Springer Nature Switzerland AG 2020
I. O. Pappas et al. (Eds.): I3E 2019 Workshops, IFIP AICT 573, pp. 103–115, 2020.
https://doi.org/10.1007/978-3-030-39634-3_10

challenges, aiming for increased gender balance. This study is based on data from the preparation project, gathered through 2 different mini-workshops that were carried out with upper secondary school students in Norway and Iceland. The goal was to identify factors that might increase the interest of young females in considering studies and careers within game development and creative IT studies.

The paper is organized as follows: I first present an insight into previous research and theory. I then briefly describe the methods and introduce the data, followed by a presentation and a discussion of the findings. As this study is based on experimental workshops from a preparation project, the conclusions of this paper are first and foremost an indicator for further areas of focus and investigation.

2 Background

It is sometimes said that the core values of a culture are reflected through its most popular games [4]. If there is any truth in this, our culture has a long way to go, as women are still vastly underrepresented in video game content, in spite of some positive signs of change in later years [5]. The underrepresentation of women in game content seems to correlate with a sexist gamer culture and the underrepresentation of women in the programming, game development and creative IT workforce [2, 6]. Women in these disciplines frequently experience discrimination. The 2014 #gamergate controversy, among other things, brought this to light, as female game designers and game critics came under unfair scrutiny and suffered severe personal and professional harassment [7, 8]. This situation, as well as widely accepted assumptions about digital games being a male-oriented and male-dominated domain, make it as important as ever to emphasize inclusion when designing digital games [2, 9]. Diverse teams, with regard to such factors as age and gender, have further been proven to contribute to the efficiency and success of software development projects [10].

Gender stereotyping has not proven successful in the commercial video game industry [1]. Nowadays women play about as much, or possibly even more digital games compared to men [11, 12]. The current target customer is not the stereotypically assumed young, single, white male, but a wide range of individuals of all ages, genders, racial identities, marital statuses etc. Furthermore, designing designated "girl games" has not always turned out well, as using stereotypical gender roles as a foundation for engaging game play can be quite a bit of a challenge and can have a discouraging effect on the intended consumers [1, 13]. Evidence indicates that the gaming preferences of males and females overlap to a large extent [13]. At the same time women dislike heavily gender-stereotyped characters [14]. Constructing video game audiences through marketing may influence which groups get to be represented in the games, at the same time as shaping who identifies as a gamer [1].

A report from the Norwegian Media Authority in 2018, titled "Children and media" indicates that gender influences a variety of surprisingly different variables. For example, there are gender differences with regard to how many 9-18 year old children report playing digital games – 63% of girls vs 96% of boys. Although at 9 years old equally many girls and boys report playing, 93%, the number decreases with age. Boys also report playing more often and for longer periods at a time. Although boys and girls share a fondness for some games, such as Minecraft, there is quite some difference in titles and genres between the genders. Gender also seems to have an impact on what kind of equipment is used for playing, how much the parents know about gaming and how many games with a (too) high age limit are played, to name some examples [15]. A comparable report from 2013 in Iceland shows similar trends. While only 72% of 9 – 15 year old Icelandic girls played digital games, 86% of 9 – 15 year old boys played digital games [16]. A new, unpublished report, suggests even higher numbers in total, indicating that 94% of children aged 6–12 play video games regularly, as well as 86% of children aged 13–17 [17]. Like in Norway, the boys also played more frequently and for longer periods than the girls. Only 24% of the Icelandic boys felt that their parents were well informed about the games they were playing, as opposed to 32% of the Icelandic girls [16].

Other research further demonstrates gender difference in behavior and relationships towards digital games. For instance, girls name a larger variety of games that they play in their free time, in spite of playing less in general than boys [18]. In some cases, girls seem to employ and stress not having skills in the domains of digital media or gaming, to assert their femininity [19]. Steinkuehler [20] draws to our attention a possible correlation between the fact that while boys seem to play more video games than girls they also seem more challenged in some aspects of school and education than girls. In Norway, girls in lower secondary schools score higher than boys in international comparisons of pupil's ICT skills [21]. At the same time, parents are commonly concerned with possible risks with regard to their children's online activities and tend to regulate girls' internet use more than boys' internet use [22].

Computer technology and related fields are traditionally seen as masculine sectors in Norway and Iceland, as in many parts of the Western world. In some other parts of the world, such as in Malaysia, the same sectors are considered feminine [23, 24]. In order to address this technological gender gap, a number of initiatives have recently and currently focused on recruiting girls to game coding courses and programs, aiming to increase their interest, motivation & self-efficacy [25–27].

Code clubs are volunteer organizations, aiming to teach children basic coding skills through play and exploration. A 2015 study of gender proportions in code clubs in Norway revealed that in 7 code clubs across the country girls represented under 20% of the participants, with only one exception where the proportion reached 35%. It also indicated that the dropout rate was significantly higher amongst girls than boys [3]. Another study, from 2016, suggests that the code clubs focus more explicitly on recruiting girls [28].

The recruitment of women to IT studies at Nord University (former HiNT) has remained relatively low from the beginning of the studies, some 30 years ago – in spite of some peaks as a result of early campaigns to recruit more women. Recent numbers for the current Games and Entertainment Technology bachelor program at the same university confirms that the dropout rate amongst female students is considerably higher than for males [3].

Universities are currently not meeting the needs and demands of the growing IT sector, when it comes to educating enough professionals. Amongst those who do graduate, the proportion of women is alarmingly low [29]. A research amongst college students in USA showed that women had significantly lower interest in CT fields than their male counterparts. There is evidence that young women give up on IT and computing before they graduate from secondary schools [29, 30].

In 2016, women were only 13% of the workforce in the Norwegian Game industry. Furthermore, there are « reasons to believe that women are overrepresented in administrative positions and that the proportion of women game developers is thus even lower" [31]. In the flourishing Swedish game industry, female video game developers are considered to have insight into women gamers' preferences. This is seen as their primary advantage to their male counterparts, rather than their professional skills. While this belief is used to justify womens' participation in the game industry, it also ties them to a "specific gendered domain of expertise" [2].

While Norwegian authorities are reporting increasing need for individuals with IT- and engineering competencies [32], representatives of both the Norwegian and Ice-landic IT-sector alike have in recent years highlighted a growing need for more women in the sector [33, 34]. In both countries, several measures have been taken in order to increase the participation of women in the gaming industry, IT and other technological professions [35, 36]. A similar trend can be seen in Sweden [2]. and in other parts of the Western world [37, 38].

There is some disparity in research when it comes to the importance of role models. Several studies have supported the widely acknowledged assumption that women role models are important when it comes to career aspirations and attitudes of female candidates to science, technology, engineering and mathematics [39, 40], and that female role models are a key factor in recruiting women to game studies [41] and other IT fields [42]. Research has even suggested that role models can help to improve womens' performance in male dominated studies [40]. According to one study, on the other hand, male and female role models are equally effective for female recruits [43]. Another study concluded that the gender of a computer science role model had no effect on women's interest in their field, while whether or not the role model was a stereotypical representative of computer science turned out to have both an immediate and lasting effect. To explain a bit further, a stereotypical computer science repre-sentative, for instance, claimed having these hobbies: "video games, watching anime, and programming" and "Electronic Gaming Monthly" as a favorite magazine – as opposed to the non-stereotypical representative who's hobbies were "playing sports, hanging out with friends, listening to music" and the favorite magazine was "Rolling Stone" and so on. The study concludes:

> "Women who encountered a role model who embodied computer science stereotypes were less interested in majoring in computer science and felt less belonging in the field compared to women who interacted with a non-stereotypical role model or no role model [44].

Motivating and empowering young women to consider seeking studies and careers within creative IT is thus widely supported. Not only is the sector in growing need of workforce [32, 40] but also benefits from diversity in terms of efficiency and success [10]. A diverse workforce may also provide role models to attract even more diversity [39, 40]. Diversity is further assumed to potentially lead to inclusive content, catering to a more diverse audience [9] which again likely leads to profit [1].

3 Methods

This study is based on a Nordplus project that bears the title Girls Just Wanna Have Fun-damental IT-skills. The project aims to empower female students in upper secondary schools and to motivate them to consider studies and careers in game development and other creative IT studies in the Nordic Countries. Nord University (Norway), Reykjavík University (Iceland) and Aalborg University (Denmark) as well as several upper secondary schools, organizations and institutions in the three countries cooperated to prepare a more substantial 3-year project. In the pre-project the participating universities had, among other things, two experimental workshops, to test out ideas on how to engage and motivate potential female applicants in the fields of creative IT and game development. Other project partners that were directly involved in the experimental workshops of this study were the Centre for gender equality in Norway (KUN) in the Norwegian workshop, and /sys/tur – a network for female students of computer science at Reykjavík University in the Icelandic workshop.

The data were gathered in the workshops, and consist of survey responds of a total of 25 upper secondary school pupils who identified as girls, in Norway and Iceland in the winter of 2017–2018, participation observation in workshops, field notes and informal and formal interviews. The goal of the workshops was to have the participants try out some creative and playful approaches to IT. As a research method workshops are a good approach to inspire new insight into a research domain, preferably in combination with other empirical approaches [45]. In addition, field notes from informal interviews or discussions with the groups of participants and an interview with one of their teachers also provided valuable data.

There were 17 participants in the workshop in Norway and 8 participants in the workshop in Iceland. They were aged 16–19, with a majority of 20 within the younger two years, 16 and 17 years old. They were pupils at a total of three upper secondary schools, one in Norway and two in Iceland. All had chosen some subjects that somehow relate to creative use of IT and/or media technology. The teacher who was interviewed is an Icelandic woman in her early fifties who teaches visual art and has considerable experience within digital art.

The workshops lasted for just under 2 h and consisted of short presentations and practical assignments. In the first workshop, in Norway, the program started with a short introduction and an inspiring talk by a member from the Centre for gender equality, followed by a group activity using a coding game (Box Island), a quick price ceremony, another short and inspiring talk, a survey, group discussion and final words. The project partners from Nord University in Norway served both as facilitators and as participant observers in the Norwegian workshop.

Similarly, the program for the workshop in Iceland consisted of a short introduction and an inspiring talk by female students of the /sys/tur network, a group activity using a tool for coding music (Sonic Pi) where the /sys/tur network members assisted the upper secondary school pupils. In Iceland, the partners from all three project partner universities took on the roles of participant observers.

After the workshops, the participants were presented with a survey, a brief group discussion and concluding words. The adults present in the Norwegian workshop, were a total of 2 women and 3 men, including 2 male upper secondary school teachers. In the Icelandic workshop, the present adults were 7 women, including one of their teachers, 4 computer science students from the /sys/tur network and 2 men.

The surveys were short and were presented towards the end of each workshop. All the 17 participants from each workshop in Norway responded. The surveys consisted of a total of 6 topical questions, of which 2 were open-ended, and 2–3 background questions. The background questions varied slightly between the two countries, as some improvements were made from the first to the second version of the survey. The topical questions all sought to reveal the participants' views and opinions regarding creative IT and how to get girls more interested and motivated. The participants could choose to be completely anonymous, or to provide their contact information in the surveys. In either case the data was treated confidentially.

The informal discussions with the groups of participants, as well as informal chats before and after the workshops were centered around similar themes as the survey. Notes were taken during the workshops and further processed those into short reports after the workshops. A telephone interview with a teacher aimed to look further into some of the topics. The teacher teaches at an upper secondary school that four of the Icelandic pupils attended. The phone interview was recorded and key points were summarized in a written form.

As the survey was short and the participants few, the survey data do not provide for a statistical analysis. However, the survey contents, including the answers to the open questions were roughly analyzed and coded, alongside the qualitative notes and interview. All the data was, in other words, viewed as interconnected. It was processed and interpreted simultaneously as a whole.

The data may have certain biases, as all the participants in the workshops have some experience with school subjects related to creative IT and all of the participants signed up for the workshop on their own initiative. It should also be noted that in addition to this bias the total number of participants in this study was simply too low to facilitate any sort of generalizability. The findings can thus not be viewed as anything more than an indication.

4 Findings

On a 5 point Likert scale, thirteen of the twenty-five participants reported finding it "rather" or "very likely" that they would consider working with media technology or creative IT in the future. A total of six respondents found it "neither likely nor unlikely". None of the girls replied that it was "very unlikely". Six of the participants, all of whom had attended the Norwegian workshop, answered that they found it "rather unlikely". A chat with the group of participants before the Norwegian workshop revealed that several of the participants had already firmly decided what to study in

University. The fact that 8 of the Norwegian participants came from a preparatory program for university studies in their upper secondary school, may have been a factor here. The Icelandic teacher noted that she feels that the girls need more preparation and motivation than boys do, when it comes to considering careers within creative IT.

The participants were presented with a list of focus areas and asked to pick all the options that they would consider working with, if they were to choose to work with creative IT or media technology in the future. The list consisted of: Game development, robotics (toys, health, industry etc.), programming, TV production, visual effects, animation, 3D art, sound production, film production, film editing, web page design, graphic design, VR/AR productions, artificial intelligenc and "other".

The most frequently picked subject for the Norwegian participants was Film production (nine out of seventeen chose this option). The most popular subject for the Icelandic participants was Web page design (five out of eight chose this option). Group discussions revealed that several of the Norwegian participants have attended a course on film production. None of the Icelandic participants reported having worked with film production, and only one Icelandic participant picked this option in the survey. At the same time, several participants from Iceland reported having had an introductory course in web design and their teacher confirmed this on behalf of one of the schools.

The overall most popular options for possible future occupation were visual effects and animation, picked by a total of eleven pupils each. 10 participants picked film production, web page design and game development. The third most popular options were programming, 3D art and graphic design. The least popular subject was sound production, picked only by one participant, from the Norwegian workshop (Fig. 1).

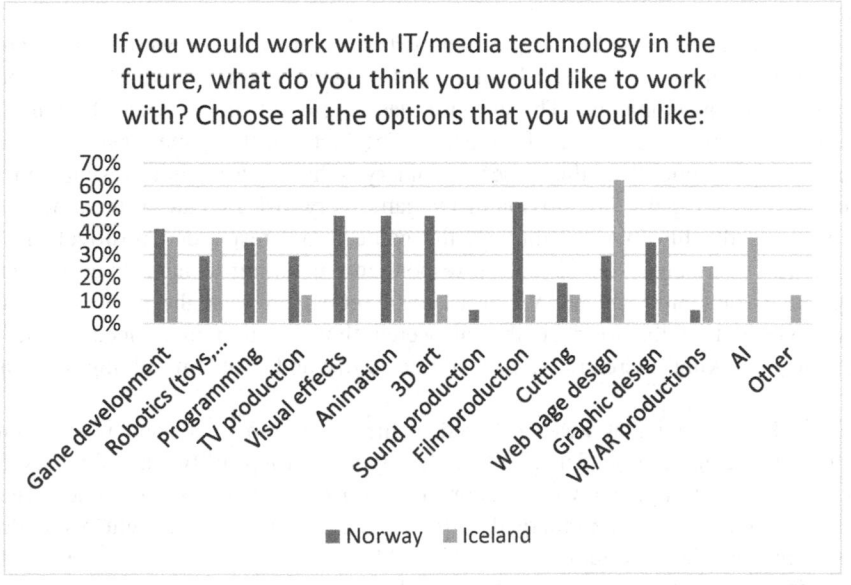

Fig. 1. The percentage of participants from each country that chose each option

When asked what would make them "even more interested" in creative IT/media technology, eleven participants wrote open answers. While the answers presented a variety of views, five of them had a common theme. They revealed that the girls found that information and opportunities regarding their creative IT/media technology options were lacking. One Norwegian participant phrased her comment this way: "I wish we got more information about media technology, then I'd definitely be more interested" while an Icelandic participant wrote "If one could get to try out more and get to see what it is like to work with this and what kind of jobs there are". Interest in learning more about what the students of game development and other creative IT studies do in their day to day life at the university was also mentioned in this context in a group discussion with the Norwegian participants. They also expressed an interest in participating on some of the activities of the university students to gain a better insight.

During the workshop, the participant were all focused on their tasks and seemed highly emerged when trying out the creative and playful approaches to IT. The final topical question was "Did this workshop influence your opinion about working in creative IT/media technology in the future?", to which answers were presented on a 5 point Likert scale, from "yes, very positively" which 15 Norwegian participants picked – to "yes, very negatively" which 1 Norwegian participant picked. While the Norwegian participants thus leaned towards the most assertive options, the Icelandic participants centered around the more neutral center of the scale. Six Icelandic participants claimed neutrality, but only 1 Norwegian participant. One Icelander chose "yes, rather positively" and another one picked "yes, rather negatively". In an interview after the workshop, their teacher confirmed that the students had enjoyed the workshop and that it had opened new horizons for them. At the same time she commented that it had been a little too short to be likely to have any permanent effect on their future choices.

The tools that were used in the practical parts of each workshop were very different. In the Norwegian workshop, Box Island, a coding game that is aimed at a very young audience [46] was employed. The purpose was to present the strategic thinking that underlies programming, in a playful manner. The fact that the game was directed at a younger target group than the upper secondary school participants resulted in the participants finishing the free version of the game very fast. In spite of this, they were deeply engaged while playing through the game - and responded positively in the survey, with fourteen of the seventeen respondents claiming to have liked the game "very much" or "fairly much". When asked to reflect on what the game had taught them, seven out of the fourteen that answered that question mentioned "logic" or "strategical thinking". Creativity, cooperation skills and problem solving were also listed.

Sonic Pi, the tool that was employed in the workshop in Iceland is sufficiently suited to mature age groups. The participants played in groups of two and three. At first they seemed a bit shy, but with encouragement from the female computer science students, they soon became emerged in the activity. Seven out of eight respondents reported having liked the tool "very well" or "fairly well". As for what the tool had taught them, two simply commented that they had learned that the program itself, Sonic Pi, was "fun". One respondent commented "that anything can be achieved through programming, such as composing music".

A group chat with the Norwegian participants at the end of the workshop brought to light that they had been pleasantly surprised to learn that several women had contributed to the advancement of modern technology. In the introduction and an inspiring talk, a representative of KUN centre for gender equality had presented several women pioneers of technology, such as Ada Lovelace, Hedy Lamarr, Grace Hopper and more. This turned out to have made a strong impression on the participants who claimed to not have been aware of the contributions of women to such technological development, prior to the workshop. They furthermore highlighted the importance of female role models and when asked which ones of them had any women role models within creative IT and media technology areas in their family or surroundings, only one out of the seventeen Norwegian participants raised their hand. The Icelandic teacher also mentioned the importance of role models. She observed that having volunteers from the network for female students of computer science seemed to influence the workshop participants in a positive way, as they were relatively close to the participants in age. She also commented that they since the volunteers had come across as pleasantly "casual and laid back" and answered and guided the upper secondary school girls openly and with a friendly and encouraging attitude, this too was a motivating factor.

5 Discussion and Conclusion

The participants in this study expressed fairly positive general attitudes towards creative IT. When asked if they would consider working with media technology or creative IT in the future, a rough half of the respondents considered it likely and six more respondents took a neutral stand. When it came to considering subjects to work with in the future from a list of preselected creative IT and media technology subjects, the participants seemed to favor subjects that they had already had some experience with. The most popular options were visual effects, animation, film production, web page design and game development. Differences in preferences between the countries seemed to correlate with which subjects the participants were familiar with from their upper secondary schools. Although the participants of the Icelandic workshop got to experiment with the sound programming environment Sonic Pi and expressed a positive attitude towards it, none of them chose sound production as a possible future occupation.

The participants identified lack of information about creative IT as an obstacle in the way of making them more interested in the field. They regretted not having received more insight into the field throughout their schooling, more knowledge of the actual tasks and activities of students of game development and other creative IT-subjects as well as more practical information about relevant job opportunities in the field. In spite of the experimental workshops being very short, and while the Icelandic participants expressed a somewhat more doubtful attitude in this respect, the attitude was generally positive and a majority claimed that the workshop had influenced their opinion about working in creative IT/media technology in the future in a positive way. Another key fact to highlight is they were both positively inclined towards the tools that they had gotten to try out in the practical workshop sessions – and reflective about their purposes.

Female role models within technology turned out to be important to the participants. They were intrigued to learn about some of the women pioneers of modern technology and emphasized the importance of female role models in their own environments. Their teacher also noted a positive effect of the presence and participation of female computer science students as role models in the workshop. Although the teacher's assertion may contradict the conclusion of Cheryan, Drury and Vichayapai [42], that the gender of a role model does not matter, it may also support their conclusion that counteracting stereotypes may work, as she described the young women from the / sys/tur network were fairly "casual", "laid back" and "friendly".

As the two experimental workshops were only short and were attended by pupils who were already more positively inclined towards creative IT subjects than average students, the Girls Just Wanna Have Fun-damental IT-skills project has some challenge ahead when it comes to finding effective ways to appeal to the average female upper secondary schools pupil. The findings of this study of the preparatory project do however provide some valuable indications that will be processed further in the main project.

While creative IT-workshops seem to have some positive effects on the participants' views, the identified obstacles of lacking information and role models draw attention to the importance of the education system. With increasing need for women's participation in creative IT, the education system may need to step up their game and cater to the seemingly lower technological interest of girls in ways that inform, motivate and inspire. The lessons learned from the preparatory project have resulted in the planning of frequent creative IT seminars for upper secondary teachers in the main project, where the aim is to equip and inspire teachers to address this need.

References

1. Shaw, A.: On not becoming gamers: moving beyond the constructed audience. Ada: J. Gend. New Med. Technol. **2** (2013). https://doi.org/10.7264/n33n21b3
2. Styhre, A., Remneland-Wikhamn, B., Szczepanska, A.-M., Ljungberg, J.: Masculine domination and gender subtexts: the role of female professionals in the renewal of the Swedish video game industry. Culture Organ. **24**(3), 244–261 (2018). https://doi.org/10.1080/14759551.2015.1131689
3. Sigurdardottir, H.D.I., Skevik, T.O., Ekker, K., Godejord, B.: Gender differences in perceiving digital game-based learning: back to square one? In: Munkvold, R.I., Kolås, L. (eds.) Proceedings of the 9th European Conference on Games-Based Learning, pp. 489–498. Academic Conferences International Limited, Steinkjer (2015)
4. Egenfeldt-Nielsen, S., Smith, J., Tosca, S.: Understanding Video Games. Routledge, New York (2008)
5. Lynch, T., Tompkins, J.E., van Driel, I.I., Fritz, N.: Sexy, strong, and secondary: a content analysis of female characters in video games across 31 years. J. Commun. **66**(4), 564–584 (2016). https://doi.org/10.1111/jcom.12237
6. Guynn, J.: Male-dominated gaming industry failing women gamers, Google finds, USA Today (2017). http://ezproxy.uin.no:2048/login
7. Quinn, Z.: Crash override: how gamergate [nearly] destroyed my life, and how we can win the fight against online hate. Public Affairs, New York (2017)

8. Weststar, J., O'Meara, V., Gosse, C., Legault, M.J.: Diversity Among Game Developers 2004–2015 Summary Report (2017). https://static1.squarespace.com/static/551ac4c9e4b003 8a33ecc74e/t/59c956e49f8dcee22ff666dd/1506367206466/Summary+Diversity+Report_FI NAL.pdf
9. Prescott, J., Bogg, J.: Segregation in a male dominated industry: women working in the computer games industry. Int. J. Gend. Sci. Technol. 3(1), 205–227 (2011)
10. Altiner, S., Ayhan, M.B.: An approach for the determination and correlation of diversity and efficiency of software development teams. South Afr. J. Sci. 114(3/4), 69–77 (2018). https:// doi.org/10.17159/sajs.2018/20170331
11. E. S. A. Essential Facts about the Computer and Video Game Industry (2014). https://www. isfe.eu/sites/isfe.eu/files/attachments/esa_ef_2013.pdf
12. Osborn, G.: Male and Female Gamers: How Their Similarities and Differences Shape the Games Market (2017). https://newzoo.com/insights/articles/male-and-female-gamers-how-their-similarities-and-differences-shape-the-games-market/
13. Lazzaro, N.: Are boy games even necessary? In: Kafai, Y., Heeter, C., Denner, J., Sun, J. (eds.) Beyond Barbie & Mortal Kombat - New Perspectives on Gender and Gaming, pp. 199–216. The MIT Press, Cambridge (2008)
14. Hartmann, T., Klimmt, C.: Gender and computer games: exploring females' dislikes. J. Comput.-Mediated Commun. 11(4), 910–931 (2006). https://doi.org/10.1111/j.1083-6101. 2006.00301.x
15. Medietilsynet: Barn og dataspill- tall Barn og medier-undersøkelsen 2018 og Foreldreundersøkelsen 2018 i forbindelse med lanscring av (2018). www.snakkomspill.no. 7 februar 2018. https://www.medietilsynet.no/globalassets/publikasjoner/barn-og-medier-undersokels er/dataspill-tallgrunnlag-februar-2018.pdf
16. Heimili og skóli. SAFT könnun á netnotkun barna og unglinga, May–August 2013 (2013). http://saft.is/wp-content/uploads/2017/09/Barnak%C3%B6nnun_4022745_SAFT_170314. pdf
17. Jónsson, B.Þ.: 66% Íslendinga spilar tölvuleiki – 41% spilar reglulega. Nörd Norðursins (2019). https://nordnordursins.is/2019/02/66-spilar-tolvuleiki/
18. Beavis, C., Muspratt, S., Thompson, R.: 'Computer games can get your brain working': student experience and perceptions of digital games in the classroom. Learn. Med. Technol. 40(1), 21–42 (2015)
19. Thornham, H., McFarlane, A.: Discourses of the digital native. Inf. Commun. Soc. 14(2), 258–279 (2011). https://doi.org/10.1080/1369118X.2010.510199
20. Steinkuehler, C.: Digital literacies: video games and digital literacies. J. Adolesc. Adult Literacy 54(1), 61–63 (2010)
21. Utdanningsspeilet: Utdanningsspeilet 2015 - Tall og analyse av barnehager og grunnopplæringen i Norge (2015). http://utdanningsspeilet.udir.no/2015/wp-content/uploa ds/2015/06/Utdanningsspeilet_2015.pdf
22. Nikken, P., Jansz, J.: Developing scales to measure parental mediation of young children's internet use. Learn. Med. Technol. 39, 250–266 (2013)
23. Lagesen, V.A.: A cyberfeminist utopia? Perceptions of gender and computer science among malaysian women computer science students and faculty. Sci. Technol. Hum. Values 33(1), 5–27 (2008). http://ezproxy.uin.no:2048/login
24. Orupabo, J.: Kompetanse – en symbolsk markør. Kjønn, etnisitet og aspirasjoner i overgangen mellom utdanning og arbeidsmarked (Unpublished Phd dissertation). University of Oslo, Oslo, Norway (2013). https://www.duo.uio.no/bitstream/handle/10852/39116/ PhDAvhandling_Orupabo.pdf?sequence=1&isAllowed=y
25. Abdul-Matin, I.: Girls Who Code and Bridge the Tech Gender Gap. PC Magazine, pp. 39–41 (2014)

26. Cunningham, C.: Girl game designers. New Media Soc. **13**(8), 1373–1388 (2011)
27. Denner, J., Campe, S.: What games made by girls can tell us. In: Kafai, Y., Heeter, C., Denner, J., Sun, J. (eds.) Beyond Barbie & Mortal Kombat - New Perspectives on Gender and Gaming, pp. 129–144. The MIT Press, Cambridge (2008)
28. Corneliussen, H.G., Prøitz, L.: Kids Code in a rural village in Norway: could code clubs be a new arena for increasing girls' digital interest and competence? Inf. Commun. Soc. **19**(1), 95–110 (2016). https://doi.org/10.1080/1369118X.2015.1093529
29. Appianing, J., Van Eck, R.N.: Gender differences in college students' perceptions of technology-related jobs in computer science. Int. J. Gend. Sci. Technol. **7**(1), 28–56 (2015)
30. Klawe, M., Whitney, T., Simard, C.: Women in computing—take 2. Commun. ACM **52**(2), 68–76 (2009)
31. Oslo Economics/Ove Skaug Halsos. Den norske spillbransjen - Utredning for Kulturde-partementet (2018). https://www.regjeringen.no/contentassets/a9e2f52dc18f4ef5a11c8f44f9 5dc7f9/den-norske-spillbransjen—utredning-fra-oslo-economics-februar-2018.pdf
32. Fallmyr, S.S.: Antall arbeidssøkere fortsetter å synke. Talentmedia (2018). https://tale ntmedia.no/antall-arbeidssokere-fortsetter-a-synke/
33. Borgersen, V.: Det er for få kvinner å velge mellom til IT-jobbene. Aftenposten. https:// www.aftenposten.no/okonomi/i/AaqM5/-Det-er-for-fa-kvinner-a-velge-mellom-til-IT-jobb ene. Accessed 19 Mar 2017
34. Morgunblaðið. Skortur á konum stendur upplýsingatækni fyrir þrifum (2015). https://www. mbl.is/vidskipti/frettir/2015/09/22/skortur_a_konum_i_upplysingataekni/
35. Finnsson, K.: Þörf á konum í tæknigreinum. Viðskiptablaðið (2014). http://www.vb.is/frettir/ thorf-konum-i-taeknigreinum/103174/?q=ccp
36. Leyton, D.: Ikke snakk om å tvinge jenter inn i en gutteklubb: Ved Høgskolen i Østfold jobbes det med å øke den lave kvinneandelen i norsk IT-bransje ved å lokke flere jenter til å velge studier innen IT. StudentTorget.no (2016). https://studenttorget.no/index.php?show= 3931&artikkelid=11887
37. Chen, Y., Mora, A., Kemis, M.: Recruiting and retaining women in information technology programs. New Dir. Commun. Coll. **2017**(178), 79–90 (2017). https://doi.org/10.1002/cc. 20255
38. Gose, B.: Rebooting Recruiting to Get More Women in Computer Science. Chronicle of Higher Education, p. 1 (2012). http://ezproxy.uin.no:2048/login
39. Young, D.M., Rudman, L.A., Buettner, H.M., McLean, M.C.: The influence of female role models on women's implicit science cognitions. Psychol. Women Q. **37**(3), 283–292 (2013). https://doi.org/10.1177/0361684313482109
40. Herrmann, S.D., Adelman, R.M., Bodford, J.E., Graudejus, O., Okun, M.A., Kwan, V.S.Y.: The effects of a female role model on academic performance and persistence of women in STEM courses. Basic Appl. Soc. Psychol. **38**(5), 258–268 (2016). https://doi.org/10.1080/ 01973533.2016.1209757
41. Fullerton, T., Fron, J., Pearce, C., Morie, J.: Getting girls into the game: towards a "Virtuous Cycle". In: Kafai, Y., Heeter, C., Denner, J., Sun, J. (eds.) Beyond Barbie & Mortal Kombat: New Perspectives on Gender and Computer Games. MIT, Cambridge (2007)
42. Tapia, A.H., Kvasny, L.: Recruitment is never enough: retention of women and minorities in the IT workplace. In: Trauth, E., Weisband, S. (eds.) Proceedings of the 2004 ACM SIGMIS CPR Conference, SIGMIS CPR 2004, pp. 84–91 (2004)
43. Drury, B.J., Siy, J.O., Cheryan, S.: When do female role models benefit women? The importance of differentiating recruitment from retention in STEM. Psychol. Inq. **22**(4), 265–269 (2011). https://doi.org/10.1080/1047840X.2011.620935

44. Cheryan, S., Drury, B.J., Vichayapai, M.: Enduring influence of stereotypical computer science role models on women's academic aspirations. Psychol. Women Q. **37**(1), 72–79 (2013). https://doi.org/10.1177/0361684312459328
45. Ørngreen, R., Levinsen, K.T.: Workshops as a research methodology. Electron. J. ELearn. **15**(1), 70–81 (2017)
46. Hour of code, 2017. Box Island (2017). https://boxisland.io/hourofcode

ATMF: A Student-Centered Framework for the Effective Implementation of Alternative Teaching Methods for CSEd

Anastasios Theodoropoulos[✉]📷, Costas Vassilakis,
Angeliki Antoniou, Manolis Wallace, and George Lepouras

University of Peloponnese, Tripoli, Greece
ttheodor@uop.gr

Abstract. The dynamic development of Informatics introduces new educational and pedagogical challenges, including the instructional design of teaching and learning. How can we teach our students better in such a growing and demanding field? Moreover, how can we motivate them and together have better learning results? This paper aims to give answers to these questions, through a student-centered framework for effectively encompassing alternative teaching methods within CS. The proposed framework (ATMF) summarizes the benefits of alternative teaching methods in contrast with known issues of traditional teaching. In addition, ATMF is built upon empirical evidence and concludes that alternative practices, if used under the right conditions, can provide increased motivation for learning and better learning outcomes.

Keywords: Computer science education · Teaching framework · Alternative teaching methods

1 Introduction

Informatics -also termed as "Computer Science" (CS)- is on the brink of an enormous possible growth and therefore it draws great interest from governments, businesses and other organizations as a top educational priority. Moreover, the dynamic development of the field introduces new educational and pedagogical challenges, including the instructional design of teaching and learning. How can we teach our students better in such a growing and demanding field? Furthermore, how can we motivate them and together consume better learning results?

Alternative Teaching Methods (ATM) that support students' active involvement in the learning process, according to the constructivism and constructionism principles, could be very helpful [1]. Alternative is considered everything that is relating to activities that depart from or challenge traditional norms[1]. Therefore, ATM refers to providing students with different approaches/strategies to learning the same information. There are several instructional methodologies used by educators and researchers

---

[1] Cambridge Online Dictionary: http://dictionary.cambridge.org/dictionary/english/alternative, last accessed June 2019

© IFIP International Federation for Information Processing 2020
Published by Springer Nature Switzerland AG 2020
I. O. Pappas et al. (Eds.): I3E 2019 Workshops, IFIP AICT 573, pp. 116–127, 2020.
https://doi.org/10.1007/978-3-030-39634-3_11

in order to deal with the complexity and the needs of various cases. Nevertheless, using them could be adapted in more approaches with similar features. As Morrison, Ross [2] state, instructors at any level of education should implement various pedagogical approaches and teaching methods when the discipline and learning tasks vary.

However, most instructors have little practice or experience with teaching methods other than traditional lecturing [3]. Some have a particular teaching style that they use in every teaching context, regardless of the type or level of student learning they expect. Others, because of the CS discipline, may already use various technology applications, but their decisions may not be based on student-centered pedagogy [4, 5]. Finally, a number of instructors are concerned that students will respond negatively to teaching and learning activities that are new to them [6]. Thus, any of these factors can hinder the reframing of teaching to a student-centered perspective. It becomes apparent that there is a need for a clear and easy-to-adopt, student-centered framework encompassing alternative teaching concepts.

One may argue that several models exist, standards, curriculum guidelines or frameworks that can be used for teaching and learning purposes. However, most of them refer to teaching in a general scope [7] or teaching in a specific discipline different from CS, like frameworks from math, science, and technology education. Therefore, the existing frameworks neither consider the identity and particularities of CS Education (CSE), nor prescribe suitable alternative teaching strategies. For example, within the CS field, the "K–12 Computer Science Framework", describes the foundational literacy in CS, aiming to show that CS is essential for all students [8]. This framework includes standards, curriculum, course pathways and even professional development suggestions for all K–12 grade levels, but it does not include any specific teaching guidelines. Other national frameworks, describe CS concepts and practices that students should know, but do not focus on alternative teaching methods. Finally, other well established frameworks in higher education, like the Advanced Placement CS Principles curriculum framework and the ACM's curriculum guidelines for undergraduate CS programs [9], provide standards for students and curricula, but not for teachers who want to teach students. Additionally, although a teaching framework could be based on existing research and well-established practices, it should also be evolving, taking into account new empirical studies. The lack of empirical research on best practices in CSE has led researchers to repetitively ask similar basic questions without clear progress toward resolving them, although current practical research shows promise [10].

Given the above-mentioned research motivations, it is clear that there is potential for learning achievement to be improved in CSE through the effective design and use of new methods, strategies and approaches. Thus, the aim of this study is the development of a student-centered framework for teaching that can provide shared understandings, which can help improve the quality of instructional design, course and lesson planning, learning and assessment.

The next section maps a territory of topics encountered in CSE. The third section presents the proposed framework and the fourth section presents briefly the empirical studies that were conducted during its formulation. Finally, we summarize this article in the fifth section.

2   Background Work

2.1   The CS Discipline

CSE is learning about CS and focuses on teaching the fundamental concepts of the discipline, just as core Mathematics and Physics courses do. Nevertheless, confusion arises when trying to distinguish between the most common areas of computing education offered in schools like CS, IT and Educational Technology [11]. There are many different aspects of CSE. To the same reason, there is an ignorance about the core concepts and characteristics that students are taught through CSE. This reflects to the wider ignorance by the general public about the nature, methodologies, and contributions of the field in the modern world.

However, through CS learners can acquire many valuable skills and characteristics, beyond the narrow scope of programming. Coding is an indispensable tool for CS, enabling the creation of software, but CS is a broader field covering many different concepts that go well beyond coding. Through CS, one can develop logical reasoning and gain awareness of the resources required to implement, test, and deploy a solution, and how to deal with real-world constraints. All these skills are applicable in many contexts, from science and engineering to the humanities and business, and they have enabled deeper understanding in these and other areas.

2.2   Traditional Strategies Issues

Probably the main argument posed against traditional classroom styles involves how little it truly engages students [12]. In addition, traditional, lecture-based structures serve particularly adroit conduits for rote learning and memorization. Another issue with traditional strategies involves teacher bias. Most subjects are not objective, and since the instructor stands as the highest authority in the room, the more strict, rote structure only presents some perspectives on the matters at hand [13]. The most effective educational settings are more active and allow students to consider content from multiple angles and form multiple opinions, rather than adopting what teachers transfer [12]. Moreover, not every teacher is good at public speaking. Poor communicators and speaking anxiety can seriously screw over different learners, even if they typically benefit from traditional lecture structures [14]. It is crucial that teachers understand where their public speaking limitations lie and alter their styles accordingly for maximum educational achievement [14].

Furthermore, traditional strategies may suit better some students than others and strengthen a limited number of skills. The highly dynamic field of CS demands that learners must be empowered with reflective lifelong learning skills in order to be successful. They need to develop skills such as CT, problem solving, teamwork, communication, critical thinking, and creativity. The traditional teacher-centric pedagogy is focused on the course content and only on transferring knowledge to the students whereas a learner-centric view is focused on assisting students to develop or build knowledge [15]. In CSE a move to a learner-centered design is recommended [16], because active elements of a 21st century education receive little attention.

Therefore, reliance on the traditional lecture as the main mode of student learning has been criticized and new alternative strategies are needed.

2.3   Alternative Teaching Methods

In addition to traditional teaching, educators and curriculum designers must consider learning activities and instructional techniques that aim to student motivation and learning. There are many parameters that need to be considered, like the students' age and experience on technology matters or the learning goals. There are also several methods used by educators and researchers in order to deal with the complexity and the needs of various cases. Table 1 gives a summary of the ATMs used in CSE by the time this article was written.

Table 1. Alternative teaching methods used in CSE.

1	Peer learning	11	Non-textual programming
2	Problem-based learning	12	Contextualized learning
3	Project-based learning	13	CS unplugged
4	Studio-based learning	14	Subgoal learning
5	Inquiry-based learning	15	Programming puzzles
6	Process oriented guided inquiry learning	16	Extreme programming
7	Team learning	17	Program visualization
8	Game-based learning	18	Competency-based learning
9	Educational robotics	19	Social networks learning
10	Physical computing	20	Emerging technologies

3   The ATM Framework

Learning different CS concepts more effectively, requires the development of a multi-level framework that could be applied in different contexts using different teaching approaches to a multitude of application domains. This article proposes a framework for the effective implementation of ATM in CS.

3.1   A New Conceptual Framework

This new framework is called the ATMF (Alternative Teaching Methods Framework). ATMF is a broad description of the context, characteristics, content and sequence of learning expected of all learners - but not at the level of detail of grade-by-grade standards or, at the course description and standards. Figure 1 illustrates the five phases of the methodology that was adapted in order to develop the ATMF. The current literature on ATM, has provided the theoretical framework for the studies reported in this paper. The proposed framework is intended as a guide to instructors (formal or informal settings) as well as for curriculum designers, assessment developers, researchers and professionals responsible for CSE. Thus, it describes the major concepts, and disciplinary core ideas that all instructors should be familiar with in order to enhance their teaching with alternative strategies, and providing an outline of how these practices, concepts, and ideas should be developed across different settings. ATMF was based both on previous theoretical frameworks and models as well as empirical guidelines.

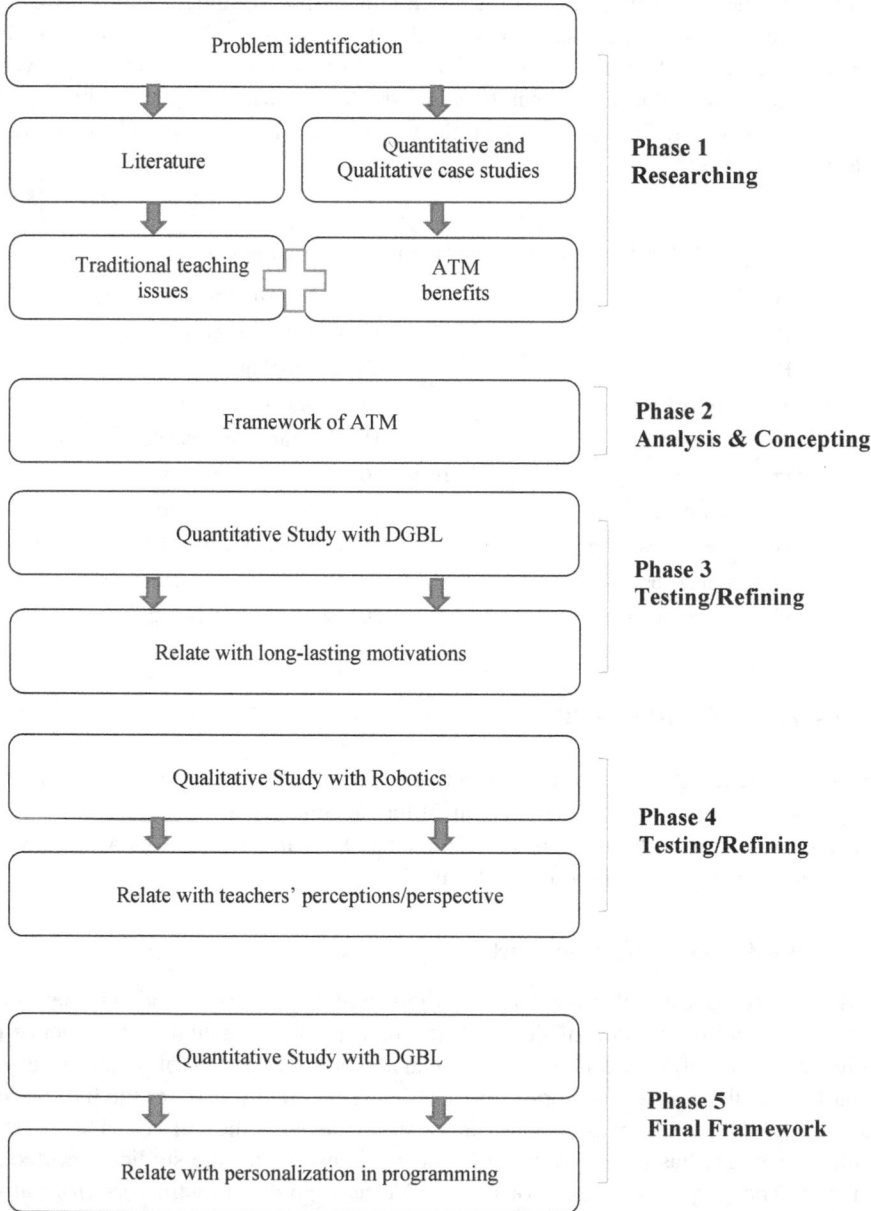

Fig. 1. The five-phased methodology adapted for developing the ATM framework.

Phase 1: We researched alternative teaching methods within CS, other frameworks and contacted two initial empirical studies with quantitative and qualitative data. Background expert work from well know educational models and frameworks was reused. The process on one hand revealed the teaching issues that the traditional teaching methods have and on the other hand highlighted the key advantages of ATM.

Phase 2: We analyzed the concepts used at the ATMF. In this phase the framework was initially shaped through literature review and the initial empirical research.

Phase 3: We tested and refined the ATMF. In this phase the framework was examined and enhanced with additional elements through another empirical research study with Digital Game-Based Learning (DGBL).

Phase 4: We tested and refined the ATMF. In this phase the framework was tested again and enhanced with additional elements, though another empirical research study.

Phase 5: We tested and shaped the final ATMF. In this phase the framework was tested once more, enhanced with additional elements and finalized.

3.2   Analysis - Concepting

The ATMF comprises the need to consider context, content, pedagogy, instructor and the learner as part of the design process, so-called dimensions. Dimensions contain components, where each component defines a distinct aspect of a dimension and components are consisted of elements that describe specific features.

Table 2. Components end Elements of Dimension 1.

Dimension 1: context		
Component **1a**	Education level	
	Element 1	Formal education/type of school/level
	Element 2	Informal education
	Element 3	Non-formal education
Component **1b**	Environment (physical)	
	Element 1	Infrastructure (availability)
	Element 2	Supporting resources
Component **1c**	Educational system	
	Element 1	Policies
	Element 2	Compulsory curriculum
	Element 3	CS standards
	Element 4	General public attitudes
	Element 5	Time restrictions

In particular, in advance of planning a lesson with the use of ATMF, it is suggested that a comprehensive learning analysis be produced that sufficiently covers the following standpoints:

Dimension 1. Context: The components in this dimension describe the surrounding environment around the learning process (Table 2). This dimension deals with the need to consider the educational level and the place where learning is taking place, the resources available (e.g. access to laptops/computers, mobiles, technical support), and the disciplinary context (e.g. in school, in ICT lab, in a university, at home, in the workplace). The components establish the environment that supports the learning and are not directly associated with the learning of any particular content, instead, they set the stage for all learning processes. The specific elements of the learning environment are captured in three categories: Teaching Level, Classroom Level and Educational System.

Dimension 2. Participants: This dimension describes the participants' characteristics in two main components, learners and instructors (Table 3). The environment including the relationship between instructor and learners and the cultural norms (characteristics) play a significant role in what can and does occur during the teaching and learning. Both learner and instructor characteristics are important for instructional designers as they allow them to design and create tailored instructions for a target group.

Table 3. Components end Elements of Dimension 2.

Dimension 2: participants' characteristics		
Component **2a**	Learner-related	
	Element 1	Age
	Element 2	Gender
	Element 3	Cultural background
	Element 4	Socioeconomic status
	Element 5	ICT use
	Element 6	ICT experience
	Element 7	Attitudes
	Element 8	Personality traits
Component **2b**	Instructor-related	
	Element 1	Age
	Element 2	Gender
	Element 3	Teaching experience
	Element 4	Academic characteristics
	Element 5	Skills - abilities
	Element 6	Attitudes
	Element 7	Personality traits

Component 2b also contains instructors' attitudes (element 6) about alternative ways of teaching. For instance, teachers that prefer traditional teaching believe that it gives better learning results and hesitate to include active-learning methods in their teaching, although they see some advantages in them.

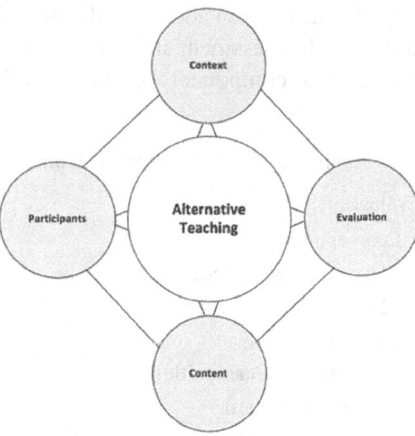

Fig. 2. The ATM Framework for CSE.

Finally, personality traits (element 7) relate to such things as actions, attitudes and behaviors that determine different personality styles like cognitive style and intelligence type. Being positive and upbeat can influence learners around an instructor, and so can negativity. The personalities of both instructor and learner interacting with one another and with the content create a unique environment. It is expected that by taking into account the participants' characteristics can be designed and developed more efficient, effective and motivating instructional materials.

Dimension 3. Content: The components of this dimension reflect process workflows from teaching and learning theories and from the ATMs. Those components describe how an instructor organizes the content that the students are to learn and how he/she designs instruction (Table 4). Component 3a comprises of five elements, related to what is the content to be taught. Elements 1 to 3, refer to lesson planning and effort to answer queries like: What is the subject to be taught? What are the objectives and goals that instructor aims to achieve? Does the lesson planning refer to short or long-term features? etc.

Table 4. Components end Elements of Dimension 3.

Dimension 3: content		
Component **3a**	Learning	
	Element 1	Subject
	Element 2	Objectives
	Element 3	Short-term & long-term planning
	Element 4	Expectations for learning
	Element 5	Relations to other subjects/disciplines
Component **3b**	Teaching	
	Element 1	Lecture-based
	Element 2	ATMs

Dimension 4. Evaluation: This dimension addresses the outcomes of the teaching and learning processes, which deal with assessment and evaluation. The outcomes (direct or indirect) are examined in two main components as shown at Table 5.

Table 5. Components end Elements of Dimension 4.

Dimension 4: Evaluation		
Component **4a**	Learner-related	
	Element 1	Knowledge/performance
	Element 2	Motivation
	Element 3	Skills
	Element 4	Metacognition
	Element 5	Beliefs
Component **4b**	Instructor-related	
	Element 1	Assessment criteria/method
	Element 2	Monitoring of learning (learning analytics)
	Element 3	Feedback to learners
	Element 4	Long-term evaluation
	Element 5	Teaching evaluation

3.3   Shaping the ATMF

Figure 2 (above) provides the visual description that was used to for the ATMF. This visual recognized the importance of multiple dimensions of: context (describing the setting, curriculum, policies and infrastructure), participants (describing the instructors and learners' characteristics), content (describing the subject matter, purposes and values, pedagogy and strategies) and evaluation (describing the outcomes for both learners and instructors). Those four dimensions are presented as being a complex and interconnected whole with ATM at the hub connecting all the dimensions. ATM is in the center of all the process in order to emphasize that instructors have to think about and reflect upon the multiple dimensions as they investigated each topic or assignment of implementing ATM. The overall goal is to guide instructors in developing an integrated, interconnected knowledge for implementing effectively ATM in their teaching.

4   Experience with the ATMF

Figure 3 provides a graphical overview of the empirical studies conducted in several Greek educational settings to help formulate the proposed framework. This model consists of three interrelated levels: Initially the key characteristics that were researched for every empirical study are reported. Next, is shown the alternative teaching approach that was implemented for each study. Finally, at the bottom of this visualization, are presented the proposed framework's stages corresponded with the previous approaches and studies.

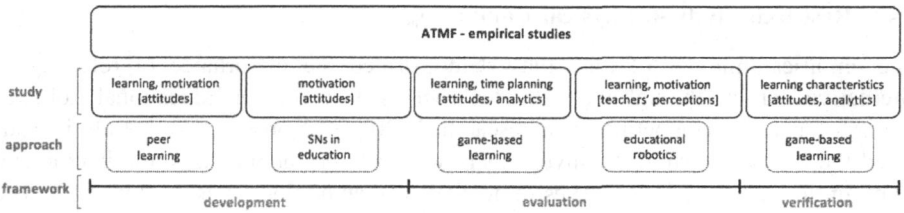

Fig. 3. A map of the empirical studies within ATMF.

All the studies described in this section, are all previously reported elsewhere in peer-reviewed publications and therefore are presented briefly.

4.1 Research Study 1: Peer Learning

Initially, we conducted an experiment using Peer Learning and Collaboration techniques comparing them to traditional teaching, to secondary education students [17]. The learning from these techniques was assessed and students' attitudes towards the alternative teaching were researched through quantitative data ($n = 57$ students). In addition, teachers' opinions about that way of teaching and learning were explored through means of qualitative data. The empirical findings of this study confirmed the positive effects of student-centered learning techniques at CSE. The study was used as an input during the design of the ATMF and provided evidence that the specific ATM had better learn results and increased motivation by learners.

4.2 Research Study 2: Social Networks in Education

Secondly, we researched Social Networks (SN) for assisted learning, through an observational study with undergraduate students [18]. Facebook was used as a teaching tool in higher education and ways that SNs can be used in teaching and learning were investigated. Both qualitative and quantitative data were gathered ($n = 66$ students) through one academic term. The results reported that students were highly motivated to participate in the lesson through the Facebook page although there seem to exist some personalities, cultural and gender differences about the usage. This study was also used as an input for the ATMF while it confirmed the positive effects of SNs in promoting learning and motivation.

4.3 Research Study 3: Game-Based Learning

Next, we examined the Game-Based Learning method (GBL), in order to teach basic programming concepts to primary school pupils [19]. The empirical findings of this study (quantitative data from $n = 94$ students gathered) confirmed the positive effects of GBL in promoting basic programming principles to young children. Empirical findings derived from this analysis provided valuable information games and pupils' satisfaction and willingness to use them for acquiring programming knowledge. In addition, Pair Programming method was students' choice for learning programming. However, the short activity of this study did not have long term results and motivation at children and thus the element of long-term planning was added to the ATMF.

4.4 Research Study 4: Physical Computing

The empirical findings of this study demonstrated the importance of referring to alternative learning through the instructor's views. In particular Educational Robotics through a national competition was researched [20]. This observational study investigated the benefits of students' involvement with robotics about skills, motivation and learning through the teachers' eyes (a qualitative methodology was used $n = 18$). The results showed that there are numerous benefits for students: they increased their collaboration, problem solving and creativity skills; understand STEM concepts about CS and engineering and especially gaining programming knowledge. Therefore, the ATMF was enhanced with the instructors' perspective about the learners' knowledge and motivations.

4.5 Research Study 5: Personal Learning Characteristics

Finally, the empirical findings of this research identified different personality traits and especially cognitive style as an important factor in programming learning through serious games. This study investigated students' attitudes (quantitative data gathered from $n = 77$ students) from gaming activities to reveal the quality of their learning experience and correlated it with their cognitive profile to reveal potential differences [21]. In addition, through an empirical way it was revealed the GBL effectiveness and next it was compared to students' cognitive styles. Cognitive style was found to be a significant learning characteristic that should be taken into consideration when using digital games to learn programming. This study was used to finalize the ATMF and provided evidence that personality traits may affect both teaching and learning.

5 Conclusion

In this paper, we present ATMF, a conceptual framework for CSE that allows teachers to continuously experiment with and improve their teaching. The proposed framework is about student-centered teaching pedagogy trying to address issues around learning and teaching of CS concepts. The ATMF is implemented based on the perspective that learning is a socially embedded cognitive process and knowledge is socially constructed through interaction and activity with others. The main objective of the ATMF is to promote motivation and enhance learning. It proposes that this model can be used in examining instructors' CS lessons of any level and any context and in designing experiences for teachers on the integration of student-centered practices in CS teaching.

The proposed framework for teaching with the use of alternative methods can make teaching both more effective and more efficient, by helping create the conditions that support student learning and minimize the need for revising materials, content, and policies. While implementing these principles requires a commitment in time and effort, it often saves time and energy later on. However, more work needs to be done. We consider that the framework itself is robust and therefore it will not change. Likewise, we expect that for ATM some practices may change and new ones may be added.

References

1. Theodoropoulos, A., Antoniou, A., Lepouras, G.: Students teach students: alternative teaching in Greek secondary education. Educ. Inf. Technol. **21**, 1–27 (2014)
2. Morrison, G.R., Ross, S.J., Morrison, J.R., Kalman, H.K.: Designing Effective Instruction. Wiley (2019)
3. Yadav, A., Gretter, S., Hambrusch, S., Sands, P.: Expanding computer science education in schools: understanding teacher experiences and challenges. Comput. Sci. Educ. **26**(4), 235–254 (2016)
4. Cuny, J.: Transforming high school computing: a call to action. ACM Inroads **3**(2), 32–36 (2012)
5. Yadav, A., Hong, H., Stephenson, C.: Computational thinking for all: pedagogical approaches to embedding 21st century problem solving in K-12 classrooms. TechTrends **60**, 565–568 (2016)
6. Stes, A., Gijbels, D., Van Petegem, P.: Student-focused approaches to teaching in relation to context and teacher characteristics. High. Educ. **55**(3), 255–267 (2008)
7. Danielson, C.: Enhancing Professional Practice: A Framework for Teaching. ASCD (2011)
8. K-12 Computer Science Framework Steering Committee: K-12 Computer Science Framework, p. 307. ACM (2016)
9. Joint Task Force on Computing Curricula, Association for Computing Machinery, IEEE Computer Society: Computer Science Curricula 2013: Curriculum Guidelines for Undergraduate Degree Programs in Computer Science, p. 518. ACM (2013)
10. Porter, L., Simon, B.: Retaining nearly one-third more majors with a trio of instructional best practices in CS1. In: Proceeding of the 44th ACM Technical Symposium on Computer Science Education. ACM (2013)
11. CSTA Standards Task Force: CSTA K-12 Computer Science Standards, ACM - Association for Computing Machinery (2011)
12. Felder, R.M., Brent, R.: Teaching and Learning STEM: A Practical Guide. Wiley, Hoboken (2016)
13. Ary, D., Jacobs, L.C., Irvine, C.K.S., Walker, D.: Introduction to Research in Education. Cengage Learning (2018)
14. King, P.E., Finn, A.N.: A test of attention control theory in public speaking: cognitive load influences the relationship between state anxiety and verbal production. Commun. Educ. **66**(2), 168–182 (2017)
15. Wright, G.B.: Student-centered learning in higher education. Int. J. Teach. Learn. High. Educ. **23**(1), 92–97 (2011)
16. Guzdial, M.: Learner-centered design of computing education: research on computing for everyone. Synth. Lect. Hum.-Cent.Ed Inform. **8**(6), 1–165 (2015)
17. Theodoropoulos, A., Antoniou, A., Lepouras, G.: Students teach students: alternative teaching in Greek secondary education. Educ. Inf. Technol. **21**(2), 373–399 (2016)
18. Antoniou, A., Theodoropoulos, A., Christopoulou, K., Lepouras, G.: Facebook as teaching tool in higher education: a case study. Int. J. Adv. Soc. Sci. Hum. **2**(3), 43–56 (2014)
19. Theodoropoulos, A., Antoniou, A., Lepouras, G.: The little ones, the big ones and the code: utilization of digital educational games in primary school pupils. In: 7th Conference on Informatics in Education (CIE 2015). Greek Computer Society (GCS), Piraeus, Greece, pp. 40–49 (2015)
20. Theodoropoulos, A., Antoniou, A., Lepouras, G.: Educational robotics in the service of CSE: a study based on the PanHellenic competition. In: Proceedings of the 11th Workshop in Primary and Secondary Computing Education. ACM (2016)
21. Theodoropoulos, A., Antoniou, A., Lepouras, G.: How do different cognitive styles affect learning programming? Insights from a game-based approach in Greek schools. Trans. Comput. Educ. **17**(1), 1–25 (2016)

Framework for Pupil-to-Student Transition, Learning Environment and Semester Start for First-Year Students

Omid Mirmotahari$^{(\boxtimes)}$, Gunnar Rye Bergersen, Yngvar Berg, Kristin Bråthen, and Kristin Broch Eliassen

Department of Informatics, University of Oslo, Oslo, Norway
omidmi@ifi.uio.no

Abstract. For several years, the Department of Informatics at the University of Oslo has welcomed large student groups: over 450 new students at the start of studies in August, divided into five study programmes. This is a demanding job involving many people and challenges with coordination of information. Over the past three years, we have worked systematically on various measures to promote a good learning environment for students throughout their first year. In this paper, we present a framework that has evolved through several years of work on semester startup and other measures during the first year of study. Using an evaluation form and interviews through several semesters, we have collected data for semester startup. We highlight in what way the measures contribute to (1) increased collaboration among students, (2) improving study progress and (3) reduced drop-out.

Keywords: First year student · Semester start · Learning environment · Mentor week · Programme seminar · Pre-course · Pupil-to-student transition

1 Introduction

For many students, the transition from high school to university is challenging. Both in Norway and internationally, there is a great interest in pupil-to-student transition [1,2], and the first-year experience (FYE). Both the experiences the students have through their first year of study and the experiences they receive from student reception during their first few days are important for academic achievement. The literature describes many challenges, including encountering a new social environment, misunderstandings regarding study requirements and high work pressure [3–6]. The research highlights the importance of a combination of various academic and social activities that support students' dedication to the subject-specific approach to knowledge as well as their preparation for new role as a student in higher education. A holistic approach that supports

© IFIP International Federation for Information Processing 2020
Published by Springer Nature Switzerland AG 2020
I. O. Pappas et al. (Eds.): I3E 2019 Workshops, IFIP AICT 573, pp. 128–139, 2020.
https://doi.org/10.1007/978-3-030-39634-3_12

academic, social and emotional measures is what seems to be beneficial for a good learning environment [7, 8].

Interaction and social belonging are important for learning. [9] claims that the amount of interaction with fellow students has far-reaching effects in almost every aspect of the learning environment, student learning and personal development. [10] conclude that creating space and opportunities for students to be able to interact with the subject teacher and to get to know fellow students is a powerful tool to promote student affiliation and sense of mastery. [11] emphasise social and cultural factors in student transition, and focus in particular on colloquium groups as an approach that promotes learning while also providing increased motivation for study. [12] show that students who spend too little time studying often find alternative strategies for passing courses with less focus on achieving learning outcomes [13–15]

The learning process includes phases of confusion and disorientation [16] and, accordingly, care should be taken to prevent first-year students from being left alone with their challenges. New students may lack the meta-cognition needed to reflect on their own knowledge, skills and working methods; thus, misunderstanding may potentially hinder further study [17].

For several years, the Department of Informatics at the University of Oslo has welcomed large student groups: over 450 students, organised in five study programmes[1] from 2017 and in four study programmes in previous years. Receiving many students is a demanding task which involves many people and the coordination of much information. Over the past three years, we have worked systematically on various measures to promote a good learning environment for students throughout their first year. We have involved students in this process through collecting data using evaluation forms and interviews. In this paper, we present a framework and a number of measures that are perceived by the students as motivational and learning-enhancing.

This paper is organised as follows: in Sect. 2 we describe the work process and framework. The method we have used to obtain the results is presented in Sect. 3. The paper concludes with results and a discussion in Sect. 4.

2   Work Process, Measures and Framework

The work to establish a good learning environment is a continuous process throughout the first year. In recent years, we have worked systematically on various measures through the students' first year of study. Our experiences have been gathered systematically to form a framework for future years. The preparation of this framework has been ongoing work over several years, which has mainly been achieved by utilising data collected through surveys and interviews with students. There are several motivations for having such a framework, especially the need for information flow to all parties involved, which are:

---

[1] The five study programmes are: (1) design, use and interaction, (2) digital economy and management, (3) programming and system architecture, (4) robotics and intelligent systems and (5) language technology.

departmental management, study administration, academic staff, subject teachers, tutors, students and technical administrative staff. There are up to 750 people to be simultaneously coordinated and provided with information. Such a tool for project planning provides good opportunities for co-writing and sharing across the organisation.

There are several activities that are carried out in relation to the learning environment, but in this paper we will only include the activities that the department arranges. Hence, we will discuss the following work processes:

- The design process
- Start of studies and student reception
- Pre-course
- Programme seminar

2.1   The Design Process

The framework is highly valuable in the design process. Using a timeline provides valuable coordination of the various tasks. All tasks are based on a model of coordination and mutual dependence, making it easy to keep track of progress. The planning starts in February, when all the key players – the study administration and the tutors – meet for a joint exchange of experiences from previous year. In this meeting, any changes and new actions will also be discussed. After this meeting, all parties have a common outline for this year's plan; especially important are the start of the semester and student reception. We will not go through the framework's 26 parts with sub-items in detail, but will highlight the most important elements in the following sub-sections.

2.2   Start of Studies and Student Reception

The most important action is the programme for the semester start, which consists of a number of activities to facilitate a good learning environment. The focus is the first week in the autumn semester – one week prior to the first lectures. Previously, this week has been called the tutor week, but the name has been changed to reflect the fact that the week contains more than just tutor activities. It is important to promote the academic content of the week and the interaction with social events. In order to create a good synergy and collaboration between the different stakeholders, the first week is carefully planned in terms of both the social events, which are organised by the tutors, and the academic events, which are organised by the department. Student reception at the start of the week involves all new students attending an opening ceremony (35 min). In order to strengthen the affiliation to the department, it is important to have an auditorium that is large enough to accommodate all students, but at the same time it is important to organise it so that local affiliation for each study programme is achieved. Figure 1 shows an example where the students are organised into different seating areas for each programme.

In the opening ceremony, the department's management and the leader of the tutors welcome the students, which also reinforces the connection between academic and social aspects of both the study start week and the rest of the semester. Next, the students get a professional presentation on what informatics is; this is done in order to reinforce the students' awareness and confirmation of what they will study in the next few years. A brief presentation of some important deadlines from the administration team helps to emphasise the students' responsibility for their own learning. The ceremony concludes with a pep-talk which gives students confirmation that they have made the right choice and initiates the process of helping increase students' pride in their study.

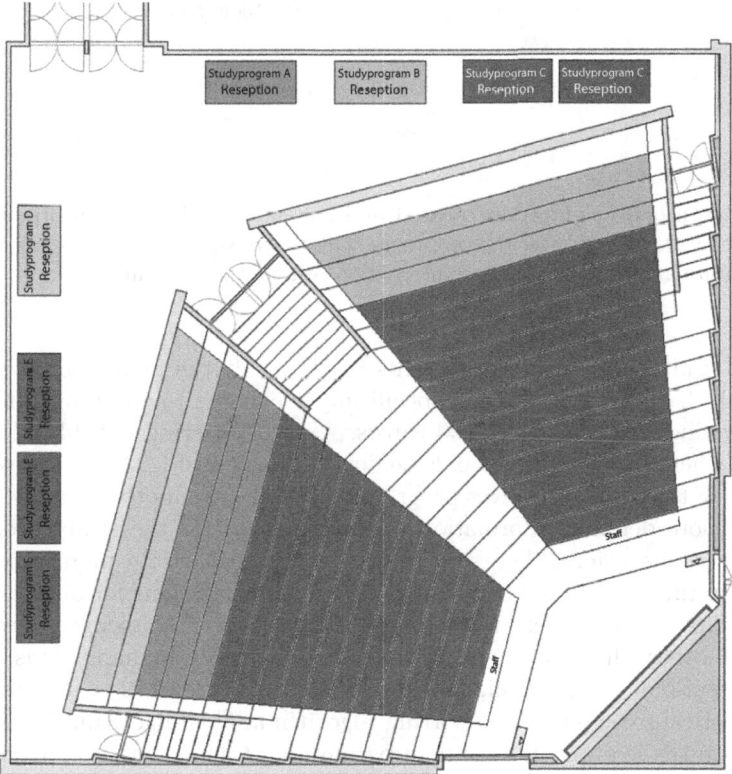

Fig. 1. The distribution and the collection of students in the auditorium for the respective study programmes.

After the opening ceremony, the students follow the programme council leader for the study they are admitted to. To strengthen the social aspect, we have chosen to include the tutors as early as possible. Already when the students leave the auditorium, all the tutors are ready to mingle with the students in the respective study programmes. Figure 2 illustrates how the tutors stand in

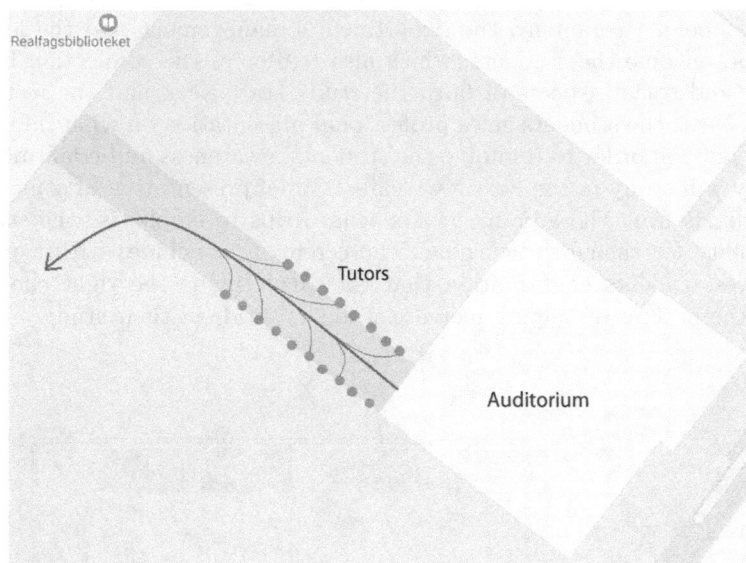

Fig. 2. The tutors (mentors) are located in a column outside the auditorium that all the new students attend after the ceremony. The tutors will continuously mix with the student group and help to promote interaction among the students.

a column and merge with the students as they exit the auditorium; it is very important that this is organised specifically so that all actors are informed – especially since there are over 100 tutors. A tutor meeting is held one week in advance, where this is clarified and the details shown in Fig. 2 are reviewed. The next part of the agenda involves programme-specific events that mainly give the students more detailed information and motivation for the study programme they have chosen. Here, there will also be information from more experienced students in the programme including their recommendations for obtaining good study habits. Before lunch, the students will receive a challenge: they should greet each other while sorting themselves alphabetically by name. It is a simple kind of team-building method, and in addition to approaching each other, they get a practical experience of a sorting algorithm. This algorithm is reinforced and used in the lectures during the programming topics. Once the students are sorted by name, they are personally handed a citizen certificate from the programme council leader. This citizen's certificate is proof that they have been admitted to the study programme with the university's seal, which also helps to strengthen the sense of pride and identity.

> *'It is wonderful to get a citizenship letter.'*
> (Student #nor18-2-15)   **Q:1**

The department serves lunch to all new students, tutors and teachers with the objective of creating a space for socialisation. The tutors gather their participants in groups during lunch, and the tutors have their own activities for socialising during the lunchtime. After lunch, students meet in their respective study programmes and receive a review of expectations to confirm and/or reject their own expectations. The first day ends with a joint departure to the official welcome ceremony of the university arranged by the university management.

During the following days there are various activities that are organised by both the tutors and the administration. Figure 3 shows a concrete overview of how the first week of the year is organised.

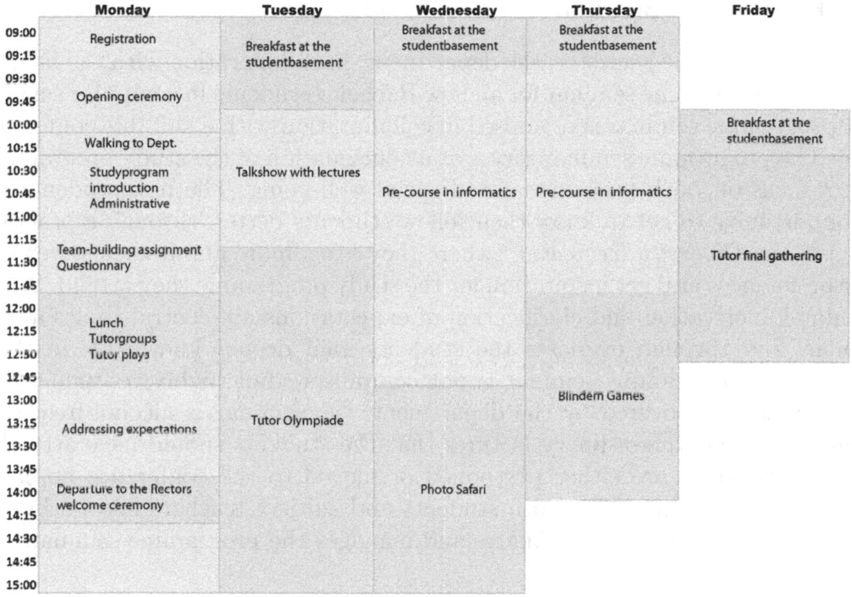

Fig. 3. Time schedule for the study start. The orange blocks represent the department's 'ownership', and the green ones are run by the tutors. (Color figure online)

2.3   Pre-course

The first pre-course at the department was given in 1997. At the end of the 1990s, many started the computer science programme without any prior experience of using a computer, and this was especially true of the girls. The purpose of the course was therefore to give inexperienced students, both boys and girls, practical experience in using computers. A teacher talked about how to use computers and the student association provided practical training by creating tasks and providing guidance. The course was a great success and has been given every year since.

The content of the course has changed over the years. Today, all new students are somewhat experienced computer users, but very few have knowledge of, for example, the Linux operating system, which is widely used at the department and throughout the study programme. The focus of the course is therefore to prepare the students for the challenges they will meet in the coming semester: computers with both Windows and Linux, suitable software to use their own computer, connection to the university's computer network, practical problems around user accounts, use of e-mail, course information, etc. The student organisation at the department is responsible for the preparation and revision of the exercises and tasks used in the course.

2.4   Programme Seminar

A few weeks into the semester, the department, in collaboration with the faculty, arranges a programme seminar for all new Bachelor students in computer science. This programme seminar is organised in collaboration with a suitable conference hotel. The programme seminar serves as a continuation of the study programme, with a focus on both professional and social well-being. The new students get the opportunity to get to know their fellow students better, through a practical exercise, the *Diversity Icebreaker*[2] where they learn more about themselves and their preferences and get inspiration for the study programme they attend. Study technique, motivation and clarification of expectations are central topics at the seminar, and through exercises the students gain deeper knowledge in these aspects. The programme seminar is not compulsory but highly recommended, and all costs are covered by the department; the seminar is alcohol-free. It is organised so that the ordinary lectures that the students should have attended on these two days are either postponed or moved to the conference hotel. In practice, joint transport for both students and subject teachers laid on by the faculty, which organises, coordinates and manages the programme seminars.

3   Method

In order to evaluate the actions, in this paper we consider students admitted to the Department of Informatics for autumn 2017, where a total of 499 students attended the first day of study. Figure 4 shows an overview of students and gender for the five study programmes.

During the first week of study, 40 of the students were selected at random and interviewed by a student assistant employed by the department. However, many of the aspects of interest, e.g. well-being or drop-out, require implementation in several semesters before major results can be generated. We therefore supplement the analysis of the 2017 students with a result from the well-being and learning environment survey conducted in the spring of 2017 for the students who started in the autumn of 2016.

---

[2] https://diversityicebreaker.com/.

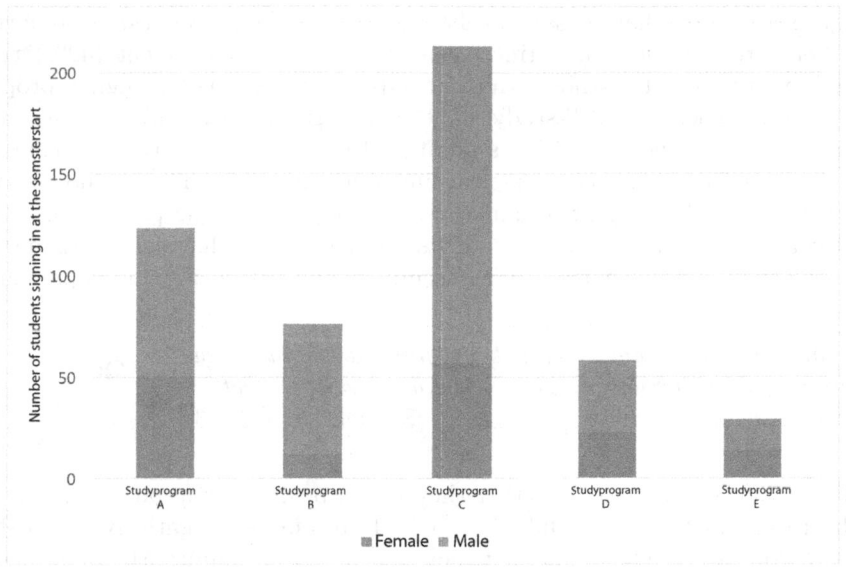

Fig. 4. Overview of the number of students who attended the first day of study, and distribution over the associated study programmes broken down by gender.

A well-being and learning environment survey was carried out in 2017 for the first time. The survey was published after the Easter holiday. The response rate was 18% (n = 87) of the 462 students who were invited to respond to the survey. The students responded to the survey in one of two ways: anonymously (n = 40) or as part of a continuous research study where we follow students throughout the entire study period and into working life (n = 47). The questions dealt with students' degree of participation in the programme seminar, the study start and whether they considered themselves an active student or non-active student. They were also asked about general well-being aspects in addition to several questions from the larger and periodically conducted national surveys such as Vilje-con-valg [18], the Shot survey [19] and the Studiebarometeret[3].

During the autumn semester of 2017, 40 qualitative interviews were conducted with the students. The interviews were conducted by the same person throughout the first week, and the main purpose was to examine in more detail the results from the survey conducted from last year's student group.

4   Results and Discussion

Participation in the study start programme could be answered as 'no' (n = 11), 'yes, partly' (n = 28) or 'yes' (n = 47). Significant differences between

---

[3] https://www.nokut.no/studiebarometeret/.

the groups showed that those who did not attend the study startup reported a higher percentage of study time spent outside the department (42%) than the other groups, while those who participated ('yes') had a higher proportion of time spent on self-study at the department (22%). Students who spend too little time and effort studying often find alternative strategies to pass topics other than achieving learning outcomes [12]. Those who participated in the study start programme also participated in the programme seminar to a greater extent. Many students commented on having a high degree of satisfaction with the programme seminar and on seeing its importance.

> 'The seminar at Sundvollen (ed. Programme seminar) was very good for linking social ties – just as good, if not better, than semester start.'   (Student #sh12-9-3)

Q:2

Participants were asked whether they had a positive or negative experience of the reception (n = 79). Only 5% (n = 4) responded negatively ('no'), but common for these students was that they also reported significantly lower degree of general well-being, study progress this semester, satisfaction with the tutor scheme and satisfaction with the social student environment. None of those who answered 'no' used quiet reading rooms, which would also substantiate that they did not participate in the learning environment. The tutors play a central role in the students' experience of the first day, especially in the coordination of academic and social aspects. The student quotes below emphasise the tutor's contributions.

> 'The study start week was very helpful for me to get to know other students, and I was well received.'
>   (Student #sh12-8-5)

Q:3

> 'The tutors were very kind and willing to answer questions about studies and help if needed.'   (Student #sh12-9-1)

Q:4

> 'Good tutors who influenced how well you got to know the other new students.'   (Student #sh12-8-2)

Q:5

As a consequence of not feeling well received, students may choose not to participate in the environment of the study programme, which in turn leads to the fact that they spend more time outside the department during the following semester.

A total of 79% of the students reported that they participated in the programme seminar. In addition to reporting that they had more friends and better study progression in this and the previous semester, they also reported a higher proportion of time spent on lectures and group lessons (30%) than those who responded 'no' or 'yes, partial' (20%) on this question (n = 17). Lecturers in the first-semester courses experience a significant change in student participation before and after the programme seminar. They reported higher levels of student activity and engagement in both lectures and group teaching. As the student statement below expresses, it is important to organise students into student groups for a good learning environment.

'The programme seminar really helped to get friends and people you could work with.'   (Student #sh12-10-2)   **Q:6**

The level of satisfaction was investigated using eight aspects from the Study Barometer[4]. Satisfaction was examined on a specific scale where the endpoints 'not satisfied' and 'very satisfied' are coded as 1 and 5, respectively. By using numbers from Computer Education for 2016 as a comparison, it appears that overall satisfaction was about the same as for the Study Barometer for social student environment, environment between academic staff and students, academic environment among students, equipment and aids in teaching, and administration. However, somewhat higher satisfaction than in the Study Barometer was reported for premises for teaching and study work, library and ICT services.

The overall results show that experiencing pleasure in studying computer science and a high degree of security in this choice are significant factors for well-being. Social conditions, such as satisfaction with the student environment and many friends at the study centre, also seem to help increase overall satisfaction. Unclear expectations of the individual student appear to be the main reason for lower well-being.

Overall, there is also an indication that some students reported a higher degree of expected satisfaction from completing the programme combined with a higher degree of anxiety of failing to perform on the programme, compared to other computer science programmes. Such concerns, and similar factors such as unclear expectations, seem to be present to a greater extent for those who answered anonymously on the survey. Further work will therefore be needed to compare the performance of those participating in the continuous study with those who did not participate to reveal whether or not the strongest students are generally over-represented on such studies.

In this paper, we have presented the main features of a framework for a good study commencement, which can exploited to facilitate an engaging and inclusive learning environment for first-year students at the Department of Informatics at the University of Oslo. This project will be continued, and more qualitative

---

[4] https://www.nokut.no/studiebarometeret/.

studies will be provided to support the preliminary results. Cooperation and exchange of experience at local and national level is also desirable.

The underlying research methodology is based on both quantitative and qualitative methods, however the sampling rate and the number of participants are relative low related to the total number of students ($n > 500$) eligible. Generally, it is quite difficult to obtain high n when it comes to involve students and to get their responses. The qualitative interviews are conducted with structured questions and are based on the quantitative results from previous years. One might argue that the sample size is small, but to our defence the qualitative interviews has been quite unanimous on several topics.

Acknowledgement. The preparation of the framework has been an initiative of individuals at the Department of Informatics with financial support from the Faculty of Mathematics and Natural Sciences at the University of Oslo.

References

1. Moesby, E.: From pupil to student - a challenge for universities: an example of a PBL study programme. Global J. Eng. Educ. **6**(2), 145–152 (2002)
2. Roderick, M., Holsapple, M., Kelley-Kemple, T., Johnson, D.W.: From high school to the future: getting to college readiness and college graduation. Soc. Res. Educ. Effectiveness 8 (2014)
3. Cherif, A.H., Wideen, M.F.: The problems of the transition from high school to university science. Catalyst **36**, 10–18 (1992). Fall(September 1992)
4. Beichner, R., et al.: Case study of the physics component of an integrated curriculum. Phys. Educ. Res. Am. J. Phys. Suppl. **67**(7), S16–S24 (1999)
5. Balloo, K., Pauli, R., Worrell, M.: Undergraduates' personal circumstances, expectations and reasons for attending university. Stud. High. Educ. **42**, 1373–1384 (2015)
6. Karataş, F., Bodner, G.M., Unal, S.: First-year engineering students' views of the nature of engineering: implications for engineering programmes. Eur. J. Eng. Educ. **41**(1), 1–22 (2016)
7. Nelson, K., Clarke, J., Kift, S., Creagh, T.: Trends in policies, programs and practices in the Australasian First Year Experience literature 2000–2010: The First Year in Higher Education Research Series on Evidence-based Practice No. 1. Brisbane, Australia: Queensland University of Technology (2011)
8. Naylor, R., Baik, C., James, R.: Developing a critical interventions framework for advancing equity in Australian higher education. Technical report, Centre for the Study of Higher Education, The University of Melbourne, Melbourne, April 2013
9. Astin, A.W.: What matters in college: four critical years revisited. J. High. Educ. 74–75 (1993)
10. Micari, M., Pazos, P.: Fitting in and feeling good: the relationships among peer alignment, instructor connectedness, and self-efficacy in undergraduate satisfaction with engineering. Eur. J. Eng. Educ. **41**(4), 380–392 (2015)
11. Maunder, R.E., Cunliffe, M., Galvin, J., Mjali, S., Rogers, J.: Listening to student voices: student researchers exploring undergraduate experiences of university transition. High. Educ. **66**(2), 139–152 (2013)
12. Kolari, S., Savander-Ranne, C., Viskari, E.-L.: Do our engineering students spend enough time studying? Eur. J. Eng. Educ. **31**(5), 499–508 (2006)

13. Kember, D., Jamieson, Q.W., Pomfret, M., Wong, E.T.: Learning approaches, study time and academic performance. High. Educ. **29**(3), 329–343 (1995)
14. Baeten, M., Dochy, F., Struyven, K., Parmentier, E., Vanderbruggen, A.: Student-centred learning environments: an investigation into student teachers' instructional preferences and approaches to learning. Learn. Environ. Res. **19**(1), 43–62 (2016)
15. Holmegaard, H.T., Madsen, L.M., Ulriksen, L.: Where is the engineering I applied for? A longitudinal study of students' transition into higher education engineering, and their considerations of staying or leaving. Eur. J. Eng. Educ. **41**(2), 154–171 (2016)
16. Biggs, J., Tang, C.: Teaching for Quality Learning at University Third Edition Teaching for Quality Learning at University, volume 3th edition (1th edition 1999). Open University Press (2007)
17. Kolari, S., Savander-Ranne, C.: Will the application of constructivism bring a solution to today's problems of engineering education? Glob. J. Eng. Educ. **4**(3), 275–280 (2000)
18. Schreiner, C., Henriksen, E.K., Sjaastad, J., Jensen, F., Løken, M.: Vilje-con-valg: Valg og bortvalg av realfag i høyere utdanning. In: KIMEN 2010, no. 2 (2010)
19. Nedregård, T., Olsen, R.: Shot 2014 (2014)

CROwd-Powered e-Services - CROPS

CROPS 2019 Workshop – Message from the Chairs

Crowdsourcing is a model in which individuals or organizations obtain goods and services from a large, open, and rapidly-evolving group of Internet users. The idea of dividing work between participants to achieve a cumulative result has been applied successfully in many areas, from biology and linguistics to engineering and cultural heritage. As a particular branch of crowdsourcing, crowd computing (also known as "human computation") systematizes the intertwining of human intelligence with artificial intelligence (AI), aiming to solve tasks that are hard for individuals or computers to do alone. Breaking down tasks in smaller parts and collaborating with humans or computers means a shift in the very nature of the work, which implies further scientific study. The key principles include (i) automation: machines do noncreative and repetitive work, providing a cascade of knowledge for humans to evaluate; (ii) microtasking: work is broken into small tasks that are easier to complete by humans chosen specifically on the grounds of their expertise; and (iii) mixed crowd: a greater volume of work, and of greater value, can be completed when specialists and open communities work together.

The CROPS workshop seeks to become a forum to discuss broad, interdisciplinary research about human-in-the-loop intelligent e-services, human-AI interaction, and techniques for augmenting the abilities of individuals and communities to perform whichever tasks. We invited researchers and practitioners to submit theoretical contributions or practical uses of crowdsourcing and crowd computing models in any domains of application. All aspects of crowdsourcing/crowd computing theory and techniques were welcome, including algorithm design, collective knowledge, human-AI interaction, incentives to collaboration, intellectual property, psychological and emotional aspects of crowd involvement, self-organization, quality control, and task assignment.

From the received contributions, the workshop Program Committee selected three for presentation at the workshop, which are good representatives of the current state of the art and innovations to come in the near future and function as a good basis for reflection. We thank all the members of the Program Committee, the authors, and the local organizers for their efforts and support. Now we look forward to organizing a new edition of CROPS in 2020, opening to a broader community in basic research and applications in such areas as digital humanities, economy, education, health, journalism, software engineering, tourism, and urban data collection.

September 2019

Martín López-Nores
Ioanna Lykourentzou
Angeliki Antoniou

CROPS Organization

Workshop Chairs

Martín López-Nores   University of Vigo, Spain
Ioanna Lykourentzou   Utrecht University, The Netherlands
Angeliki Antoniou   University of West Attica, Greece

Program Committee

Ioannis Anagnostopoulos   University of Thessaly, Greece
Antonis Bikakis   University College London, UK
Sylvain Castagnos   University of Lorraine, France
Ahmed Dahroug   Arab Academy for Science and Technology, Egypt
Lidia Gryszkiewicz   The Impact Lab, Luxembourg
Vassilis-Javed Khan   Eindhoven University of Technology, The Netherlands
Sébastien Laborie   University of Pau and IUT de Bayonne et du Pays Basque, France
Yannick Naudet   Luxembourg Institute of Science and Technology, Luxembourg
José Juan Pazos-Arias   University of Vigo, Spain
Vladimir E. Robles-Bykbaev   Universidad Politécnica Salesiana, Ecuador
Tuukka Toivonen   University College London, UK
Nicolas Tsapatsoulis   Cyprus University of Technology, Cyprus
Manolis Wallace   University of Peloponnese, Greece

Crowd-Based Assessment
of Deformational Cranial Asymmetries

Kathrin Borchert[1]([✉]), Matthias Hirth[2], Angelika Stellzig-Eisenhauer[3],
and Felix Kunz[3]

[1] University of Würzburg, Würzburg, Germany
kathrin.borchert@informatik.uni-wuerzburg.de
[2] TU Ilmenau, Ilmenau, Germany
matthias.hirth@tu-ilmenau.de
[3] University Hospital Würzburg, Würzburg, Germany
{stellzig_a,kunz_f}@ukw.de

Abstract. Crowdsourcing allows collecting subjective user ratings promptly and on a large scale. This enables, for example, building subjective models for the perception of technical systems in the field of quality of experience research or researching cultural aspects of the aesthetic appeal. In addition to research in technical domains, crowdsourced subjective ratings also gain more and more relevance in medical research, like the evaluation of aesthetic surgeries. In line with this, we illustrate a novel use-case for crowdsourced subjective ratings of deformational cranial asymmetries of newborns. Deformational cranial asymmetries are deformations of a newborn's head that might, e.g., result from resting on the same spot for a longer time.

Even if there are objective metrics to assess the deformation objectively, there is only a little understanding of how those values match the severity of the deformational cranial asymmetries as *subjectively perceived* by humans. This paper starts filling this gap by illustrating a crowdsourcing-based solution to collect a large set of subjective ratings on examples of deformational cranial asymmetries from different groups that might have a different perception of those deformations. In particular, we consider pediatricians, parents of children with cranial deformation, and naive crowdworkers. For those groups, we further analyze the consistency of their subjective ratings, the differences of the ratings between the groups, and the effects of the study design.

Keywords: Crowdsourcing · Subjective assessment · Medical data · Deformational cranial asymmetries

1 Introduction

Crowdsourcing gives easy and cost-effective access to a large and diverse group of people. Therefore, crowdsourcing has become an established tool to acquire

The authors of this chapter have provided an addendum which is available in the correction to this chapter at https://doi.org/10.1007/978-3-030-39634-3_16

© IFIP International Federation for Information Processing 2020, corrected publication 2020
Published by Springer Nature Switzerland AG 2020
I. O. Pappas et al. (Eds.): I3E 2019 Workshops, IFIP AICT 573, pp. 145–157, 2020.
https://doi.org/10.1007/978-3-030-39634-3_13

participants for surveys and user studies. Besides collecting objective information, e.g., shopping behavior, crowdsourcing surveys are also often used for collecting subjective ratings, e.g., to investigate the quality of technical systems from the user's perspective or to analyze differences in the perception of the aesthetic appeal depending on the cultural background of participants.

One major field of application for those large-scale subjective surveys is quality of experience (QoE) [6] research that targets at understanding, modeling, and optimizing the user's perceived quality of a technical system. In addition to research in technical domains, the usage of crowdsourced subjective studies also gains more and more relevance in medical research, like the evaluation of aesthetic surgeries. Today, objective measurements and metrics for biometric data are well studied and discussed. Therefore, disease patterns can be objectively classified and quantified. However, besides this objective perspective, human perception also needs to be considered in the evaluation of the outcome of treatments. One illustrative example of this are deformational cranial asymmetries. Deformational cranial asymmetries are a deformation of newborn's head caused by always resting on the same spot, for example. This leads to a flattening of the shape of the head as the head is malleable during the first month after birth. While the deformations can be quantified using modern 3D scanners and several objective metrics, no commonly agree thresholds for those metrics exist when to start or stop therapies. Further, it remains unclear when a head is *perceived* to be asymmetric by the general public.

Large-scale online user studies, similar to existing works in QoE research, can help to solve these open questions. Still, running those studies to analyze the perception of experts and non-experts with medical data, leads to new challenges including privacy issues due to the sensitivity of the data or new challenges while displaying the data online, due to the unique data formats used for storing medical data or their pure size.

In this work, we introduce a novel medical use-case for the collection of subjective ratings, namely the large scale subjective assessment of deformational cranial asymmetries. We develop an online user study that displays complex medical data and still preserves the patients' privacy. With the help of this tool, we collect assessments of the deformation severity from different groups of participants. Based on the collected data, we evaluate if the perception varies between people with different background and knowledge about deformational cranial asymmetries. In detail, the ratings of pediatricians, other physicians, laypersons including crowdworkers and non-crowdworkers as well as affected persons, i.e., parents of children with deformational cranial asymmetries, are analyzed and compared. Further, the impact of the study design on the ratings is evaluated.

The remainder of this work is structured as followed. Section 2 provides the background of deformational cranial asymmetries and the objective measurements used to quantify the deformations. Further, an overview of the usage of crowdsourcing in medical research, especially for collecting subjective ratings, is given. Section 3 describes the data set used in our study and details on the study design. The evaluation of the study results is given in Sect. 4. Section 5 concludes this paper.

2   Background and Related Work

In this section, we first provide background about de-formational cranial asymmetries, then give an overview of the usage of crowdsourcing for medical research, especially about the collection of subjective ratings.

2.1   Deformational Cranial Asymmetries

The head of a newborn is malleable, and therefore its shape is deformable, e.g., by resting on the same spot over a long time or due to prenatal reasons. Such deformations are also known as deformational cranial asymmetries [12]. If the deformation is more advanced, a therapy for aesthetic and medical reasons is necessary. There exists several objective metrics to classify [2] and to quantify the severity of the deformation, e.g., including biometrical information like characteristics of the neck muscles [3]. In this work, we use 3D-stereophotogrammetric scans obtained by using the methodology introduced by Meyer-Marcotty et al. [9]. Here, the non-invasive 3D scans are created with a special scanner[1]. By using the software Cranioform Analytics[2], metrics about the shape and volume of the head are determined. These metrics include, e.g., the Cephalic Index (CI) which defines the ratio of the maximum width to the maximum length of a head, the ear shift as well as the anterior and posterior cranial asymmetry index (ACAI/PCAI). The indexes ACAI and PCAI represent the ratio of the volumes of different quadrants of the head.

However, even if there are objective metrics to quantify the deformation, these are not fixed thresholds when to start or to stop the medical treatment [19]. This is mainly because the subjective perception of the grade of deformation is not fully understood yet and may even differ between experts, e.g., physicians, and affected people, e.g., parents of newborns with deformational cranial asymmetries, as well as non-experts. Crowdsourcing is one possibility to acquire a large number of subjective assessments for deformational cranial asymmetries from a diverse set of participants. These assessments can then help to gain an understanding of the perception of the deformations and ultimately be used to derive guidelines for therapies.

2.2   Crowdsourcing and Medical Research

There is a large community focusing on the usage of crowdsourcing in the context of medical research [10,13,17]. The fields of application are ranging from the area

---

[1] http://www.3dmd.com/ Accessed Jun. 2019.

[2] https://www.cranioform.de/fuer-aerzte/medizinische-informationen.html Accessed Jun. 2019.

of machine learning, e.g., labeling medical big data [15] or improving automatic speech recognizer [14], to recruiting participants for medical user studies [5, 11]. Further, the crowdworkers could also provide medical diagnosis [1]. For example, the work of Meyer et al. [8] introduces the platform CrowdMed that gives crowdworkers access to data of patients with undiagnosed illnesses and Li et al. [7] focusing on the reliability of such crowdsourced diagnosis.

Besides the collection of diagnosis, the collection of subjective assessments of medical images concerning aesthetic aspects is also a possible use-case. The study of Vartanian et al. [18] focuses on the definition of the ideal thigh proportions. Therefore, the authors analyze the ratings of crowdworkers concerning the perceived attractiveness of thighs shown on photographs. While this work only discusses mostly medical aspects, the work of Tse et al. [16] also consider the reliability of crowdsourced ratings and compare them to assessments provided by experts. Here, the aim of the study is the evaluation of the aesthetic outcome of treatments for unilateral cleft lip. The results of the study show that the ratings of crowdworkers are reliable and well correlated to the assessments of the expert group.

Even if the study of Tse et al. discusses and compares assessments of crowdworkers and an expert group, they did not consider the group of affected persons and their friends or family members. Furthermore, there is only a small amount of research about the comparability of crowd-based assessments and expert ratings in the context of aesthetic, medical cases. Thus, it is unclear if these results are transferable to other medical fields. In this work, we do not only discuss assessments of crowdworkers and specialists, but we also consider the perception from affected people, i.e., parents of children with deformational cranial asymmetries, as well as from a non-crowdsourcing layperson group and a group of physicians who are no pediatricians.

3 Study Description

In this section, we describe the design of the user study. Additionally, we detail on the preprocessing of the medical data as well as the conduction of the study.

3.1 Medical Dataset

Our dataset consists of 3D scans from 51 newborns' heads that exhibit different severities and types of deformational cranial asymmetries. In addition, different objective asymmetry metrics are available for each patient, e.g., the Cephalic Index. While it is desirable to collect subjective rating for the whole dataset, this is not reasonable for this preliminary test. To perform a comparison of the ratings of the different groups of test-takers, a larger number of ratings per stimulus and group is necessary. While affected parents might be tolerant against a long-lasting subjective test that includes all scans, practitioners that participate voluntarily might not be willing to spend too much time on this research task. Further, paid crowdsourcing tasks should also be kept short, as long tasks fatigue workers and workers might start to rush through the task instead of performing it thoroughly. Another option would be to split the dataset into smaller subsets. However, as the number of practitioners and parents are highly limited in our case, we decided to focus on a larger number of ratings per scan, instead of a large number of annotated scans.

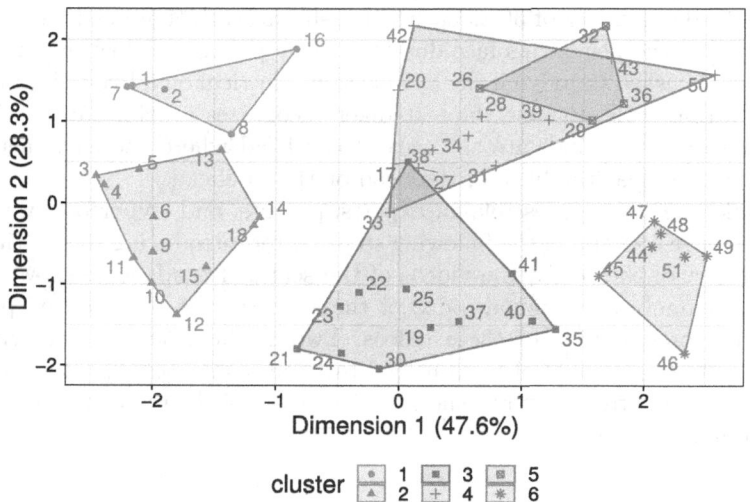

Fig. 1. Clustering of the 3D scans based on the patients medical data.

We use clustering to minimize the number of annotated samples but still test a diverse and representative set. In our specific case, we decided to cluster the patients with the Partitioning Around Medoids (PAM) algorithm, as the PAM algorithm identifies data points as cluster centers instead of calculating theoretical cluster centers like, e.g., k-means [4]. As the distance metric, the Euclidean distance is calculated. The objective medical metrics of the participants' heads, described in Sect. 2, are normalized to have zero mean and unit variance and are used as features for the clustering. An elbow plot is used to identify a suitable number of clusters for initializing the process. Further, the clustering is evaluated by using silhouette coefficients, and based on the results, the optimal number of clusters is identified as six. Figure 1 shows a two dimensional representation of the final clustering.

Based on the clustering, we select a representative patient for each of the six clusters. These representatives are as distinct as possible concerning their characteristics. Four additional patients are added based on the suggestion of medical experts. This results in a dataset of 10 different patients for the evaluation. To further evaluate if an asymmetry on the left or right side of the head is perceived differently, we also generated mirrored versions of all scans.

3.2 Study Design

The original 3D scans are produced with the methodology described by Meyer-Marcotty et al. [9] that allows viewing the scan from different perspectives interactively. However, in order to make the scans accessible to a large group of persons, we have to guarantee that they can be viewed on all types of devices with a minimum amount of user preparations. Therefore, we decide to convert the scans to short videos of 30 s. Each video shows a rotating head omitting the frontal view of the newborn's face due to privacy policies. Below the video, the test takers are asked to judge if the head is asymmetrical on a five-point absolute category rating scale. In case the test taker recognizes a deformation, the test taker is also asked to indicate the area of the head where the asymmetry has been noticed, e.g., at the back of the head or the forehead.

To make the study accessible for experts, parents, and laypersons, we realize it as a web page containing the following steps. After introducing the participants to the subject of the study, the videos of the scanned heads were shown to the test taker, namely the original video of the scans of the ten selected patients and the mirrored version of these videos. Two of the videos are shown twice to evaluate the constancy of the ratings. In total, each participant watches 22 videos in random order. Figure 2 shows a screenshot of the realization of the web page containing a video.

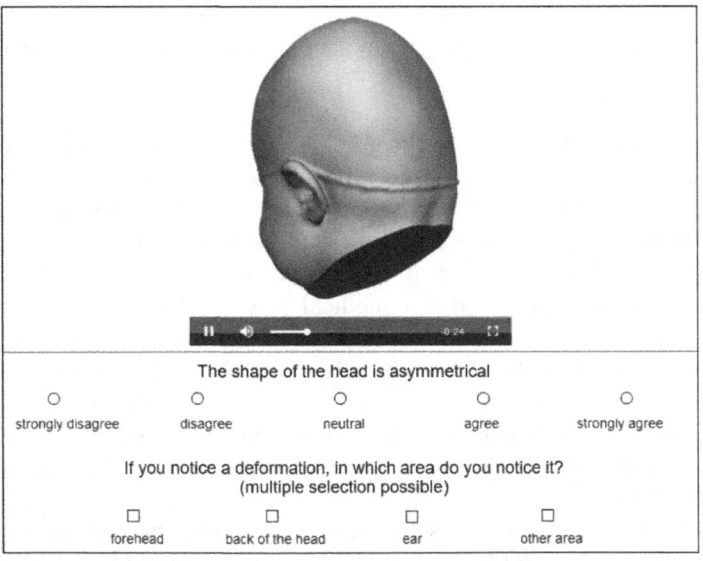

Fig. 2. Mockup of the web page showing a video of the rotating head.

After rating all videos, the participants are asked to provide additional demographical information, like age and gender. Further, we collect information if the participant works in health care, if so in which area as well as if the participant has children in the age between zero to six years. At the end of the survey, the participant has the option to give additional feedback.

3.3 Study Conduction

The group of crowdworkers has been recruited via the crowdsourcing platform Microworkers[3] in March and April 2017. We limited the study to users from the United States, Canada, and the United Kingdom to prevent misunderstandings concerning the instructions due to language barriers. Further, the limitation reduces side effects due to demographic or cultural differences, e.g., aesthetic aspects. The payment per participation was $0.50. The participants of the other groups, i.e., pediatricians, physicians, and parents, as well as the other non-experts, have been invited via e-mail between July and September 2017. Here, participation has been voluntary.

Table 1 presents an overview of the groups of participants. We only consider participants who answer all questions. Overall, 54 crowdworkers take part in our study. Those workers are on average 32 years old, and 46.3% of the group is female. The average age of the parents (38 years), other non-experts (42 years) and other physicians (42 years) is slightly higher than in the group of crowd-workers. Further, the group of pediatricians is the oldest (50 years) with the lowest share of female participants (25.1%), while the group of parents has the highest share of female members (76.7%).

Table 1. Overview about age and gender of the groups of participant.

Group	N	∅ Age	Female [%]
Pediatricians	31	50	25.1%
Other Physicians	27	42	48.1%
Parents	73	38	76.7%
Crowdworkers	54	32	46.3%
Other Non − Experts	54	42	61.1%

4 Results

In this section, the constancy of the provided ratings is analyzed. Further, we compare the ratings of the groups of participants and discuss factors which may influence the perception of the groups.

---

[3] https://microworkers.com Accessed Jun. 2019.

4.1 Constancy of Ratings

To evaluate the constancy of the answers given by the participants, we compare
the ratings of the videos which are shown twice within the study, i.e., the video
of patient 1 and patient 17. We analyze if the ratings of the first and the second occurrence of the videos originate from the same distribution by using the
Kruskal-Wallis rank sum test. The test results in a rejection of the null hypothesis ($\chi^2 = 28.83, df = 4, p < 0.001$). A pairwise comparison of the samples per
group using the Wilcoxon rank sum test with Bonferroni correction shows significant differences between the crowdworkers and the other non-experts ($p < 0.01$),
parents ($p < 0.001$), pediatricians ($p < 0.01$) and other physicians ($p < 0.01$).
We found no significant differences between the other groups ($p > 0.05$). By
comparing the mean, standard deviation and quantiles of the answers of each
group, a higher divergence between the ratings provided by the crowdworkers
and the other groups are seen (see Table 2).

Table 2. Statistical parameters of rating differences of videos shown twice during the
study.

Group	Mean	SD	90% Quantile
Pediatricians	0.29	0.49	1
Other Physicians	0.25	0.44	1
Parents	0.32	0.52	1
Crowdworkers	0.80	0.93	2
Other Non − Experts	0.32	0.51	1

Especially, the 90% quantile indicates that the crowdworkers' ratings for
watching a video the second time often differ for more than one point on the
rating scale. This effect may be explainable by a training phase that is more
noticeable for the crowdworkers. If so, the participants should be more precise
in rating the asymmetry of later shown videos especially for the copies, i.e., by
answering with the option *(strongly) agree/disagree* instead of selecting the neutral one. Therefore, the correlation between the absolute position of the copied
videos and the distance of the selected options to the neutral option is analyzed.
Other than expected, we found no significant relationship between these values by using Spearman's rank correlation. This result indicates that on the one
hand, there are other crowd-specific factors which may lead to different ratings
for some participants. On the other hand, it may be an indicator that these
participants are inattentive.

  In the following evaluations, we only consider participants who submit constant ratings. This means we exclude participants providing ratings of the videos
shown twice, which are not identically or are not located next to each other in the
rating scale. Overall, 21 crowdworkers, two other non-experts, four parents, and
one pediatrician are filtered out. Further, the assessments of the copied videos
are omitted from the evaluation.

4.2   Comparison of Asymmetry Ratings

To evaluate potential effects on the perceived asymmetry caused by the background, e.g., previous knowledge about deformational cranial asymmetries, we analyze the assessments of the participants per group and compare the mean opinion. A rating of 1 represents the option *strongly disagree*, the value 3 corresponds to a neutral rating while a rating of 5 means that the participant *strongly agrees* that the shown head is asymmetrical. In the following evaluation, we omit the mirrored version of the videos to prevent biases caused by side effects.

To analyze differences in the ratings between the groups, we run a one-way ANOVA. The test shows a significant effect of the group on the ratings ($F(4, 2075) = 93.81$, $p < 0.001$). Bonferroni's post-hoc test revealed significant differences between the crowdworkers and all other groups ($p < 0.001$). By analyzing the ratings in detail, we observe that 62.2% of the crowd-based ratings (strongly) agreed that the shown heads are deformed. In comparison to the other groups with a percentage of agreements ranging from 7.7% to 14.2%, the amount is by far higher. Other than expected, this indicates that the crowdworkers perceive weak deformations as more critical than the other groups. An explanation may be crowd-specific, additional influence factors on the assessments, e.g., the participants are less attentive due to distractions or rushing through the test. Alternatively, the phrasing of our question might induce bias, and the workers might assume that they are *expected* to identify an asymmetry.

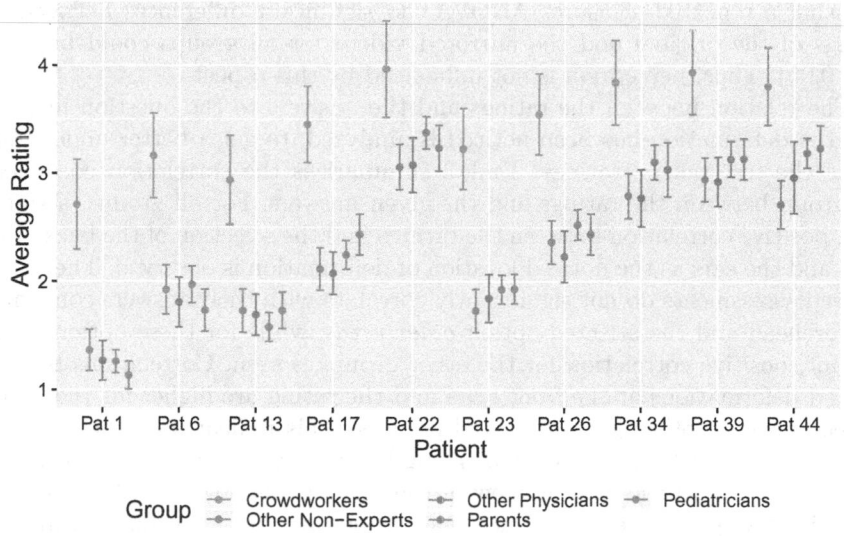

Fig. 3. Mean of the ratings with 95% confidence intervals per group.

As the observation may be invalid on a per patient basis, the assessments are also evaluated on a patient level. The average ratings per patient, including the 95% confidence intervals, are shown in Fig. 3. While the average ratings for the groups of other non-experts, parents, pediatricians, and other physicians are quite similar with mostly overlapping confidence intervals, the crowdworkers rate more often neutral or agreed to notice a deformation. This leads to higher average ratings with a constant offset of approximately one point on the rating scale for each patient. This observation corresponds to the result of a one-way ANOVA per patient, which shows a significant difference between the ratings of the groups for all patients ($p < 0.001$). By using the Bonferroni post-hoc test again, a significant difference between the assessments of the crowdworkers and those of all other groups is revealed for all patients ($p < 0.05$). Between the other groups, we found no significant differences except for *patient 44*. For this patient, there is a significant difference between the group of other non-experts and the parents ($p < 0.01$) as well as other non-experts and pediatricians ($p < 0.05$).

The different findings for the patients indicate that for unique characteristics of deformation the perception differs between experts (physicians and parents) and laypersons. We further analyze this aspect by evaluating the assessments of the mirrored and original videos as well as the provided answers concerning the areas where the participants noticed the deformations.

4.3   Influence Factors on the Perceived Asymmetry

As it may influence the perception if the deformation is located on a head's left or right side, the assessments of the original and the mirrored scans are evaluated. By using a repeated-measures ANOVA, no significant differences between the ratings of the original and the mirrored videos for all groups could be found ($p > 0.05$). Thus, perception is not influenced by this aspect.

The relation between the ratings and the answers to the question in which area the deformation has been noticed is analyzed, to get a better understanding of the test takers' ratings. Table 3 summarizes the correlation coefficients per group between the ratings and the given answers. For all groups, a significant, positive correlation between the ratings and the selection of the back of the head and the ears as the noticed location of deformation is observed. The crowdsourced assessments do not significantly correlate with their answers concerning the forehead and the selected option *other areas*, while for these options a significant, positive correlation for the other groups is seen. Correlations between noticed deformations at the front head and the rating are higher for the groups of pediatricians, other physicians and parents. This indicates on the one hand that for non-experts it is more challenging to identify deformations at the front of the head due to the missing view of the face of the newborns. On the other hand, it may be a piece of evidence that the groups focus on different areas of the head, which may influence the perception.

Table 3. Coefficients r of point-biserial correlation between ratings and areas of noticed deformation, i.e. front head, back of the head, ear and other areas including level of significance.

Group	r Front	r Back	r Ears	r Other
Pediatricians	0.47***	0.64***	0.48***	0.20***
OtherPhysicians	0.27***	0.57***	0.38***	0.19**
Parents	0.33***	0.64***	0.39***	0.11**
Crowdworkers	0.07	0.42***	0.30***	0.11
OtherNon − Experts	0.17***	0.49***	0.27***	0.26***

** 0.01, *** 0.001

5   Conclusion

Utilizing crowdsourcing for the collection of subjective assessments, e.g., for evaluating the perceived quality of technical systems by the users, is a commonly used approach in several research directions. Nowadays, collecting ratings for medical use cases via crowdsourcing gain more and more interest.

In this work, we introduce a novel medical use-case for the collection of ratings about the perceived severity of head deformations. We conducted a user study involving people with different background, i.e., pediatricians, other physicians, parents of children with deformational cranial asymmetries and non-experts including crowdworkers and non-crowdworkers, leading to different prior knowledge about deformational cranial asymmetries.

The results of the study showed that the perception of the crowdworkers and the other groups differ when comparing the ratings independent from the patients. While the crowdworkers more often perceived deformation of the shown heads, the other non-expert group rates mostly similar to the groups of physicians and parents. Here, the similar perception of experts, affected people, and laypersons is other than expected.

The analysis of the ratings per patient showed that some characteristics of deformations also leads to differences in the perception of the laypersons and the expert groups. Further, we found that the recognition of deformations is based on different areas of the head for people with a medical background and affected persons. Even if a frontal view of the faces is not shown, which makes it challenging to notice deformations on the forehead, they consider this area for their ratings. This observation may be an explanation of the different perception of deformational cranial asymmetries, as mentioned above.

Nevertheless, the differences concerning the focus of the participants do not fully explain the variations in the ratings of the crowdworkers and the other groups. Instead, these ratings may be influenced by crowd-specific, additional factors, e.g., inattentiveness due to distractions, biases induced by the phrasing of the instructions, or an insufficient training phase, which will be subject of future research.

Furthermore, the objective medical information could be considered to get a more in-depth insight into the relationship between the objective and the subjective data.

Overall, the results of our study encourage the involvement of a diverse group of people with different knowledge and background concerning the subject of studies. Further, our observations show the importance of carefully designing such studies when conducting them in the context of crowdsourcing.

Acknowledgment. The authors thank Veronika Cheplygina for the fruitful discussions on crowdsourcing in the context of medical images and Norman Stulier for his support during the implementation of the survey software. This work is supported by Deutsche Forschungsgemeinschaft (DFG) under Grants HO4770/2-2, TR 257/38-2. The authors alone are responsible for the content.

References

1. Alialy, R., et al.: A review on the applications of crowdsourcing in human pathology. J. Pathol. Inform. **9**, 2 (2018)
2. Argenta, L.: Clinical classification of positional plagiocephaly. J. Craniofac. Surg. **15**(3), 368–372 (2004)
3. Captier, G., et al.: Classification and pathogenic models of unintentional postural cranial deformities in infants: plagiocephalies and brachycephalies. J. Craniofac. Surg. **22**(1), 33–41 (2011)
4. Han, J., Pei, J., Kamber, M.: Data Mining: Concepts and Techniques. Elsevier, Amsterdam (2011)
5. van der Heijden, L., Piner, S.R., van de Sande, M.A.J.: Pigmented villonodular synovitis: a crowdsourcing study of two hundred and seventy two patients. Int. Orthopaedics **40**(12), 2459–2468 (2016)
6. Hossfeld, T., et al.: Best practices for QoE crowdtesting: Qoe assessment with crowdsourcing. IEEE Trans. Multimedia **16**(2), 541–558 (2014)
7. Li, Y., et al.: Reliable medical diagnosis from crowdsourcing: discover trustworthy answers from non-experts. In: Proceedings of the International Conference on Web Search and Data Mining (2017)
8. Meyer, A.N., Longhurst, C.A., Singh, H.: Crowdsourcing diagnosis for patients with undiagnosed illnesses: an evaluation of crowdmed. J. Med. Internet Res. **18**(1), e12 (2016)
9. Meyer-Marcotty, P., et al.: Head orthesis therapy in infants with unilateral positional plagiocephaly: an interdisciplinary approach to broadening the range of orthodontic treatment. J. Orofacial Orthopedics **73**(2), 151–165 (2012)
10. Ørting, S., et al.: A survey of crowdsourcing in medical image analysis. arXiv preprint arXiv:1902.09159 (2019)
11. Peleg, M., Leung, T.I., Desai, M., Dumontier, M.: Is crowdsourcing patient-reported outcomes the future of evidence-based medicine? A case study of back pain. In: ten Teije, A., Popow, C., Holmes, J.H., Sacchi, L. (eds.) AIME 2017. LNCS (LNAI), vol. 10259, pp. 245–255. Springer, Cham (2017). https://doi.org/10.1007/978-3-319-59758-4_27
12. Persing, J., James, H., Swanson, J., Kattwinkel, J.: Committee on Practice and Ambulatory Medicine, et al.: Prevention and management of positional skull deformities in infants. Pediatrics **112**(1), 199–202 (2003)

13. Ranard, B.L., et al.: Crowdsourcing-harnessing the masses to advance health and medicine, a systematic review. J. Gen. Internal Med. **29**(1), 187–203 (2014)
14. Salloum, W., Edwards, E., Ghaffarzadegan, S., Suendermann-Oeft, D., Miller, M.: Crowdsourced continuous improvement of medical speech recognition. In: Workshops at the Thirty-First AAAI Conference on Artificial Intelligence (2017)
15. Servadei, L., Schmidt, R., Eidelloth, C., Maier, A.: Medical monkeys: a crowdsourcing approach to medical big data. In: Debruyne, C., et al. (eds.) OTM 2017. LNCS, vol. 10697, pp. 87–97. Springer, Cham (2018). https://doi.org/10.1007/978-3-319-73805-5_9
16. Tse, R.W., Oh, E., Gruss, J.S., Hopper, R.A., Birgfeld, C.B.: Crowdsourcing as a novel method to evaluate aesthetic outcomes of treatment for unilateral cleft lip. Plastic Reconstr. Surg. **138**(4), 864–874 (2016)
17. Tucker, J., Day, S., Tang, W., Bayus, B.: Crowdsourcing in medical research: theory and practice. Technical report, PeerJ Preprints (2018)
18. Vartanian, E., Gould, D.J., Hammoudeh, Z.S., Azadgoli, B., Stevens, W.G., Macias, L.H.: The ideal thigh: a crowdsourcing-based assessment of ideal thigh aesthetic and implications for gluteal fat grafting. Aesthetic Surg. J. **38**(8), 861–869 (2018)
19. Wilbrand, J.F.: Transferring the assessment of cranial deformities to the affected. J. Craniofac. Surg. **28**(2), 303–304 (2017)

CuneiForce: Involving the Crowd in the Annotation of Unread Mesopotamian Cuneiform Tablets Through a Gamified Design

Martín López-Nores[1]([✉]) [iD], Juan Luis Montero-Fenollós[2] [iD],
Marta Rodríguez-Sampayo[1], José Juan Pazos-Arias[1] [iD],
Silvia González-Soutelo[3] [iD], and Susana Reboreda-Morillo[4] [iD]

[1] Department of Telematics Engineering, University of Vigo, Vigo, Spain
{mlnores,jose}@det.uvigo.es, martarodsam@gmail.com
[2] Department of Humanities, University of A Coruña, Coruña, Spain
juan.fenollos@udc.es
[3] Department of Prehistory and Archaeology,
Universidad Autónoma de Madrid/MIAS, Madrid, Spain
silvia.gonzalezs@uam.es
[4] Group of Studies in Archaeology, Antiquity and Territory,
University of Vigo, Vigo, Spain
rmorillo@uvigo.es

Abstract. We present the concept and early design of a crowd computing system that aims at involving people in the annotation of unread cuneiform tablets, in an attempt to (i) increase public awareness about the history of Ancient Mesopotamia and (ii) to supplement the shrinking force of experts in the subject with the contributions of interested individuals, who are instructed in reading from the simplest inscriptions towards more complex ones in a gamified strategy.

Keywords: Crowd computing · Serious games · Cuneiform writing · Digital Humanities

1 Introduction

Cuneiform was one of the earliest systems of writing, emerging in Sumer (modern-day southern Iraq) in the middle of 3rd millennium BC and used until the 1st century AD for the writing of the various languages used by the oldest major civilizations in the region of Mesopotamia and beyond, namely Sumerian, Akkadian, Assyrian, Babylonian, Elamite, Hittite, Urartian, Ugaritic and Achaemenid.

Mesopotamia is generally dubbed *"the first place where civilized societies truly began to take shape"*. Therefore, the study of the History of the region

© IFIP International Federation for Information Processing 2020
Published by Springer Nature Switzerland AG 2020
I. O. Pappas et al. (Eds.): I3E 2019 Workshops, IFIP AICT 573, pp. 158–163, 2020.
https://doi.org/10.1007/978-3-030-39634-3_14

plays a key role in understanding the consolidation of the earliest developments of agriculture, cities, laws, long distance trade, ... as well as the rise and fall of the first empires, and the many advances that sprung therefrom to influence posterior civilizations.

Much of what is known about Ancient Mesopotamia comes from archaeological evidence. Among the remains, it is estimated that between 0.5 and 2 million cuneiform tablets have been excavated in modern times, of which only 30 000–100 000 have been read or published [24]. Therefore, there's a wealth of knowledge awaiting to be deciphered and put into context. Unfortunately, Humanities enrolment has dropped dramatically since the early 2000s, as parents and educators around the world have encouraged students to pursue degrees in science, technology, engineering and mathematics, where employment opportunities are seemingly endless [23]. Having fewer (and older) experts in the area of Ancient Mesopotamia History entails a clear risk that most of that knowledge will remain in limbo [13].

Paradoxically enough, we believe technology can play a role in preventing this from happening. During the last two decades, the Digital Humanities have seen many successful applications of *crowdsourcing* models, in many cases pursuing the transcription of handwritten manuscripts from medieval and modern times [22]. Often, these applications fit the more specific definition of *crowd computing*, which systematises the intertwining of human and artificial intelligence, aiming to solve tasks that are hard for people or computers to do alone [11]. The key principles include the following:

- *Automation:* machines do non-creative and repetitive work, providing a cascade of knowledge for humans to evaluate.
- *Microtasking:* work is broken into small tasks that are easier to complete by humans, chosen specifically on the grounds of their expertise.
- *Mixed crowd:* a greater volume of work, and of greater value, can be completed when specialists and open communities work together.

In this paper, we present the concept and early design of a crowd computing system that aims at involving people in the reading and interpretation of cuneiform tablets, by means of a game that challenges them from the simplest known inscriptions, progressively, towards more complex and unknown ones.

2   Some Quick Facts About Cuneiform

The first writing began as a system of pictograms in the late 4th millennium BC. In the 3rd millennium BC, the pictorial representations turned to abstract shapes as the number of characters in common use became smaller. The system thus evolved into a combination of signs that, as noted above, was used for the writing of different languages over the centuries. The HZL lust of signs used in Hittite cuneiform, for example, contains a total of 375 signs, many with a few variants [19].

Because of its versatility, transliteration from cuneiform requires deciding, for almost each sign, which of its several possible meanings is intended in the original document. For example, the Sumerian sign DINGIR (✳) in an Akkadian text may represent the syllable *"an"* (as in the word *"antallum"* = eclipse), may be part of a phrase (reading *"ilum"*) and it may translate as *"god"*. This is precisely one of the challenges that we want people to address in the proposed game.

Finally, it is worth noting that cuneiform was used to record many different types of documents: laws, maps, medical manuals, religious stories and beliefs, business records, personal letters, etc. Cuneiform tablets, therefore, can convey quite a complete view of the society of their times, owing to the fact that literacy was not reserved for the elite; rather, it was common for average citizens [4]. This wide scope gives great flexibility to design the learning curve of the game, with different itineraries that may even be adapted to each user's interests and preferences.

3   The CuneiForce System: Early Design

We have started to design CuneiForce as a crowd computing system that will bring together innovative solutions in computer vision, automated reasoning, knowledge modelling and crowdsourcing (see Fig. 1). At the core of it, we aim to create (and ensure others' contributions to) a semantic knowledge base linked to the existing archives of digitized tablets (e.g. the Cornell University's Cuneiform Library[1] or the Cuneiform Digital Library Initiative[2]).

The knowledge base will rely on an ontological model created according to reference metadata standards, like CIDOC-CRM [6], with proper additions to represent arguments (e.g. CRMinf, an extension of CIDOC-CRM itself) and uncertain or inconsistent information [3,12]. Additionally, we aim to develop a neural network model like that of Word2vec [15], but for Ancient Mesopotamian languages rather than English. Both models will help to explicitly capture incomplete or inconsistent knowledge, different levels of certainty, different interpretations and arguments.

The computer vision solutions will be based on recent advances in deep learning and convolutional neural networks [20]—also on the achievements of the Transkribus system[3] with manuscripts in Latin scripts—to recognise individual wedges and to make informed guesses about their aggregations. Multiple instance learning will be combined with structured prediction and weakly supervised learning to allow automatic segmentation of the images. The automated reasoning processes will work on top of the knowledge bases to establish associations and correlations, aiming to provide humans with hypotheses about how to complete missing information or manage contradictions (if necessary). We plan to integrate mechanisms from several areas of artificial intelligence and logic:

[1] http://cuneiform.library.cornell.edu/.
[2] https://cdli.ucla.edu/.
[3] https://transkribus.eu/.

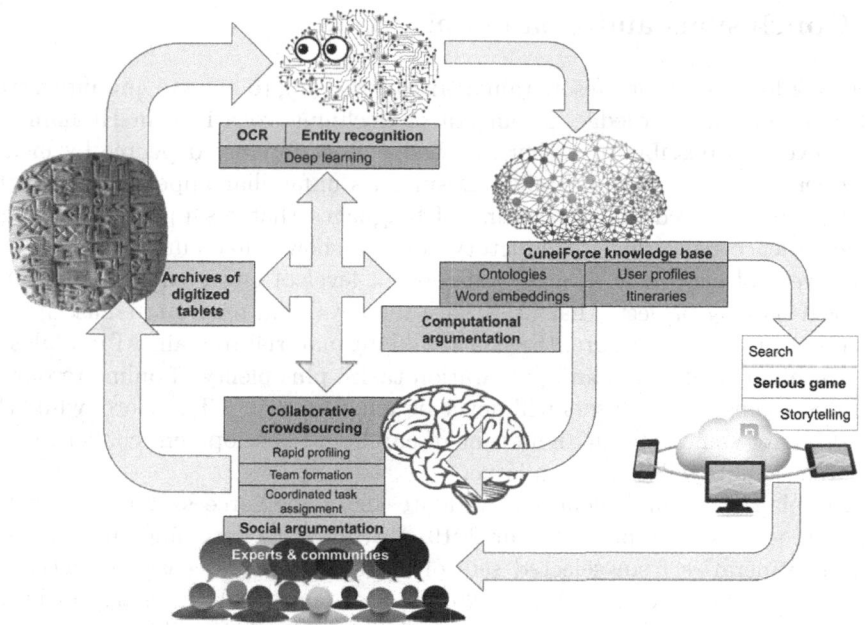

Fig. 1. Overall design of the CuneiForce system.

- Qualitative, rule-based approaches for defeasible reasoning [16,18], which allow making conclusions that could be invalidated in the light of new information.
- Quantitative, fuzzy approaches for probabilistic/statistical reasoning [5,21] needed to handle the guesses coming from the computer vision systems and the wisdom gathered from humans through social argumentation (user-generated arguments and votes on arguments).
- Abductive reasoning [10], aiming to discover new rules from incomplete sets of observations.
- Approaches based on many-valued logic for paraconsistent reasoning [8,9], needed to avoid trivialisation (any conclusion follows) from contradictory bits.

On these grounds, computational argumentation [7,17] will provide tools for modelling and reasoning about the support for/against any conclusions.

Finally, the collaborative crowdsourcing solutions will combine virtual team formation and coordination with *macrotasks* and complex problems in the shape of personalized learning paths. Since we are targeting the wider public, personalization is crucial to promote long-standing involvement, preventing dropouts due to improper learning curves, uninteresting topics, etc. Task assignments optimization will be inspired by the work presented in [2]. This approach goes beyond traditional microtasking, which typically views participating users as a fully replaceable, low-skilled and anonymous mass. Personality matching [1,14] will be used to construct teams that are highly motivated to collaborate and work efficiently together.

4   Conclusions and Roadmap

There is a lot of Ancient Mesopotamia History waiting to be read and integrated with our current knowledge. In an era of declining vocations in Humanities, we believe it is possible to gather knowledge from interested people by means of properly-designed serious games. Despite its unfamiliar appearance and the fact that it was used for the writing of languages that disappeared long ago, our experience delivering introductory courses shows that cuneiform script is attractive and accessible enough to expect a level of engagement comparable to crowdsourcing projects that dealt with medieval and modern manuscripts in the recent past. Furthermore, there is abundant material to train AI modules to aid in tablet classification and preparation tasks, plus plenty of online resources available to ensure that users will never be left wondering. Therefore, while the idea does not come without significant research and development challenges, we believe feasibility will not be an issue.

Our plan is to implement and validate the CuneiForce system within the next three years. The present year 2019 is devoted to designing the complete learning itineraries from selected sets of read tablets, and ensuring access to convenient online resources. Year 2020 will focus on the AI in charge of image processing and computational argumentation. Lastly, 2021 will primarily look at the implementation of web and mobile versions of all the user interfaces; it is also scheduled to be the year for validation experiments, not only with the open community on the Internet, but also in the context of collaborating primary/secondary education institutions.

Acknowledgements. This research has received funding from the European Regional Development Fund (ERDF) and the Galician Regional Government under agreement for funding the AtlantTIC Research Center for Information and Communication Technologies, as well as from the Ministry of Education and Science (Spanish Government) research project TIN2017-87604-R.

References

1. Antoniou, A.: Compatibility of small team personalities in computer-based tasks. Challenges **10**(1), 29 (2019)
2. Basu Roy, S., Lykourentzou, I., Thirumuruganathan, S., Amer-Yahia, S., Das, G.: Task assignment optimization in knowledge-intensive crowdsourcing. VLDB J. **24**(4), 467–491 (2015)
3. Ceravolo, P., Damiani, E., Leida, M.: Which role for an ontology of uncertainty? In: Proceedings of the 4th International Conference on Uncertainty Reasoning for the Semantic Web (URSW), Aachen, Germany, pp. 132–136 (2008)
4. Charpin, D.: Lire et écrire en Mésopotamie: une affaire de spécialistes? In: Comptes rendus de l'Académie des Inscriptions et Belles Lettres, pp. 481–501 (2004)
5. Coletti, G., Scozzafava, R.: Conditional probability, fuzzy sets, and possibility: a unifying view. Fuzzy Sets Syst. **144**(1), 227–249 (2004)
6. Doerr, M.: The CIDOC conceptual reference module: an ontological approach to semantic interoperability of metadata. AI Mag. **24**(3), 75–92 (2003)

7. Gorogiannis, N., Hunter, A.: Instantiating abstract argumentation with classical logic arguments: postulates and properties. Artif. Intell. **175**(9–10), 1479–1497 (2011)
8. Grant, J., Hunter, A.: Analysing inconsistent first-order knowledge bases. Artif. Intell. **172**(8–9), 1064–1093 (2008)
9. Hunter, A., Konieczny, S.: Approaches to measuring inconsistent information. In: Bertossi, L., Hunter, A., Schaub, T. (eds.) Inconsistency Tolerance. LNCS, vol. 3300, pp. 191–236. Springer, Heidelberg (2005). https://doi.org/10.1007/978-3-540-30597-2_7
10. Janíček, M.: Abductive reasoning for continual dialogue understanding. In: Lassiter, D., Slavkovik, M. (eds.) ESSLLI 2010-2011. LNCS, vol. 7415, pp. 16–31. Springer, Heidelberg (2012). https://doi.org/10.1007/978-3-642-31467-4_2
11. Kelley, B.: Announcing the crowd computing revolution (2014). https://braden kelley.com/2014/03/announcing-the-crowd-computing-revolution/
12. Lembo, D., Lenzerini, M., Rosati, R., Ruzzi, M., Savo, D.F.: Inconsistency-tolerant semantics for description logics. In: Hitzler, P., Lukasiewicz, T. (eds.) RR 2010. LNCS, vol. 6333, pp. 103–117. Springer, Heidelberg (2010). https://doi.org/10.1007/978-3-642-15918-3_9
13. Long, K.: As STEM majors soar at UW, interest in humanities shrinks – a potentially costly loss. The Seattle Times, January 2019
14. Lykourentzou, I., Antoniou, A., Naudet, Y., Dow, S.: Personality matters: balancing for personality types leads to better outcomes for crowd teams. In: Proceedings of the 19th ACM Conference on Computer-Supported Cooperative Work & Social Computing (CSCW), San Francisco, California, USA, pp. 260–273 (2016)
15. Mikolov, T., Chen, K., Corrado, G., Dean, J.: Efficient estimation of word representations in vector space. CoRR abs/1301.3781 (2013). http://arxiv.org/abs/1301.3781
16. Modgil, S.: Reasoning about preferences in argumentation frameworks. Artif. Intell. **173**(9–10), 901–934 (2009)
17. Moguillansky, M.O., Wassermann, R., Falappa, M.A.: An argumentation machinery to reason over inconsistent ontologies. In: Kuri-Morales, A., Simari, G.R. (eds.) IBERAMIA 2010. LNCS (LNAI), vol. 6433, pp. 100–109. Springer, Heidelberg (2010). https://doi.org/10.1007/978-3-642-16952-6_11
18. Prakken, H.: An abstract framework for argumentation with structured arguments. Argum. Comput. **1**(2), 93–124 (2010)
19. Rüster, C., Neu, E.: Hethitisches Zeichenlexikon. Otta Harrassowitz, Wiesbaden (1989)
20. Schmidhuber, J.: Deep learning in neural networks: an overview. Neural Netw. **61**, 85–117 (2015)
21. Stoilos, G., Simou, N., Stamou, G., Kollias, S.: An abstract framework for argumentation with structured arguments. IEEE Intell. Syst. **21**(5), 84–87 (2006)
22. Terras, M.: Crowdsourcing in the digital humanities. In: Schreibman, S., Siemens, R., Unsworh, J. (eds.) A New Companion to Digital Humanities. Wiley-Blackwell, Hoboken (2016)
23. Tworek, H.: The real reason the humanities are 'in crisis'. The Atlantic, December 2003
24. Watkins, L., Snyder, D.: The digital hammurabi project (2003). http://www.jhu.edu/digitalhammurabi/

Exploring Self-organisation in Crowd Teams

Ioanna Lykourentzou[1]([✉]), Antonios Liapis[2], Costas Papastathis[3], Konstantinos Papangelis[4], and Costas Vassilakis[3]

[1] Utrecht University, Utrecht, The Netherlands
i.lykourentzou@uu.nl
[2] Institute of Digital Games, University of Malta, Msida, Malta
antonios.liapis@um.edu.mt
[3] University of Peloponnese, Tripoli, Greece
{cst12079,costas}@uop.gr
[4] Department of Computer Science and Software Engineering,
Xi'an Jiaotong-Liverpool University, Suzhou, China
K.papangelis@xjtlu.edu.cn

Abstract. Online crowds have the potential to do more complex work in teams, rather than as individuals. Team formation algorithms typically maximize some notion of global utility of team output by allocating people to teams or tasks. However, decisions made by these algorithms do not consider the decisions or preferences of the people themselves. This paper explores a complementary strategy, which relies on the crowd itself to self-organize into effective teams. Our preliminary results show that users perceive the ability to choose their teammate extremely useful in a crowdsourcing setting. We also find that self-organisation makes users feel more productive, creative and responsible for their work product.

Keywords: Crowd teams · Self-organization · Computer-supported collaboration · Creative writing

1 Introduction

As the nature of work is becoming more and more distributed and flexible, creating effective remote teams is becoming an increasingly pertinent problem. Recently, team collaboration has been the subject of increasing research in the crowd work domain. The reason is simple: as the problems that task providers want to delegate to the crowd increase in complexity, individual contributions are not enough and it becomes evident that people from the crowd need to collaborate. Complex problems where crowd collaboration has proven valuable range from mass scale scientific research and article authoring [16], to designing software prototypes [12], and from writing stories [7] to collaborative idea generation [14].

Creating an effective team is well-known to be a problem involving multiple challenges. In a typical workplace setting these include balancing the need

© IFIP International Federation for Information Processing 2020
Published by Springer Nature Switzerland AG 2020
I. O. Pappas et al. (Eds.): I3E 2019 Workshops, IFIP AICT 573, pp. 164–175, 2020.
https://doi.org/10.1007/978-3-030-39634-3_15

for skill diversity, personality compatibility and schedules, among other parameters [3]. Crowd team formation poses further challenges since crowd team members (i) have usually never worked together before the crowdsourcing task begins, (ii) must perform effectively in relatively little time, and (iii) cannot be assumed to share common values or loyalty to a specific firm (which may be the case when bringing together a remote team from within the same organisation). These challenges mean that the typical methods of team formation, which usually involve pre-profiling team members (in regards to skill, personality etc.) and then placing them to work together, may not suffice in a crowd setting. Instead, new methods are needed to form crowd teams fast and efficiently. In our previous work we proposed "team dating": a method for crowd team formation in cold-start conditions, i.e. assuming nothing about the profile of the individual workers or the way they will collaborate [9]. Team dating allows people to "try out" different candidate teammates for a number of rounds, before placing them into teams with an appropriate teammate of their choice, with the help of an algorithm that takes into account their in-between evaluations. This ad-hoc manner proved to help create efficient ad-hoc teams on a creative task.

Similarly to most existing algorithm-based methods for crowd management (see for example [11, 13]), our previous method suffered from one important disadvantage: not actively involving the workers in the process, but rather assigning them directly to a task or to a team. However, as latest research in management sciences [8] and also crowdsourcing [18] indicates, too close a monitoring can stifle worker creativity and initiative-taking: two features that are absolutely necessary in creative, complex teamwork.

In this work we explore a new concept: *self-organisation*, which aims to empower crowd workers with the opportunity to choose their teammates, and "guide" the algorithmic process of team formation. Self-organisation is a well-known concept in domains such as Open Source Software Development, or online content co-creation communities like Wikipedia. To the best of our knowledge, however, self-organization has never been explored in a crowd setting. In this first study, we aim to explore how people behave in such a setting, what choices they make, and how.

The rest of this paper is organised as follows. First, we present related literature, focusing on team formation algorithms for crowdsourcing, and findings from management literature on the nature of self organisation. Then we present our methodology, including the description of the interface and algorithm we used to explore crowd team self-organisation, as well as our data collection method. Next we present our preliminary experimental results, focusing on the way people behave when given the choice to select their teammate. We conclude this paper with limitations and future work.

2   Related Work

This paper builds on algorithmic methods for forming teams in a crowd setting but also no self-organization methods for team management. The most critical related work on these two topics is covered below.

2.1   Team Formation Algorithms

Team formation in crowdsourcing is often managed by algorithms. Whereas in a traditional work setting a human manager is often enough to decide which person should work with whom in the context of a task, the scale of crowdsourcing often necessitates automation. A number of algorithms managing the crowd team formation process have emerged recently, which can be mapped to two broad categories: (i) *crowd team building algorithms*, which select which worker should collaborate with whom before the task begins, and (ii) *crowd team coordination algorithms*, which control the team processes after the task has begun.

Crowd team building algorithms, such as the ones proposed in [11], view team formation as a mathematical optimisation problem. They tap on the scale of crowdsourcing, which makes it impossible for traditional methods (e.g. a human manager) to put together an effective team. Assuming a large pool of workers with known profiles (e.g. skill level) and a varied pool of tasks, the objective of crowd team building algorithms is to match each task with a group of workers so as to accomplish the task optimally within given constraints (deadline, upper budget threshold etc.).

Crowd team coordination algorithms come to play after the task has begun. For example, the algorithm proposed by Salehi *et al.* [13] rotates workers across teams based on their viewpoint diversity, in an effort to achieve idea cross-fertilisation and thus increase the innovation capacity of the participating collective. Workers however are not asked whether they would like to switch teams or not, and the rotation decision is only taken by the algorithm. Other works in the area are those by Valentine *et al.* [17] and Kim *et al.* [7], who use computational methods to assign crowd workers to specific parts of the work, either in teams or individually, according to a top-down decision manner and pre-defined roles.

The problem with team management algorithms like the above is that they largely micro-manage the workers by assigning them directly to a team. This approach is indeed appropriate for microtask crowdsourcing, where the crowdsourcing task can be clearly delimited to discrete parts and given to specific workers with specific roles. However, when it comes to more complex work, which is usually the type of work that crowd teams are called to address, such algorithms can stifle creativity and initiative-taking, as indicated by recent research in management sciences [8] and crowdsourcing [6,18].

2.2   Self Organization for Team Building

Self-organisation is a management term often used to describe the functionality of software development teams, either within a company or in Open Source Software Development communities. As part of the Agile Manifesto [1], it is defined as a process followed by teams that manage their own workload, shift tasks based on needs and best fit, and participate in the group decision making [4]. It has been found to improve the performance of participating teams as it "brings the decision making authority to the operational level, thus increasing speed and accuracy of problem solving" [10].

Self-organizing teams have certain characteristics [15]. First, they are driven by "zero information", where prior knowledge does not apply. This enables the team members to challenge existing knowledge status quo and have the potential to create something truly novel. Second, they exhibit autonomy, as they do not have a top-down appointed leader; leadership is a property that emerges as the team members divide their roles [5]. Third, the team pursues ambitious goals (self-transcendence), and fourth, team members have a variety of backgrounds, viewpoints and knowledge (cross-fertilization).

In crowd teams, not a lot of works currently exist giving workers the option to self-organise. An early attempt is the work by Lykourentzou et al. [9] who partially delegate the team building process to the crowd workers themselves, by enabling them to try out different candidate teammates, evaluate them, and then make crowd teams based on these indications. Although this work does take worker preference into account, it does so indirectly.

In this paper we start exploring the notion of self-organisation for crowd teams. Given the effectiveness of the approach on other types of teams, such as corporate ones, we experiment with allowing individuals from the crowd to explore the "space" of candidate teammates available to them, discover those with whom they might work best, through a trial-and-error approach, and finally directly indicate their preferences.

3   Methodology

This section describes the task for which team self-organization is tested, along with the user interface and self-organization algorithm that facilitate it.

3.1   Interface Design

Current crowdsourcing platforms do not encourage collaboration, let alone self-organisation and choice of who to work with. Therefore, to explore the properties of self-organisation, and how people behave in this context, we designed a tailor-made framework and interface, outlined in Fig. 1.

The task given to the crowd workers is a creative writing challenge inspired by the exquisite corpse method [2], where participants co-create a story by gradually building on each others' contributions. To give a sense of competition and inspire motivation, the framework has been designed as a game, played in three rounds. Before the start of the game, a pre-authored story is presented to all users. Then during each round, users work in teams of two and collaboratively write a possible continuation to this story. At the end of the round, individuals vote for the best story (they cannot vote for their own team's story), and decide whether they would like to continue with the same teammate or not. In case they want to change, they can indicate their preference for another person, choosing from the list of all possible candidate teammate profiles. The most voted story is then appended to the main story, the team that wrote it receives an award (a score bonus), and a new round begins. In the next round, teams are formed with the help of a self-organisation algorithm, which attempts to best satisfy each user's desired (or undesired) teammate. Each team will have to continue the main story, as it was formed in the previous round(s). This cycle repeats until, at the end of the third round, the final main story is presented, and the user with the highest score is the winner of the challenge. More details on the specifics of the interface, process, and solicited user feedback are presented below.

(a) Initial player profiles

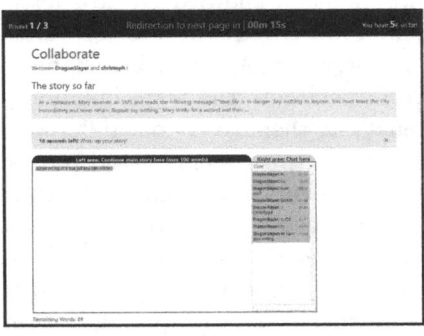

(b) Team collaboration interface

(c) Assessing a player's team-mate

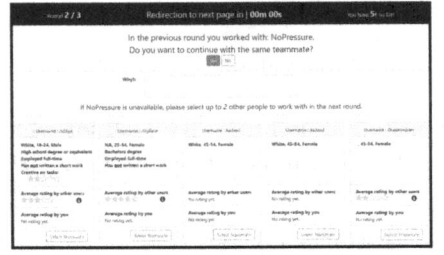

(d) Updated player profiles

Fig. 1. Screens from the user interface

Start of the Game: Once the system is synchronized to all players, the instructions of the game are presented. Afterwards, players are asked about their demographic information, measuring: age, gender, ethnicity, education level, employment status, whether they have won or participated in a similar writing task before and their self-perceived creativity level. Then, each player is presented with the start of the pre-authored story and is asked to individually write a continuation for it. We use this input as a "writing sample", and add it to the profile of the individual, for other users to see.

Teammate Selection: Once players have submitted their individual story writing sample, they choose their first teammate from the list of all players' profiles. A player's profile at this stage consists of the player's username, demographic data, as well as their writing samples (Fig. 1a). In the following stages, when players have already collaborated with and have rated one another, profiles will be enriched to include each player's ratings, both from the person looking at the profile and on average. Players can choose up to two possible teammates with whom they would like to work with. The self-organisation algorithm uses these choices to form the pairs that will be invited to work together in the next round.

Team Collaboration: As soon as the algorithm has placed users in pairs, based on their profile choices, the teams must collaborate to continue the story so far ("main story"). In the first round, the main story consists of the initial pre-authored story. Players' individual writing samples are not taken into account, since all teams must start from the same basis. However, each user is free to propose their sample to their teammate, or write something new together. The interface at this stage, shown in Fig. 1b, consists of four main parts: (1) a clock that indicates how long the team has for their collaboration, (2) a chat area, serving as their communication channel, (3) the story so far ("main story"), and (4) a collaborative text writing area, where users can see in real time what their teammate writes, and work together to continue the main story.

Peer Evaluation: Once they complete their collaborative writing, players evaluate their teammate on a Likert scale of 1 to 5 on: Skillfulness ("How skillful was [teammate's username] in continuing the story?"), Collaboration ability ("How good is [teammate's username] as a collaborator?"), Helpfulness ("[teammate's username] comments were helpful"). Players can also rate their own helpfulness level from 1 to 5. Finally, players can tick one or more options regarding how they are similar with their teammate (the options are "commitment to working hard on this task", "how we think the work should be done", "general abilities to do a task like this", "personal values"). These ratings are used to enrich each player's profile, as explained above.

Voting for Best Story: After providing feedback on their teammate, each individual player votes for their preferred story continuation (direct voting method). Given a number of P participants in the experiment, there are $P/2$ candidate story continuations to choose from. Users can vote for any story, except their team's (they cannot see it as an option). Once all players vote, the story with the most votes is presented to them along with the winning team.

Teammate Selection (Enriched). If there are more rounds remaining, users start a new round by first selecting a teammate, as described above. The only difference is that now players are also asked whether they would like to continue with the same teammate or not. This choice is critical for self-organisation: it renders players responsible for calculating the relative gain they will have from continuing with the same teammate (e.g. lower communication overhead) versus the risk of not working with another teammate that could potentially get them access to a better story in the next round.

Self-organization Algorithm: The aim of the algorithm is to assist the team self-coordination process, by matching users with those teammates that they mostly prefer working with. The algorithm does so by ranking the possible candidate teams based on their pairwise average profile ratings (affinity), and then gradually selecting those teams with the highest affinity values, until all users have been placed into teams. In case of ties, e.g. two candidate teams having the same pairwise affinity score, the algorithm selects randomly among tied options.

End of Game: After three rounds, all users are prompted to the "Final Survey" screen, which shows the final story with all winning stories appended, the ranking of the users (based on a point system rewarding each round's winning teams), and a questionnaire that users must fill regarding their overall experience.

3.2 Data Collection

As a first exploratory study, we conducted five experiments with teams of crowdworkers, using only the self-organisation team formation algorithm described above. In total, 34 crowdworkers participated. While more crowdworkers joined each experiment, they swiftly dropped out and were not part of any phase of the team-based tasks; their data is omitted without affecting the validity of the findings. Three of the sessions had 6 participants working in 3 teams, while two sessions had 8 participants working in 4 teams. The majority of participants self-identified as aged 18–24 (94%), Asian (91%), male (62%) and with a Bachelors (53%) or High school degree or equivalent (29%). While only a few participants (18%) reported some prior experience with creative writing, most of them reported being highly creative, with an average score of 3.9 out of 5.

4   Results

This section compiles the findings of the five experiments detailed in Sect. 3.2.

4.1   Research Questions

We wish to analyse the participants' opinions on self-organization as supported in this experiment and implications in their selection of team-mate, relating to the following questions:

1. Do people like being able to choose their teammate?
2. How does having the choice of teammate affect participants?

3. What matters the most when having the option to select a teammate?
4. How did players decide which team's story to vote for?

The questions are analysed at the level of the individual, using the questionnaire data that players filled in at the end of the experiment. Since we are dealing with a single population, we employ the one sample t-test and Chi-Square Goodness-of-Fit Test methods.

Table 1. Reasons for choosing a teammate.

What mattered the most when choosing teammate?	
Choosing the person that would make me win	27%
I chose randomly	13%
I chose the people whose initial story I liked the most	27%
I chose the people whose profile information I liked the most	27%
Other	6%

4.2   Player Behavior in a Self-organisation Context

RQ1: Users Find It Useful to Choose Their Teammates. We conduct a one-sample t-test on their answers to the question "How useful was being able to choose your teammate?" of the final questionnaire, against the hypothetical mean of 3.0 (denoting a neutral opinion). Results show that users show a significantly higher than neutral preference to being able to choose their teammate, with $t(29) = 2.134, p < 0.005$. A mediation analysis revealed that this preference is not affected by being in a winning team or not.

Table 2. Effects of choice.

Having the choice to select who I work with, made me...	
More productive	27%
Feel in control of my own work	13%
Be more responsible for what I write	27%
More creative	27%
More tired	3%
Other	3%

RQ2: Having the Choice to Select One's Teammates Makes Users Feel Productive, Responsible and Creative. A Chi-Square Goodness-of-Fit Test revealed that there are significant differences among the different ways that this choice could affect users, with $x^2(5) = 12.00, p < 0.005$. Specifically, having the choice to select one's teammates made users feel more productive, creative, responsible for what they write and more in control of their work (Table 2). Post-hoc binomial pairwise tests revealed statistical significant differences across all user-reported answers with at least $p < 0.05$, except between answers "more tired" and "other" where no statistically significant difference was found. No statistically significant differences were found on whether the user was in a winning team or not.

RQ3: Users Selected Teammates Based on a Variety of Reasons. A Chi-Square Goodness-of-Fit Test revealed that there are no statistically significant differences among the different ways that users select teammates, with $x^2(4) = 5.33, p = 0.26$. Player choices from our sample seem to be distributed primarily among selecting a teammate based on winning potential, writing sample and profile, and to a lesser extent randomly or for other reasons (Table 1).

Table 3. Story voting criteria.

How did you decide which story to vote?	
I always vote for the story I like the most	83%
I sometimes voted for a not good story, to have more chances to win	3%
I voted randomly	14%
Other	0%

RQ4: Users Voted for the Story They Liked the Most, Not Strategically. A Chi-Square Goodness-of-Fit Test revealed that there are very significant differences among the different ways that users select the winning story, with $x^2(3) = 133.625, p < 0.001$. The dominant reason for voting for a story is how much users liked it (Table 3). Users did not vote strategically (i.e. for a worse story in hope that their would win) or randomly. Post-hoc binomial pairwise tests revealed statistical significant differences only across the dominant reason mentioned above ("I voted for the story I liked the most") and the rest, but not among the other reasons.

4.3 Sample Session

To shed more light onto the process followed by different crowd workers when collaboratively writing in teams, we analyse an indicative session with 8 crowd workers. The session is one of the five sessions analyzed in the quantitative results section above. The winning story of the first round is the one by users *shuyuan-liu16* and *yihao15*. Interestingly, this story is very unlike to the initial writing sample that any of the two users contributed. The harmonious collaboration of this team was rewarded by other players, and the winning team chose to stay together, with both users rating each other highly (pairwise rating of 4.5 out of 5). From the other competing teams, at least one member per team declared that they wanted to change teammate. It is also interesting to note that both members of the winning team declared to have 3 out of 4 possible collaboration style elements in common ("task commitment", "way of thinking", "general abilities", differing only in the "personal values" element). In contrast, the members of the losing teams either declared no collaboration style element in common (2 out of the 3 losing teams), or they had a large imbalance in the collaboration style elements they declared (in the last team, one member declared to share no elements, while the other member declared sharing all four). This observation indicates that the dissimilarity in regards to the collaboration styles may play an important role to the perceptions of the team members and their eventual team's performance. Further research is however needed to statistically examine this observation.

Moving forward to the next rounds, we observe that the winning story of the next round is that of a newly formed team, that of users *HanbinQin* and *grizzHuang*. Similarly to the previous winning team, this team declared to share many collaboration style elements (4 out of 4) and its members rated each other highly (4.25 out of 5). From the losing teams, two out of three also shared at least one collaboration style element, and these teams declared that they wanted to continue working together, despite having lost. The members of these teams also rated each other highly (4.75 out of 5, and 5 out of 5 respectively). The losing team that expressed a wish to change teammates was the team that shared no common collaboration style element, and teammates rated each other very low (2 out of 5). This qualitative observation also indicates that there seems to be a connection between the number of collaboration style elements a team shares, their inter-team evaluations and their wish to stay together, as well as their performance. Further research is needed to confirm this observation. Given that all but one teams wanted to stay together, all four teams remained unchanged by the algorithm in the third and final round. The winning story was again by a different team, this time by the team of users *nakashimaritsu* and *Hecate*, who had rated each other highly in the previous round. The inter-team ratings and collaboration styles that the teams had declared to share in the previous round remained unchanged.

A final interesting observation with regards to this sample is the fact that the number of total user votes on the winning stories decreases from round to round. After the first round, all 8 users voted for their preferred story. However in rounds 2 and 3 only 6 users voted. This pattern seems to repeat in the other experiments. Although users declared that they did not intentionally vote strategically, this finding indicates that perhaps some of them avoided to vote, to give more chances to their team by not taking any action "against" it. Further research is nevertheless required as to the reasons why some users choose not to vote, and whether this finding is supported by statistical evidence.

5   Conclusion, Limitations and Future Work

The results of our exploratory study show that users consider being able to choose their teammates, and thus being able to affect the decision of the team formation process, extremely useful in a crowdsourcing setting. Being involved in the process—and not a mere component of it—made users feel significantly more productive, responsible for their choices and creative. These findings are fully in line with what research in organisational sciences has shown, i.e. that involving users (in this case workers) in the decision-making process helps motivate feelings of empowerment, responsibility and ownership of one's work, with eventual positive effects on team performance.

As an exploratory work, this study has a number of limitations which can eventually form part of future work. The study only explored the behavior of users in a self-organisation context, without a control condition. This is appropriate to gain insights regarding the process, but it also means that further work is needed to examine, for instance, the differences between self-organised team formation and more traditional team building methods. Moreover, the results of this study relied only on the final questionnaire that users answered. Much richer information can be extracted by quantitatively analysing their pairwise evaluations or their profile choices after each round, and this can also be the subject of future work. Such an analysis can help reveal what makes a "winning team" and if these teams share some common characteristics compared to non-winning teams. There is also a need for deeper analysis of the quality of the stories themselves (winning or not) to reveal the extent to which users may vote strategically, even without realising it. Finally, a sentiment and text analysis can be performed on the text produced during team collaboration phases, on the shared collaborative document or on the chat. Such an analysis can reveal more fine-grained elements of team collaboration, such as turn-taking styles, signs of social or cultural affinity, trust and common ground building, equality of communication etc. Exploring these elements, especially between rounds, can help reveal why some teams persist while others dissolve, and therefore help understand to a deeper level the properties of human self-organised collaboration.

References

1. Beck, K., et al.: The agile manifesto (2001). https://agilemanifesto.org/
2. Brotchie, A., Gooding, M.: A Book of Surrealist Games. Redstone Press, London (1995)
3. Gilley, J.W., Morris, M.L., Waite, A.M., Coates, T., Veliquette, A.: Integrated theoretical model for building effective teams. Adv. Dev. Hum. Resourc. **12**, 7–28 (2010). https://doi.org/10.1177/1523422310365309

4. Highsmith, J.: Agile Project Management: Creating Innovative Products. Addison-Wesley, Boston (2004)
5. Hoda, R., Noble, J., Marshall, S.: Organizing self-organizing teams. Assoc. Comput. Manuf. J. (2010). https://doi.org/10.1109/NSREC.2017.8115448
6. Jahanbakhsh, F., Fu, W.T., Karahalios, K., Marinov, D., Bailey, B.: You want me to work with who?: Stakeholder perceptions of automated team formation in project-based courses. In: Proceedings of the 2017 CHI Conference on Human Factors in Computing Systems, CHI 2017, pp. 3201–3212. ACM, New York (2017). https://doi.org/10.1145/3025453.3026011
7. Kim, J., Cheng, J., Bernstein, M.S.: Ensemble: exploring complementary strengths of leaders and crowds in creative collaboration. In: Proceedings of the 17th ACM Conference on Computer Supported Cooperative Work & Social Computing, pp. 745–755 (2014). https://doi.org/10.1145/2531602.2531638
8. Lawler III, E.E., Worley, C.G.: Designing organizations that are built to change. MIT Sloan Manag. Rev. **48**, 19–23 (2006)
9. Lykourentzou, I., Wang, S., Kraut, R.E., Dow, S.P.: Team dating: a self-organized team formation strategy for collaborative crowdsourcing. In: Proceedings of the 2016 CHI Conference Extended Abstracts on Human Factors in Computing Systems, pp. 1243–1249. ACM (2016)
10. Moe, N.B., Dingsøyr, T.: Scrum and team effectiveness: theory and practice. In: Abrahamsson, P., Baskerville, R., Conboy, K., Fitzgerald, B., Morgan, L., Wang, X. (eds.) XP 2008. LNBIP, vol. 9, pp. 11–20. Springer, Heidelberg (2008). https://doi.org/10.1007/978-3-540-68255-4_2
11. Rahman, H., Roy, S.B., Thirumuruganathan, S., Amer-Yahia, S., Das, G.: Optimized group formation for solving collaborative tasks. VLDB J. **28**(1), 1–23 (2019). https://doi.org/10.1007/s00778-018-0516-7
12. Retelny, D., et al.: Expert crowdsourcing with flash teams. In: Proceedings of the 27th Annual ACM Symposium on User Interface Software and Technology (2014). https://doi.org/10.1145/2642918.2647409
13. Salehi, N., Bernstein, M.S.: Hive: collective design through network rotation. In: Proceedings of the ACM on Human-Computer Interaction - CSCW, pp. 151:1–151:26 (2018)
14. Siangliulue, P., Chan, J., Dow, S.P., Gajos, K.Z.: IdeaHound: improving large-scale collaborative ideation with crowd-powered real-time semantic modeling. In: Proceedings of the 29th Annual Symposium on User Interface Software and Technology, pp. 609–624 (2016). https://doi.org/10.1145/2984511.2984578
15. Takeuchi, H., Nonaka, I.: The new product development game. J. Prod. Innov. Manag. (1986). https://doi.org/10.1016/0737-6782(86)90053-6
16. Vaish, R., et al.: Crowd research: open and scalable university laboratories. In: Proceedings of the 30th Annual ACM Symposium on User Interface Software and Technology (2017). https://doi.org/10.1145/3126594.3126648
17. Valentine, M.A., Retelny, D., To, A., Rahmati, N., Doshi, T., Bernstein, M.S.: Flash organizations: crowdsourcing complex work by structuring crowds as organizations. In: Proceedings of the 2017 CHI Conference on Human Factors in Computing Systems, pp. 3523–3537 (2017). https://doi.org/10.1145/3025453.3025811
18. Xia, H., et al.: No workflow can ever be enough: how crowdsourcing workflows constrain complex work. Proc. ACM Hum.-Comput. Interact. (2017). https://doi.org/10.1145/3134724

Correction to: Crowd-Based Assessment of Deformational Cranial Asymmetries

Kathrin Borchert, Matthias Hirth, Angelika Stellzig-Eisenhauer,
and Felix Kunz

Correction to:
Chapter "Crowd-Based Assessment of Deformational
Cranial Asymmetries" in: I. O. Pappas et al. (Eds.): *Digital*
Transformation for a Sustainable Society in the 21st Century,
IFIP AICT 573, https://doi.org/10.1007/978-3-030-39634-3_13

The authors of the chapter "Crowd-based Assessment of Deformational Cranial Asymmetries" have provided an addendum which is included hereinafter.

Addendum to: Crowd-based Assessment of Deformational Cranial Asymmetries

Kathrin Borchert[1], Matthias Hirth[2], Angelika Stellzig-Eisenhauer[3],
and Felix Kunz[3]

[1] University of Würzburg, Würzburg, Germany
kathrin.borchert@informatik.uni-wuerzburg.de
[2] TU Ilmenau, Ilmenau, Germany
matthias.hirth@tu-ilmenau.de
[3] University Hospital Würzburg, Würzburg, Germany
{stellzig_a|kunz_f}@ukw.de

Abstract. This Addendum presents a correction of the evaluation of the data presented in Borchert et al. [1].

The original chapter can be found online at
https://doi.org/10.1007/978-3-030-39634-3_13

© IFIP International Federation for Information Processing 2020
Published by Springer Nature Switzerland AG 2020
I. O. Pappas et al. (Eds.): I3E 2019 Workshops, IFIP AICT 573, p. C1–C4, 2020.
https://doi.org/10.1007/978-3-030-39634-3_16

1   Corrected Results

We identified an issue in the evaluation methodoloy of the original publication. Other than describe in Borchert et al. [1] (Section 4.2), the rating scale used by the participants with non-crowdsourcing background, has been a four-point scale without the neutral option. The rating scale used by the crowdsourcing participants, was a five-point scale as described in the original publication. For a corrected analysis of the perception of groups with different backgrounds, the neutral answers of crowdworkers are excluded and their remaining ratings are transformed to a four-point scale. Therefore, ratings of 4 (agree) and 5 (strongly agree) are reduced by one. Hence, a rating of 1 represents the option *strongly disagree* and a rating of 4 means that the participant *strongly agrees* that the shown head is asymmetrical. For the corrected evaluation, 12% of the crowd-based ratings have to be excluded.

1.1   Constancy of Ratings

The analysis of the constancy of the corrected ratings show no significant differences in the ratings of the first and second occurrence of a video. This is revealed by a Kruskal-Wallis rank sum test, which results in no rejection of the null hypothesis ($p > 0.05$), meaning that the ratings originate from the same distribution. Even if the average difference between the first and second rating of the same video provided by crowdworkers is slightly higher with 0.47 than the computed mean of the ratings of the other groups, the analysis establishes the constancy of the ratings.

The correction of the rating scale also has an impact on the filtering of the participants based on the discrepancy between the first and the second rating of the videos shown twice. Instead of filtering out 21 crowdworkers, we only exclude 5 participants from Microworkers from the further analysis.

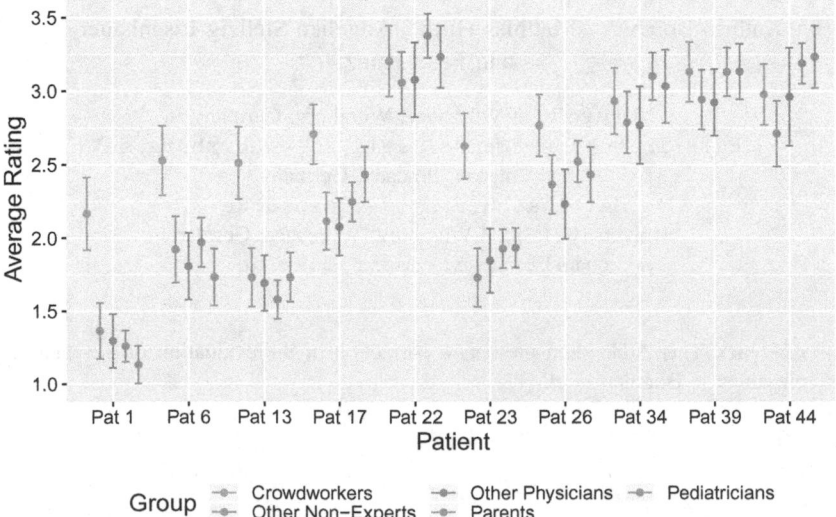

Fig. 1. Mean of the ratings with 95 % confidence intervals per group.

1.2   Comparison of Asymmetry Ratings

The corrected data still indicates that there is a significant effect of the group on the perception, i.e., the ratings. This is shown by an one-way ANOVA ($F(4,2194) = 22.19$, $p < 0.001$), and, additionally, Bonferroni's post-hoc test revealed significant differences between the crowdworkers and all other groups ($p < 0.001$). By analyzing the ratings in detail, we observe that 66.8% of the crowd-based ratings (strongly) agreed that the shown heads are deformed. In comparison to the other groups with a percentage of agreements ranging from 34.4% to 45.3%, the amount is still higher by far. These findings lead to the same conclusion as presented in Borchert et al. [1]. Crowdworkers perceive weak deformations as more critical than the other groups.

This effect is also observable when evaluating the ratings on a per patient level, shown in Fig. 1. Based on the corrected data, an one-way ANOVA per patient shows an effect of the group only for a part of the patients, namely patient 1, 6, 13, 17, 23, 26, and 44 ($p < 0.01$). These are patients with less deformed heads from the perspective of study participants with no crowdsourcing background. For patient 1, 6, 13, and 23, a significant difference between the assessments of the crowdworkers and those of all other groups is revealed by using the Bonferroni post-hoc test ($p < 0.01$). Further, for patient 17 and 26, we observe a significant effect between crowdworkers and experts, i.e., pediatricians and parents ($p < 0.05$). For these patients no effect is seen between the crowdworkers and the other groups as well as the other non-experts and experts. The effect for patient 44 is still the same as described in [1]. This findings indicates even more, that for unique characteristics of deformation the perception differs between experts (physicians and parents) and laypersons. Further, crowd-specific side effects impacts the ratings of the crowdworkers.

Table 1. Coefficients r of point-biserial correlation between ratings and areas of noticed deformation, i.e. front head, back of the head, ear and other areas including level of significance.

Group	r Front	r Back	r Ears	r Other
Pediatricians	0.47***	0.64***	0.48***	0.20***
OtherPhysicians	0.27***	0.57***	0.38***	0.19**
Parents	0.33***	0.64***	0.39***	0.11**
Crowdworkers	0.09	0.42***	0.30***	0.18***
OtherNon − Experts	0.17***	0.49***	0.27***	0.26***

** 0.01, *** 0.001

1.3   Influence Factors on the Perceived Asymmetry

Table 1 summarizes the corrected correlation coefficients per group between the ratings and the area in which deformations have been noticed. By using the corrected data set, a different result is seen for the correlation between the ratings and the option *other areas*. Now, the positive correlation is significant for all groups. Nevertheless, the conclusion drawn from the results remains the same as in [1].

Reference

1. Borchert, K., Hirth, M., Stellzig-Eisenhauer, A., Kunz, F.: Crowd-based assessment of deformational cranial asymmetries. In: Pappas, I., Mikalef, P., Dwivedi, Y., Jaccheri, L., Krogstie, J., Mäntymäki, M. (eds.) Digital Transformation for a Sustainable Society in the 21st Century. I3E 2019. IFIP Advances in Information and Communication Technology, vol. 573, pp. 145–157. Springer, Cham (2020). https://doi.org/10.1007/978-3-030-39634-3_13

Author Index

Printed in the United States
By Bookmasters